Business Crime

Business Crime

Its Nature and Control

MICHAEL CLARKE

with a chapter by Sally Wheeler

Polity Press

First published 1990 by Polity Press
in association with Basil Blackwell

Editorial office:
Polity Press, 65 Bridge Street, Cambridge CB2 1UR, UK

Marketing and production:
Basil Blackwell Ltd
108 Cowley Road, Oxford OX4 1JF, UK

ISBN 0 7456 0662 8

British Library Cataloguing in Publication Data
A CIP catalogue record for this book is available from
the British Library

Typeset in 10/11 pt Plantin
by Witwell Ltd, Southport.
Printed in Great Britain by
TJ Press, Padstow, Cornwall

Contents

Preface

This book had its origins in previous work on business crime and was further stimulated by the teaching of a course on white-collar crime to graduate socio-legal studies students at Birmingham University. The necessary attempt to give some sort of structure to a field characterized by very diverse kinds of literature pitched at widely varying levels gave rise to a feeling that business crime is in a number of ways different from conventional property crime, which gradually became elaborated into the form presented here.

Previous contact with the publishing world, however, made me cautious about writing at any length without a commission, and I am therefore very grateful to Tony Giddens and Polity Press for being willing to back my proposal with the minimum of delay and constraint. I hope that I have been able to justify his confidence.

This book could not have been completed without a period of intensive application, and I am grateful to the Department of Social Policy and Administration at the University of Birmingham for allowing me study leave to write it. I am also grateful to Sue Raybould for her speed and accuracy in producing the typescript. Finally I am grateful to David Downes and the *British Journal of Criminology* for permission to adapt material on insurance fraud published in 1989 issue 1 and 1990 issue 1 as chapter 5 of this book.

The author and publishers wish to thank the Office of Fair Trading for permission to reproduce material previously published in 'A General Duty to Trade Fairly', copyright © Office of Fair Trading Publications 1986; and D. C. Heath Publishers for permission to reproduce material previously published in H. Edelhertz and C. Rogovin, *A National Strategy for Containing White-Collar Crime*, copyright © D. C. Heath Publishers 1980.

Michael Clarke

1 Introduction

The object of this book is to present business crime as a distinctive social phenomenon. That means that it is sustained by an argument which it hopes to persuade the reader to accept. It also, however, seeks to review the evidence of various kinds of business crime through the intellectual discipline of sociology and in doing so to provide a source book for students interested in the field. The book is therefore divided into three parts.

In Part I a general analysis of the distinctive character of business crime is presented, first in chapter 2 by way of a perspective on the nature of deviance in work and business, then in chapter 3 in an account of the more specific points which distinguish business crime from conventional property crimes. The object of Part I is to convey a general analysis, though a number of moderately detailed points are made in chapter 3. The reader, especially the reader unfamiliar with the field, may find some of these points provocative. This is an inevitable consequence of attempting to analyse a field which contains so many different sectors, each internally complex and in many ways distinctive.

The argument of Part I is hence intended to become clearer when applied to the series of empirical illustrations in Part II. The topics chosen here by no means exhaust the range of those which are comprehended in business crime. They have been chosen partly as a reflection of the author's own research interests, partly because of the existence of a reasonable research literature, and partly in an attempt to give some at least illustrative coverage of the range and diversity of business crime.

The topics investigated in Part II are not, however, presented as mere instantiations of the arguments of Part I. The distinctive features of each topic have been allowed to determine the way it is treated, so that a reasonable account of the present state of knowledge is available to the reader who is interested more in the particular topic than in the field as a whole. To this end references to source material are provided at the end of each chapter. Sources cited are not intended to be exhaustive, but to provide a base for the reader who wishes to pursue inquiries further, and in many cases more comprehensive bibliographies on the topic concerned will be found in the references cited. An attempt has been made, however, to draw on sources from the wide range of disciplines which have contributed to an understanding of business crime – law, criminology, accountancy, economics, management, journalism – as well as on sources within sociology and political science, which form the basis for presentation here.

Equally, a great deal of material has not been included, either because it would take the account beyond the boundaries of feasible presentation, or because it adds little or nothing of substance to material which is used. All this reflects the fact that the field of business crime is one very widely commented upon, but very weakly organized intellectually. What is presented here does not purport to be definitive, but rather to co-ordinate material into a sociological account of the topics covered, and one which reflects what are, as is argued in Part I, distinctive characteristics of business crime. The points in Part I are hence not repeated verbatim in the chapters of Part II, but are alluded to in a considerable number of specific points. The reader whose interest is in verifying the application of Part I to one or more of the chapters of Part II will hence need to refer back to Part I, and especially to chapter 3, in the light of the evidence presented.

Part III is again analytical rather than empirical, and outlines a strategy of control of business crime which reflects its nature as identified in Part I, reinforced, it is hoped, by the evidence presented in Part II. Part III deliberately refrains from attempting a detailed blueprint however, since successful control systems will be conditioned significantly by the problems and characteristics of different kinds of business crime, and would take a considerable space to set out and justify. Rather the objective is to identify the ingredients essential to any successful control system and to argue for a distinctive set of objectives for control. Part III is intended, by being to some extent provocative though well grounded in the evidence and analysis of parts I and II, to stimulate debate and clarify some of the issues involved in the control of business crime.

A final point should also be made. This book is of an analytic and generalizing character. It is based on British material, but makes comparisons in a number of places with other countries, most frequently the United States. It is not part of its object to imply, however, that business crime is in all respects the same in different countries. There is important work still to be done in this field, which takes the development of the political economies of different nation states as its starting point and investigates the development of business crime as an adjunct of the development of business which is distinctive of that nation, and the development of controls on business crime as an adjunct of the politics of that nation. There are of course extensive similarities between nations, especially those of the industrialized west, because of their interdependent economies and trading patterns, and the increasingly extensive exchanges of personnel and communications in business affairs, but it would be rash indeed to suggest that business and business crime are the same in Japan as they are in France, or the same in Italy as they are in Britain. These are demanding and interesting issues which are necessarily largely set aside in this book.

PART I

The Nature of Business Crime

2 Business Crime and Organizational Deviance

It will be maintained in this book that crime and misconduct are endemic in business and that the key to understanding them lies in recognizing the structure that the business environment gives to misconduct, both in terms of opportunities and in terms of how misconduct is managed. In adopting this viewpoint a substantial obstacle has to be overcome: the conceptualization of business crime as exceptional and abnormal, rather than as an outcome of the normal operation of business, albeit not always routine. Business itself, naturally, likes to think of misconduct and certainly crime as exceptional. To do otherwise would be to invite a host of difficulties: public doubt about the integrity of the business or even the entire business sector, alarm at the disloyalty of the employees or fellow directors, confusion about what are acceptable standards of conduct. It makes much more sense to polarize misconduct into the rare flagrant cases demanding action as crime, and the rest as 'just business'. The media are content to go along with this polarization, for the most part, since it serves their interest in the exceptional and the dramatic instance with a clear moral character.

Academic research, however, has done almost nothing to redress this view. There are large bodies of research in many industrialized countries on industrial relations, management and the sociology of organizations, but little on business crime and, more importantly, no cross-fertilization between studies of business crime and business regulation on the one hand and the mainstream of industrial relations and management research and the sociology of organizations on the other. In consequence, research on business organizations tends to be preoccupied, directly or indirectly, with aspects of the wage-bargaining debate. The centre of concern is, in the first place, how the rewards of industrial production are to be allocated, and, in the second, how workers are to be motivated to greater productivity and management to acquire greater skills in work organization and in motivating workers. These concerns feed naturally into party political debates about the allocation of economic rewards, with parties of the left arguing for greater tax burdens on business and higher wages for workers, and those on the right for greater freedom for business and harder work and more productivity from workers.

Regrettably all of this presumes not merely the priority, but the all-encompassing character of the cash nexus. People are assumed to work to earn their living and to work only as hard as they can be cajoled, coerced and induced. Basic acceptance of industrial discipline is assumed – that all workers, high or low, devote their time to pursuing the specific objectives of the organization whilst at work and that they render themselves up to this end almost entirely. Of course they have needs, such as for food, rest and excretion, which must be accommodated, but the arrangements for doing so impose strict limitations to prevent indulgence. Management are accorded more latitude than blue-collar workers, but are expected to demonstrate a greater commitment to achieving the goals of the organiza-tion than manual workers.

Yet even a casual review of what actually takes place within work organizations reveals that the majority of workers' time – and the term is used generically here to refer to all participants from janitors to the chairman of the board of directors – is not spent in activities that directly further the aims of the organization, and it is not expected that it will be. Much time is spent in preparatory activities, travelling to appointments, setting up, cleaning and maintaining machines, asking where files are kept or about office routines. Some, as has been indicated, is spent servicing workers' recognized needs – toilet, tea and meal breaks, trade-union meetings. A considerable amount also is spent in various forms of indulgence with greater or less organizational approval, ranging from senior management's afternoon round of golf with important clients (or are they just friends?) to production line banter, gossip and horseplay.

All of these aspects of the use of organizational time put us on notice that businesses may employ labour, but they get people, who are not programmable machines. People work first and foremost because they need an income, and submit to organizational discipline to remain acceptable to the business, but they do not cease to have their other needs and interests, nor to pursue them at work.

What do Workers Seek from Work?

The attitudes and interests of individuals to work vary very widely. Some may work primarily because it is a chosen occupation using a skill which gives intrinsic satisfaction. Some may work purely calculatively because the job gives a desired level of economic reward and is itself tolerable. There are others, a significant and very diverse minority, who come to work because of the non-work opportunities it offers. Some of these are legitimized: a trade-union activist may spend more time in his/her trade-union activities than on the job, with the acceptance of management. Others are tolerated but not officially approved: the individual who goes out to buy food, who makes the tea, who organizes and administers the office sweepstake, for example. Others still are tolerated, but largely because unnoticed officially: the workplace Romeo who, finding himself in an environment with a number of desirable women, devotes his energies to chalking up as many conquests as possible. Others again are not tolerated at all if they come to the attention of authorities: the worker who runs a consultancy from his/her office using organizational resources, the individual who constantly absents him/herself on grounds of illness to pursue a hobby. Finally, there are those who directly exploit the organization's resources for personal and private ends, the most extreme example of which is embezzlement, but the much more common ones are the use of work vehicles, plant and equipment for a large variety of commercial ends and the systematic use of company time to engage in private commercial activities.

People may go to work, then, in order to earn a living, but the means by which they get some satisfaction from their work involve very varied stances to it. The solution arrived at by each person is usually very complex and may very well change over time, as she or he moves from job to job, the nature of a particular job alters, and the person's interest, age and commitments develop. In all cases a substantial degree of outward conformity to the requirements of work is necessary to avoid dismissal, but the personal adaptations are sufficiently well known for at least some roles or types to be fairly frequently identified in the informal social life of the workplace. For a vital consequence of individual adaptation is that it conditions the possibilities open to others. The role of the clown for example, the buffoon who makes others laugh and is happy to be laughed at as well as with, does not easily permit more than one person to occupy the position in a small or medium-size work group, both for reasons of competition for attention, and for fear that the entire group will degenerate into anarchic horseplay and elicit sanctions from above.

Further, attitudes and adaptations to work require social recognition in so far as they are deviant from or in conformity with the ideals and orthodoxies of work. Some people get considerable satisfaction and support from strong identification with these ideals and are therefore treated with caution by those whose adaptations are less conformist. Thus, there is the company man (or woman) who believes in and devotes him/herself to the service or the organization and may be respected for his dedication and breadth of knowledge and experience, even if derided for the lack of rewards she/he receives as a result. The blue-eyed boy is in a slightly different position, in that his overt and zealous conformity is seen to be calculated upon the expectation of advancement through the powers of his patron. The toady is a conformist, but different again in being protected by a powerful patron though with no expectations of advancement; he is feared for his willingness to sneak to superiors about his colleagues' deviance. Even conformity, in other words, is not a simple matter, and these examples by no means exhaust the possible variations. The young man in a hurry, by contrast with the three so far cited, is committed to outward conformity with organizational ideals and objectives, but is prepared to exploit and manipulate his colleagues and superiors in order to gain advancement.

Varieties of Workplace Deviance

Nor are the alternative sets of adaptations all definitely non-conformist. Many social roles exist which are accepted as socially functional whilst not devoted to the overt and publicized goals of the organization. Thus the gossip has an important communicative role in disseminating both organizational and social information about incidents and developments in the workplace, which is paralleled in a different way by the trade-union activist, whose concerns and communications are concerned more specifically with workers' rights and obligations and management initiatives and plans. The social organizer may derive great satisfaction, esteem and social support from his efforts at organizing social events based on the workplace – outings, parties, birthday treats, leaving-presents and so on. The trader and the gambler have somewhat more deviant roles in organizing activities – the sale of goods within the organization for workers' consumption which are not produced at or a part of the workplace, and the organization of sweepstakes, card games and bets. Such activities may well be tolerated by superiors in a more or less explicit way, but pose dangers in diverting workers' time and energy from work if they become too extensive, and show the potential to create parallel economies for a few individuals at the workplace, thereby undermining the basis of work discipline.

More deviant still, though still often tolerated by co-workers, are the drunk, the sexual athlete (who may be male or female) and the skiver. These roles are recognizably deviant, but require the active co-operation of at least some co-workers, and the tolerance of far more on the basis of acceptance of weakness or sympathy – 'It's not my style, but I can see why she (or he) does it.' If detected, these habits are liable to incur sanctions from superiors at least in the form of a formal insistence that such conduct will not be tolerated in the future.

The solidly deviant roles naturally require either complete privacy from colleagues, as is the case with some embezzlers, or their active connivance, as is more widely the case. Typists doing private work in office time, organized theft and pilfering of organizational materials and equipment, the use of the organization's vehicles for private projects and business, the running of a private business using work as a base are all examples. Participation in such clearly exploitative conduct varies widely in the degree of commitment which is involved. Active participants who behave in ways that if detected would warrant instant dismissal may be relatively few, but there are often many others who collude, either because of the material benefits to be gained, or at a minimum because of a lack of willingness to denounce the activity.

Scope for exploitatively deviant conduct exists at all organizational levels, but it is clearly greater the higher the level of authority involved. Not only do more senior personnel have a greater privacy and discretion, they have wider control of resources and subordinates, and activities can the more easily be not merely concealed but legitimized as acceptable or necessary in the circumstances. At the higher levels of management this discretion can be penetrated substantially by deviant conduct, but still rationalized as part of what it takes to run the organization. Thus gifts and hospitality can be exchanged as part of the normal process of negotiating contracts, tax demands from the Inland Revenue and VAT can be left unpaid in the interests of keeping enough cashflow to keep the business running, creditors can be asked to wait for improvements in trade that may never come, employees asked to work long unpaid hours to get the organization out of difficulties when a proper analysis of the books would show that the business is insolvent and that they will never be paid.

Much conduct subsequently denounced and even prosecuted as fraud, corruption, theft, perversion of the course of justice, falsification of accounts and tax evasion begins, at any rate, with this ambiguous character, even though it may conclude in deliberate criminality.

In only a relatively small minority of cases is criminal conduct the objective from the start, with the organizational form, resources and personnel systematically abused and manipulated to make it possible, and it is these cases, not surprisingly, that precipitate the greatest outrage when they are uncovered, and most regularly lead to the involvement of the police. In these cases – the setting up of a bogus charity, the establishment of a business to exploit credit (long firm fraud), the fraudulent application for a mortgage, the setting of a major fire to claim insurance indemnity – the trappings and form of a legitimate business are no more than a sham, though a sham that may have to be sustained with considerable patience and skill, and may even involve a period of legitimate business activity to bring off the fraud. Even in these cases, the organizational environment and its rules and culture must be understood and investigated in order to demonstrate the fraudulent character of the enterprise.

Business crime, then, is to be understood as very much a part of business, an intimate part of it, not separable from it, as bank robbery is clearly no part of banking. It can be analysed, and as will be later shown, controlled only by investigating its location and accepting in the fullest sense its nature as part of business. Cases, particularly publicized cases, may often seem in their later public, and especially their courtroom presentation, as though they are the work of external villains visited by force and guile upon the hapless public. Such a view is misleading, even if congenial to public authorities and representatives of business organizations. It represents as alien, calculatedly predatory and highly abnormal that which is more usually an outgrowth and shrewd exploitation of everyday business life. To adopt this sociological perspective does require a distinct shift of mental set and a conscious caution about easy moralizing. These introductory remarks have been directed to making that shift possible. Before examining in more detail the nature of the problems in different areas of business, however, it is necessary to state more precisely the differences between business crime and conventional crime.

3 The Nature of Business Crime

In 360 BC in Syracuse, Sicily, then a Greek colony, one Xenothemis and a ship-owner, Hegestratos, persuaded a buyer to advance them cash by claiming that a vessel was fully laden with corn. Maritime trade was at that time risky, and many vessels were lost at sea. Hegestratos intended to exploit this weakness three days after the ship sailed, with its hold empty, by attempting to cut through the timbers and scuttle it. He was discovered by the passengers, however, and in a panic jumped overboard and drowned.[1]

If fraud has not always been an aspect of human society, this example suggests that it has existed at least since the establishment of trade. Concern about fraud and, arising out of this, measures to control it, vary considerably with time and place. The essence of the offence remains the same, however – and it might be added that frauds very similar to that attempted by Hegestratos and Xenothemis are perpetrated regularly upon modern shipping. The essence of fraud, and indeed of almost all business crime, is deceit and violation of trust. Trade and commerce cannot operate without an element of trust. The Syracusan buyer might have gone to the harbour and verified that the ship's hold was in fact laden, but that would have done him little good. The corn could have been removed before sailing, and even if he stood on the dockside and watched the ship depart, it could have diverted en route and discharged its cargo for a quick sale before the scuttling. The employer is in no different a position as regards his staff. He must allow them some discretion to undertake their duties in the expectation that they will do so diligently and honestly. Even quite sophisticated security checks can be outwitted, and of course the more complex the system, the more time consuming and expensive it is to administer.

In the 1980s fraud has acquired a much higher profile as a public issue in western industrialized countries, many of which have undertaken special measures to combat it: special laws to make prosecution easier, increased penalties, special courts with judges trained in dealing with fraud cases, specialized investigation and enforcement agencies and police units, enhanced budgets.

In the United States public and political awareness of business crime developed rapidly in the 1970s as a consequence of the widespread abuses of office of the Nixon Presidency, which were investigated so dramatically by the press and Congress in the Watergate affair.[2] This overlapped with the revelations of bribery and political chicanery by US-based multinational corporations, most notoriously Lockheed,[3] which was eventually shown to have bribed the Prime Minister of Japan, among others, in order to ensure sales of its aircraft, and ITT, which was extensively involved in the overthrow of President Allende of Chile in 1973. These events were accompanied by a growing awareness of the penetration of legitimate business beyond the conventional area of anxiety of the gambling industry, then restricted to Nevada, by criminal syndicates (organized crime).[4] Not only were money laundering operations greatly extended, but racketeers acquired sufficient financial muscle to compromise some financial institutions besides in engaging in a variety of frauds and scams in, for example, real estate and insurance. Taken together these developments were sufficient to lead to a war on white-collar crime from the 1970s,[5] besides a number of specific pieces of legislation such as the Foreign Corrupt Practices Act and the Racketeer-Influenced and Corrupt Organisations legislation (RICO), designed to make the prosecution of criminal syndicates easier and the expropriation of their assets possible. This campaign was conducted predominantly in terms of law enforcement, with additional resources being given to the training of personnel in police and district attorneys' departments in the skills necessary to detect and prosecute business crime, and the establishment of special offices to co-ordinate their efforts.

It has been in the 1980s, however, that concern about business crime in a general sense, that is, crimes committed on a widespread basis within mainstream business, has crystalized. The 1970s could be said to be a characteristic episode of soul-searching about the morality of the political and economic leaders of the United States. The Reagan Presidency brought that sharply to an end with a return to the traditional view that what is good for business is good for America, which was given practical implementation by tax cuts and the deregulation of business, both industrial and financial. Although, as will be detailed in chapter 9, the impact of deregulation has been substantial in industry, it has been the financial sector that has captured the headlines, with banks and savings and loans institutions (Thrifts, which are equivalent to building societies) large and small becoming insolvent, sometimes amid revelations of extraordinary recklessness and malpractice.

Latterly it has been securities in investment houses that have been the centre of the debate, not only through flagrant misconduct in such matters as insider dealing, but with contested takeovers accelerating in size to $25 billion for a single bid. This has caused serious concern about the propriety of methods used at times, about distortions of the markets and about the consequences of the debt burdens on the companies involved. Matters reached an apparent head in 1988 with the acceptance of a guilty plea and a $650 million fine for various offences by Drexel, Burnham, Lambert, the vehicle of the financial iconoclast, Michael Milken. His methods of securitizing smaller companies by offering high interest rates, so called junk-bond, were the basis for the creation of a multi-billion dollar enterprise in the 1980s. The public profile of Rudolph Giuliani, the US Attorney involved in prosecuting Drexel and the Boesky and Levine insider dealing cases, has been so high that serious suggestions have been made that he should use it as a springboard to run for President.

In Britain, too, concern about fraud has been particularly stimulated by a series of scandals associated with financial institutions, for example, the series of frauds involving tens of millions of pounds against investors or 'Names' at Lloyd's insurance market; the collapse and controversial rescue by the Bank of England of Johnson Matthey Bankers; the takeover by Guinness of Distillers, and the ensuing allegations of sharp practice and breaches of the Companies Acts in the process, culminating in the dismissal of the chairman and chief executive, Ernest Saunders, and the preferment of criminal charges. The government has demonstrated its concern by sustained efforts at control. The reform of Lloyd's by Act of Parliament in 1982 has been followed by the comprehensive restructuring of the regulation of financial institutions through the Securities and Investments Board, and the subsidiary self-regulatory organizations under the Financial Services Act 1986.[6] This has been followed up by a series of initiatives on enforcement: the report by Lord Roskill, a senior judge, into the improvement of frauds trials procedure to clarify and speed them up;[7] the establishment of the Fraud Investigation Group to co-ordinate the activities of the police and non-police agencies such as the Department of Trade and Industry; and the establishment in 1987 of the Serious Frauds Office, a similar co-operative organization staffed with a range of professional expertise to deal with large and complex frauds. At the same time, the 1987 Criminal Justice Act increases penalties, provides for confiscation of assets, and allows the freezing of assets of suspected fraudsters at an early stage in inquiries, a pattern of controls explicitly compared by the responsible minister to that adopted in relation to drug dealers. 'We want the public to realise we are in deadly earnest about stamping out City fraud. The City fraudster is just as much a professional criminal as is the large-scale bank robber, and motivated just as much by greed'[8] And no doubt the minister might have said much the same about VAT swindles on gold bullion, mortgage swindles, and credit card frauds, all well-organized multi-million pound operations commanding the headlines at much the same time as his speech.

Is this concern justified, and is the reaction appropriate? On the first point there seems little doubt. The manpower of the relevant enforcement agencies, such as the fraud squad, Department of Trade Companies

Inspection Branch, Customs and Excise Investigation Units, Inland Revenue Special Offices, and Bank of England Compliance and Regulation staff, has increased steadily, albeit from a fairly low base, over the past twenty years, and the complaint continues to be that workloads are increasing faster than manpower. The amount at risk in cases currently under investigation by the City and Metropolitan Police fraud squad alone rose from £70 million in 1970 to £450 million in 1980 and £1349 million in 1985.[9] On the second point, the only issue seems to be whether the amount of resources in money and skilled manpower, and the increased freedom of action accorded to investigators – access to bank accounts, requirements to answer questions under oath, etc. – is great enough. So much seems to be implied by the nature of the cases investigated, and the prosecutions which follow and make headlines. What are involved are, in the main, carefully planned, extended and often substantial frauds involving serious losses to customers, creditors, employees and the state, and sometimes involving great suffering for the victims, such as those who entrust their savings to crooked investment agencies or franchise operators. The only appropriation recourse for such obvious villains is criminal prosecution, expropriation of assets, and imprisonment.

It will be the contention of what follows that this is true, but, for a very large part of business crime, almost entirely beside the point. Pursuing business crime as fraud, through criminal prosecution, though appropriate for a minority of cases, is irrelevant and impossible for the majority. Furthermore, if criminal prosecution is pursued as the sole or even the principal means of control, it will fail to achieve anything more than public hysteria and expense, and the jailing of a few of the less lucky or competent villains. Apart from the limited deterrent effect of a vigorous prosecution policy, its weakness, to put the point at its most general, is that it makes no contribution to prevention.

This is not to say, however, that no provisions for the prevention and management of business crime exist, but rather that they receive only limited and rather fragmented publicity. By contrast, the object of what follows is to show by argument and illustration that a great deal of preventive work is already undertaken, and that a proper understanding of its nature may enable us, first, to understand business crime and the place of fraud and criminal prosecution in it more fully, and secondly, to build upon and improve methods and institutions for preventing and managing it.

The first step towards this understanding is terminological, though, as will become apparent later, not without wider implications. Fraud is unequivocally criminal: it involves theft by deceit and trickery. It follows, therefore, that criminal proceedings are inescapably appropriate. Business crime, however, in the sense in which it is used here, covers a much wider range of misconduct, which may be none the less damaging and otherwise undesirable from resulting from duress, incompetence, negligence, lack of training, lack of clarity in the rules, opportunism, technical infraction, or sheer muddle-headedness, rather than calculated deceit motivated by greed. Consider: if an insurance salesman sells you a life policy, he obtains (or his company obtains) a commission from the insurance company. If he sold you Policy A, whose terms were inferior, rather than Policy B, because Policy A earned more commission, you might claim that he had acted wrongly, but you might also merely regret not having sought advice from more than one source before signing up. As things currently stand, the salesman will now be likely to incur sanctions if he does not offer the best available product. He would not have done so in the past. But if, on the other hand, he sold you Policy A, which was worse, as it happened, for you, than either B or policy C, because he did not realize you could get special preferential terms as a non-smoking clergyman, for example, he would just be incompetent. He may indeed have done his level best for you within his knowledge, but you would be worse off still. Further, if you bought the policy from the sales representative of the insurance company with whom you already had a policy, taking advantage no doubt of his 'special offer', but failing to inquire more widely as to what the market had to offer, you would have only yourself to blame if you did not get the best policy available.

If, therefore, we consider not in the narrow terms of calculated theft, but in terms of the legitimate interests and expectations of the parties involved, what is permissible and what is impermissible, a rather different, and, it should be said, considerably more complex picture emerges. It will be this perspective that will inform this book: the legitimate interests of the parties involved in a business transaction; the limits of what is permissible; the responsibilities of each party to have regard to the interests of others whilst, of course, for that is the essence of business, pursuing his own; and the relation of these private parties' interests to those of the public at large, or of society, represented usually by the state and its specialized agencies. Fraud, from this point of view, constitutes one extreme of behaviour: the gross, deliberate oppression of all other interests in favour of one party. As such, it is scarcely likely to be the norm – business certainly could not continue if it were. It is of the nature of business, however, that the pursuit of self-interest is legitimate – profit and fair reward are inherent in it. The competition to which this gives rise between the parties in a business transaction, and between businesses, is not only the energizing force of capitalist societies, but very hard to eliminate in any society complex enough to have a business sector. This jockeying for position, however, necessarily takes place within a framework of rules, some legal, others written but not legal, others only social expectations. All of these rules are constantly debated and modified, usually in practice before formal change. The foundation of the argument based on this perspective is that this process of rule-making, which distinguishes and sanctions business crimes and misconduct, takes place in large part at the coal-face, within business itself, and only belatedly and relatively infrequently in the courts and in Parliament. The purpose of what follows is, then, to show that business crime is already largely managed by business itself, and that it is only by understanding how and why this is achieved, and its inevitability, that the nature of business crime can be understood, and its relationship with criminal investigation and sanction be put in proper context.

But enough of generalities. It is through its more specific characteristics that business crime and its sharp difference from conventional property crimes, such as burglary, robbery and car theft, can be understood. Once the main distinguishing features have been outlined, extended examples will be discussed of the way in which business crime is managed in different areas of the economy. This will allow us to return at the end to an informed review of the way in which the effectiveness of this management can be maximized, the balance of public and private interests secured, and the role of criminal proceedings clarified.

Matters of Definition

Before doing so however, the issue of the definition of business crime should be addressed directly. In a sense, the more detailed comments that follow on the characteristics of business crime are an extended definition, but there will no doubt be readers who require something more succinct. Two points which are part of a definition have so far been made about business crime. It is in the first place misconduct that takes place in a business environment. To this it might be added, by way of modification, that business crime is that which takes place in the course of legitimate business. It is, hence, to be distinguished from the activities of criminal syndicates, which at times adopt the appearances of legitimate business for enterprises that are wholly criminal. Thus the use of pizza parlours as a front for the distribution of heroin would fall beyond business crime into conventional crime. This aspect of the definition cannot be precise in all cases however: human conduct is too diverse and inventive. Criminal syndicates have, for example, dominated refuse-collection contracts in some American cities. They have used their coercive powers to overcharge for the contracts, but they have not necessarily failed to provide the service contracted for on a businesslike basis. Similarly, long firm frauds have at times been established by criminals with the sole purpose of defrauding creditors, but there are other cases where businessmen decide to run up their credit when they realize their business is about to fail, and others still in which criminals approach ailing businesses with offers of financial aid and then operate them for a credit fraud.[10]

So what really matters here? What matters in business crime is the extent to which the business context structures the opportunities for misconduct and the ways in which misconduct is dealt with. A key feature of business crime is the legitimate opportunity it provides for exploitation and the key consequence of this is the contestability of the offence. Take an example of apparent theft. Two men approach industrial premises in the early hours of the morning in a large empty lorry. They cut the locks on the gates and on the warehouse and proceed to select goods which they load into the lorry. The police are called and the men stand their ground. They claim they have committed no offence as the goods are theirs, because they were supplied on credit to the business, which is now in liquidation. As chapter 7 (on liquidation) shows, this kind of incident is by no means unusual, and the police response is to call the liquidator and suggest a civil resolution to the problem, though they may of course contemplate prosecution for breaking and entering.

If the first aspect of the definition of business crime is that it is misconduct that takes place within a predominantly legitimate business environment, the second is then that this environment provides business crime with a contestable character. In so far as the business context can be used to debate the legitimacy of the conduct in question and is not readily denounceable as a cover for conventional crime, a contest will ensue about the degree to which the conduct is to be categorized formally as an abuse and about the appropriate mode of sanction. As was remarked above, criminal categorization and sanction is only one mode, involving a small proportion of the misconduct included in business crime. There are many other modes of sanction, formal and informal, including the use of the civil law, the actions of professional bodies and trade associations, management decisions to dismiss or otherwise sanction employees, votes of boards of directors to expel their colleagues, and recourse to the media to make damaging allegations.

In the case of business crime, therefore, it is not merely criminal behaviour that is at issue but the wider anathematization of misconduct by a variety of routes, all of which necessarily involve the mobilization of resources and most of which will be resisted.[11] Put in a slightly different way, it is a process of labelling conduct as deviant.

The view presented here hence has its origins in the insights of the symbolic interactionist approach to the sociology of deviance. It differs from that body of research and theorizing, however, as a result of its focus on subject matter which was, curiously, never considered by the labelling school. The symbolic interactionist studies of deviants were concerned typically not merely with conventional crimes, but with those committed by the weakest and most vulnerable in the population, where stigmatization was straightforward for the criminal justice process and its agents. Thus the burden of their message was the demonstration of the selection of the incompetent for criminal sanction and the co-ordination of various agencies – police, courts, social work and probation agencies and others – to this end. Implicit was the suggestion that the competent conventional criminals – rarely studied incidentally – usually escape sanction, and that the relatively powerful, competent and socially respectable in society almost invariably do so. Sympathy for the underdog and the class bias of criminal justice were the reigning moral ideas.[12]

A principal objective of the present work is to show that business crime is covered by sanctions, but predominantly not by criminal ones, and indeed that the criminal justice approach is largely inappropriate and ineffective. Thus the labelling theorists were correct in their insinuations that middle- and upper-class deviants largely escaped criminal sanction, but not in their conclusion that they therefore escape all sanction. They were also correct in pointing to the privileges enjoyed by business offenders in resisting stigmatization: legitimate business does provide the resources to contest allegations that conduct is wrong and to resist sanctions. The process of interaction for many business offences is hence not merely founded upon much more diverse institutions including those of business itself and specialized regulatory bodies, rather than a monolithic criminal justice system; it is also, in many cases, a much more open contest. Business crime involves a political struggle over labels and sanctions, where the odds are not stacked in favour of the stigmatizers, but this does not mean that a more open contest results in no sanctions being applied.

The Characteristics of Business Crime

Privacy

The most consequential feature of business crime is the private context in which business crimes are committed. This is true almost as much of organizations in the public sector, such as schools and hospitals, as it is of private-sector business. The differences lie in the service ethic which predominates in the public sector, as against the profit orientation of the private, and in the greater penetration of public-sector organizations by oversight and funding agencies in the state hierarchy – area health authorities, local education authorities, and beyond them the relevant government ministries. Private businesses are subject to the shareholders and non-executive directors in the case of companies with shares held by the public, neither of which groups have easy access to the detail of the companies' activities, and are easily deceived, not so much by the refusal of relevant information as by not knowing the pertinent questions to ask. Both companies with public shareholders and those where shares are held privately are subject to audit by external accountants, but, as a number of decisive court cases have shown, auditors are not required as part of their inquiries into whether the company's accounts constitute a true and fair view of the company's affairs, to ensure that they check for possible malpractices; and accountants who ask awkward questions and provoke embarrassing cover-ups may not be engaged for the following year's audit.

The principal points about privacy for present purposes – others will emerge later – are first, that members of business organizations are protected from detection by the veil of privacy. This is formally and legally the case in respect of the limited company form, which is designed to protect commercial confidentiality and not to give information away to competitors. But privacy is also inherent in the relatively complex and specialized work and context of the organization. The minutely organized, bureaucratized division of labour which characterizes modern business renders its activities opaque to outsiders, even outsiders to the section, unit, office or division within a large organization, who measure its success and probity by its inputs and outputs, not by a detailed scrutiny of its working routines. It is thus only too easy for individuals or groups within an organization to shield misconduct from prying eyes and to manipulate outputs so that all appears to be normal.

Secondly, therefore, privacy means that business offenders are legitimately present at the scene. Offences consist of violations of the trust implicit in them as officers of the organization and exploitation of the resources of the organization for personal gain. The scope for such exploitation and the ease with which it can be covered up vary partly because of chance aspects of organizational structure – individuals or groups may happen to find themselves in a position in the organization where it is particularly easy to steal organizational property or funds, where others, located elsewhere, would find this very difficult. More systematically, however, opportunities vary with discretion, autonomy, and access to a range of organizational resources, and these of course increase as one ascends the organizational hierarchy. Delivery drivers, for example, may be able physically to divert goods from their vehicles, but will probably need the co-operation of the warehousing and despatch departments to reconcile the necessary paperwork. Similarly, clerks in accounts departments may have no difficulty making use of company telephones, postage and photocopying, but, although dealing with company cheques, receipts and invoices, may find it very hard to embezzle without a collective effort. The accounts manager, by contrast, has less need to communicate such misdeeds to others, and much greater discretion, and probably also has the knowledge of the company and the expertise in accounting necessary to enable him to embezzle company funds and to manage the paperwork to disguise the fact.

This disguise of even serious offences can continue successfully for long periods and, no doubt in some cases, especially where the misconduct ceases undetected, offences are never discovered. The chief executive of the Grays Building Society was discovered in 1978 to have embezzled £2 million over a period of 40 years, successfully deceiving the auditors, with whom he enjoyed a good relationship, and his staff, by always making up the books himself, sometimes working late to do so. He was discovered only because the auditors were changed on the retirement of the accountant after 27 years.[13] Similarly the chief accountant at Pitman's Secretarial College admitted in 1987 to stealing £1.4 million over twenty years, at a rate in later years of £50,000 per annum, mostly in cash fees paid by students. He was discovered only as a result of a company reorganization and special audit, in the course of which he was made redundant.[14]

Unlike conventional crimes, such as burglary and robbery, therefore, in the case of business crime there is not necessarily an immediate complainant. Those whose interests have been damaged may not be aware of it, or, as in the case of shops which write off stock losses through shoplifting, staff theft and accidental damage under the one heading 'stock shrinkage', not fully aware of it. Business crime is certainly not victimless, but the principal objective of the offender is to prevent the victim recognizing the loss. For, in the case of business crime, it is the offence which is difficult to discover because it is hidden by the normality of the organization's functioning and by the legitimacy of the offender's presence in the organization. Of course, some major offences emerge because their extent is so great as to cause the financial breakdown of the organization. Once the offence is uncovered, however, it is usually relatively simple to establish who committed it or at least colluded in it, as a result of checks back on individuals' actions and responsibilities. This is the reverse of the case of conventional crime, where the householder who is burgled is immediately aware of the fact of the loss but finds it extremely difficult to detect the offender precisely because he had no legitimate access to the premises.

Lack of Public Order Violation

A consequence of this is that public order is not violated in business offences as it is in conventional crime. There is normally no violence to persons or property, and the conduct in question takes place in private not public places, between people with a pre-existing and usually continuing relationship, not between strangers. This in part accounts for the much less threatening character of business offences: not only do they not involve violence, but they become possible at all only if citizens enter into a situation where they can be deceived and defrauded. Whilst there is a substantial contemporary debate on the citizen's reasonable expectations, on which more below, there is also some expectation of caution and self-protective measures against deceit. Trust is necessary between employer and employee, businessman and customer, creditor and debtor, but trust has to be established, not merely taken for granted.

This explains the relatively limited interest of the police in business crime. Its privacy and complexity make it difficult to investigate; the pre-existing relationships between victim and offender make for the likelihood of claim and counter-claim as to who occupies which role; and in many cases the police may take the view that their victims have only themselves to blame for their lack of caution, or have the necessary resources to remedy the situation by civil action. Indeed, in legal terms, the whole field of business crime is beset by ambiguity as to whether offences are to be dealt with by the criminal or the civil route. Disputes between private parties are normally dealt with through civil litigation, and the public authorities are often reluctant to act, even where a criminal offence has clearly been committed, if matters can be settled privately. As the chapters illustrating practice in a variety of areas of business crime will show, there is a strong tendency for matters to be dealt with privately, and thus for the question whether the misconduct was criminal never to be formally raised. This is reflected in the disposition of manpower in the police forces: about 5 per cent of detective manpower and 0.5 per cent of overall police personnel nationally, totalling 588 police in the UK, were allocated to the fraud squads in 1987. The police see their primary responsibility as the maintenance of order in the public realm, and the pursuit of conventional crimes which violate it as well as damaging the interests of private citizens. In addition, the police and other public agencies can normally gain access to premises to pursue inquiries only where they have reasonable grounds to suspect that a criminal offence has taken place. Restraints upon the power of public authorities in a liberal democracy act to protect the accessibility of private domains.

As will become clear below, however, this tendency for business crime to be dealt with privately and often non-legally is not a matter for alarm but rather an inevitable outcome of its character. Certainly it is much more effective and flexible in coping with what are in most cases quite ambiguous patterns of conduct. Research, even on embezzlers, the most obviously criminal of business offenders, suggests a pattern not of calculated villainy but of opportunism, financial stress, and at times an intention to repay embezzled money well before being stimulated to do so by detection. In many other areas the issue is precisely: Has an offence been committed, or is it at worst error or misunderstanding, or more often a loss that the victim must accept as legitimate, as 'just business'?

Internal Detection and Control

It is evident from the foregoing that the detection and control of business crime is primarily, and at least in the first instance, internal to the organization, and hence private. It is up to those with a direct interest in the business to decide how much effort they devote to ensuring that probity is maintained and wrong doing is detected and sanctioned, and as to how they define wrongdoing: does it include arriving five minutes late for work, using company phones to call home, or giving lifts to friends in company vehicles for example? When misconduct is detected or suspected, however, the mobilization of resources to deal with it internally is potentially very great. Here the privacy, enclosure, and the official allocation of tasks of the business environment act to the advantage of control. The existence of rules and routines, of task responsibilities and specialized competencies, of authority clearly delimited, and of extensive record-keeping and accounting makes the tracing of misconduct and its pinning down to individuals possible in a way that is immensely difficult in the case of conventional crimes. Membership of the organization requires the constant generation of evidence of activities in discharging job responsibilities, evidence that has as its counterpart the meagre traces left to scene-of-crime officers in conventional offences, which only in the fictional cases of such as Sherlock Holmes routinely provide anything like a substantial lead to the offender.

This advantage to internal control once suspicion is aroused is further enhanced by the range of sanctions available. Ideally proof and confession, and hence the introduction of effective remedies against repetition, are desirable, but even suspicion that is not cleared can be followed by, for example, the transfer of individuals to other duties, or a simple failure to promote them. Suspicions which are confirmed can be sanctioned not only by dismissal, but by demotion, involving of course recurrent loss of pay, and at worst perhaps by public exposure outside the organization, involving loss of occupational standing. In the case of professionals this may include loss of professional accreditation, but for all employees dismissal for specified misconduct will make re-employment in any position of trust very difficult. All of this is at the discretion of the organization, and its procedures for implementing investigation and imposing sanctions, while subject to the powers of the trade unions and to legislation such as the Employment Protection Acts, usually combine the formal and the informal. The scope for the control of the employee if the organization wishes to exercise that control is hence very great, and the great majority of misconduct in organizations is dealt with in this way, by procedures ranging from a reprimand from an immediate superior to formal inquiry and arraignment before a special disciplinary panel.

The position of the employee is hence very much weaker than that of the employer. Where the employer engages in abuses, his staff have to organize strongly if their interests are affected, and may still find it difficult both to gain access to information essential to proof of misconduct, and to resist selective or even collective dismissal. Outside interests such as customers, creditors and the Inland Revenue may find all the privileges of private enterprise deployed to frustrate them: information is refused, lies are told, meetings postponed, correspondence unanswered, worthless promises made and managing directors become inaccessible. One enters what might be called Checkpoint country where Roger Cook in his radio days thrust a microphone under the noses of recalcitrant businessmen 'to record an interview with you now to answer questions from a number of customers about your management of X Ltd'.[15]

The Limited Role of the Law

The obvious recourse of those suffering from recalcitrant and fraudulent businessmen is to the public domain of the law, usually by suing for damages or bankruptcy, or by calling on the Department of Trade to investigate the affairs of the company. As has already been remarked, the police are by no means always ready or able to act, and usually do so only if clear evidence of a criminal offence is presented to them, or where the number of complaints becomes substantial. The victims, however, are caught in a dilemma. The law is slow, uncertain, and expensive; worse still, at the end of the day its use may well have the effect of closing down the business, leaving little behind but debts. This may be in the public interest in not ensnaring any more people as victims, but it does nothing to secure the interests of existing victims in recovering their money, whether this consists in repayment of the debt, the provision of goods not supplied, or supplied but defective, or in continuity of employment. There is therefore a powerful incentive for the victim to keep matters in the private realm, and to attempt to negotiate a solution. In practice recourse to the law and the public agencies is usually indicative of despair and a thirst for vengeance on the part of the victims. It is hence in the interests of the offender to continue negotiations for as long as possible by making offers, promises and part-payments.

This set of incentives is not confined to the victims of a recalcitrant company. The employer is in a similar position in relation to his employee. Not only does he want his money back, he also wants to know how the trick was pulled, to try to ensure that it does not happen again. He may therefore negotiate extensively with the employee about disclosure and reparation, and agree not to call in the police. He may even agree not to dismiss the employee, and to give him a good reference when he leaves, both as part of the bargain, and in order to avoid potential damage to the public reputation of the organization.

The private and the informal hence tend to prevail over the public and the formal, even arguably at the expense of the public interest in protecting others from the depredations of rapacious employees and businessmen, and in having criminals brought to justice as a deterrent example to others. Any effective strategy of control of business crime must take this into account. This is a matter to which we shall return in the conclusion.

The Ambiguity of Business Crime

A point which has already been alluded to but needs stating more fully is the ambiguity of business crime, which ranges from calculated and single-minded fraud to hotly debated misconduct. It includes, as has been remarked, losses consequent upon incompetence, naïvety and negligence, as well as deliberate misappropriation; and misappropriation itself may be opportunist or pressured, as well as sheer, cold theft. The most comprehensive study to date of the most classically criminal of frauds, the long firm credit fraud, in which the perpetrator builds up his creditworthiness with prompt payments for a time, and then takes as much credit as he can obtain before disappearing, shows that a substantial proportion were not the unaided efforts of habitual criminals. Some cases, it is true, involve criminals financing 'front men' to set up businesses with the sole objective of building up credit and then maximizing the fraud on suppliers. Many, however, involve businessmen who have fallen on hard times and who, despairing at last of ever recovering – a corner shop squeezed out of the market by the arrival of a supermarket for example – decide that years of honest trading deserve some substantial reward, and decide to go bankrupt for a large amount rather than a small one. Sometimes too, professional criminals prey upon such businesses by offering loans to get them through a difficult period, and then take over the business and use the proprietor as a 'front man'.

The ambiguities of business crime extend also to the corner-cutting and sharp practice from which almost no great modern business organization and business tycoon has been free at some point in their careers. Doubts and complexities here are legion. If your competitor does not realize the weakness of his position, is it your job to inform him? Is it illegitimate to obtain contracts by offering lavish entertainment to clients and key personnel? In some circumstances this may fall foul of the Corrupt Practices Acts in others not. Goods ordered are not available and others are supplied in their stead. How does this affect the contract in respect of quality, performance and price? Are professional services to be charged at their cost plus a reasonable rate per hour, or at whatever the client can be persuaded to pay, and at what stage does this constitute fraudulent misrepresentation?

One has also to recognize the readiness of a very large sector of the public to collude in or connive at some illegal and underhand practices. Who voluntarily insists on paying VAT when they have their car serviced, their plumbing fixed or their windows repaired? Who will refuse the offer of a friend to run off some photocopies on the office machine, or do some calculations on the office computer? Who will resist the offer of the company van to move furniture or other heavy goods, or the offer of a load or 'cheap' tarmac to improve their drive? Recent careful research has concluded that the best estimate of the size of the black economy is about 3–5 per cent GDP.[16] Although less than many more publicized claims, this is a very substantial sum, and more importantly it involves the acceptance by very large numbers of people of failure to pay taxes, purchase of stolen goods, and misappropriation of company goods, services, specialized machines, vehicles, time and expertise, since the same research showed that few in the black economy make more than a little money from it.

Behind this widespread collusion in impropriety and misappropriation lies a powerful ideology, the strong form of which asserts that only a mug pays the full price for anything. Anyone with self-respect knows someone who can get it cheap. In its weak form this ideology becomes the bargain-hunting of the citizen consumer, encouraged by special offers, sales, discount warehouses, free credit offers and the like, always to seek maximum value for money. This view implies that goods and services have no value calculable in relation to the costs of their production and supply, and that their price is determined by the battle of wits between the businessman, ever eager to extract an extortionate profit, and the consumer, always wanting something for nothing.

Within business the complexity and rapid rates of change in many areas result in accepted rules and practices being constantly outdated, and the businessman is left to determine what is fair, what is good practice, what is taking advantage, and what is a rip-off. Of course it remains true that the businessman who carefully reflects on a regular basis whether the interests of all parties with whom he is involved, customers, creditors, suppliers and employees, are being fully respected will, mistakes and confusions apart, come up with acceptable answers and practices. But people in business are often under pressure, are close to their job and not privileged to stand back and contemplate, and are preoccupied with active trading and making ends meet (a profit). Innovation, ingenuity, and new angles, and profit based on them, are rewarded not just financially, but by expansion and social esteem. Profit and competitive ability is the name of the game, and financial success is a demonstration of virtue in the market-place. This business ideology is of course tempered by respect for giving value for money, but where the product, the service, the means of delivery or the market niche are new, what constitutes value for money? The role of the market is that competitive supply will pare down excessive profits, but everyone knows that most markets today are imperfect, and even perfect ones take time to perform their equilibrating function.

The ambiguity of business crime is hence profound and pervasive, and furthermore there is no prospect of eliminating it. Whether it can be tempered or reduced is a matter to which we shall return in the conclusion, but it seems safe to say at this point that debate about how acceptable conduct is to be distinguished from unacceptable must be informed by the practice and practitioners of business itself.

Business Offences as Politics

It follows from this that business crimes have an essentially contested character. They are basically political offences, not in the parliamentary sense of the term, but in that they involve the mobilization of power to make the accusation of wrongdoing stick. Where conventional crimes are self-evidently so, business crimes, as has been outlined above, have to be shown to be crimes and not something else. The compilation of evidence and successful denunciation require the mobilization of sufficient powerful interests to overcome the offender, who will naturally secrete or destroy damning evidence, interpret his actions as legitimate (if perhaps mistaken), and counter-claim malevolence on the part of his accusers. Because he is inside the organization and may remain close to the scene of the offence, he has maximum opportunity to resist exposure, and he will of course mobilize the support of friends and colleagues if possible. Above all it is difficult to prove *mens rea* (malign intent) in business offences, even though the evidence of the records may easily show wrongful conduct. It is hard for the surprised burglar to explain forced entry, but the business, offender is in the reverse position, and will use it to deny, not that he was the offender, but that the offence was an offence. Even the embezzling employee may deny theft, on the grounds that it was only a loan that he intended to repay. No burglar can credibly make such a claim; the employee's may be doubtful but not necessarily entirely so.

Political mobilization may also be evident in a cruder fashion. In the employer–employee relationship, the employee may use his trade union and workplace solidarity to protect himself and bargaining may ensue, not about the nature of the offence, but about the extent of sanctions, with an industrial dispute threatened if he is dismissed, but perhaps a readiness to accept his transfer within the organization. Where accusations occur further up the organizational hierarchy, office politics will come into play, with friendships, unrepaid obligations and old scores featuring in the struggle to control evidence and muster support and testimony.

If the issue enters the public realm as a result of claims by customers or creditors of an organization, or allegations between businesses, or between businesses and the state, the political character of the struggle becomes more immediately obvious. Just as civil litigation involves claim and counter-claim, proof of documents introduced in evidence, and contests as to the facts at every stage, so the Inland Revenue, for example, will attack a reluctant taxpayer with demands for proof, un-willingness to accept claims on trust, and heavy assessments requiring disproof, to be countered with a welter of receipts, calculations and accountants' opinions. Bankruptcy and receivership follow a similar pattern of examination of evidence, or at any rate such evidence as the individual or organization has left behind for officials to seize and scrutinize, accompanied by vigorous and extensive cross-examination, one side attempting to disclaim debts, liabilities and dishonesty, the other to establish them. Into this process intervene professional advisers of various kinds, offering expertise on how to attack and resist, particularly lawyers and accountants. This struggle is frequently a protracted one, culminating, many conclude, in little more than a good living for the officials and professionals involved.

Finally, when accusations reach their most public, they become political in the conventional sense of headline news and ministerial intervention. The Guinness affair will be discussed in a more appropriate context later, but the political embarrassment of the scandal over alleged improprieties, and the illegitimate tactics in Guinness's hotly contested takeover of Distillers, were painfully evident in the context of the preceding years of the reform of City regulation, with ministers expressing determination to 'get the handcuffs on the culprits' at Guinness before the 1987 general election. To cite another example, the investigation by *The Sunday Times* in 1983[17] of the operation of doctors' deputizing services in south-east England led to a conflict between the paper, the medical profession and the Ministry of Health. The paper claimed that the deputizing services were being used for all weekend and evening visits by some doctors, and that some of the services were seriously defective, resulting in deaths which clearly should have been prevented. In the debate which followed, the BMA stoutly defended the right of doctors to use deputizing services, though there was wide support for improvements in the quality of care offered by some services. The Ministry of Health resisted the wholesale use of deputizing services, and claimed that GPs should do at least some weekend and evening visits themselves. What was at issue was on the one hand the maintenance of standards of health care, and on the other attempts by GPs to improve their working conditions by increasing their free time. Such improvements might have been negotiated through the normal channels and provision made in doing so for the enforcement of minimum standards in deputizing services. What actually took place was an extended public political row, and a number of unnecessary deaths, resulting in damage to the reputation of the medical profession.

Sanctions

It should be evident from the above and from earlier remarks that the sanctions imposed at the end and in the course of the struggle over business offences are of a much greater diversity than those under criminal law. Those which the offending employee risks have already been referred to, and the preceding point adds to that the odium and embarrassment of more or less public political debate and discredit. To this must be added the possibilities of civil litigation and damages awards and legal costs, personal bankruptcy and its attendant disabilities, disqualification from pursuing a profession or from acting as an officer or director of a company, and, under the regime envisaged under the 1986 Financial Services Act, disqualification from pursuing many careers in the financial sector. There may also be spin-off effects in terms of indebtedness, forced sale of assets including homes, and loss of position in the local community, for example as a magistrate, a member of the Rotary Club and so on. These features of 'public disgrace' are sometimes cited in litigation where criminal conviction is also involved. There is little rational measure in the way in which such sanctions apply once business offences or allegations of them move from the private to the public domain. One of the difficulties as things presently stand is that it may be argued that too much remains for private negotiation between directly interested parties or some of them to the exclusion of the public interest, yet when cases do become public, the lust of the media for scurrilous and titillating information can give credit to wild and irrelevant allegations. Whilst it might be said that there is at present no control on 'trial by the mass media' it should be recognized, however, that it is the few cases which give rise to media scandals which are often of greatest importance in clarifying standards of business conduct.[18] And it may also be observed that those at the centre of such scandals are frequently not without resources, personal, financial and political, with which to defend themselves.

Consumerism and Business Accountability

As has been implicit in what has been said above, business crime and its control is also political in a wider sense, inasmuch as societies take a greater or lesser interest in it, and may vary from detailed regulations and specialized enforcement by state intervention or sponsorship of self-regulation, to detached *laissez-faire*. The historical trend throughout the course of industrialization has been towards greater regulation, and this has expanded markedly in the post-war years, particularly from the 1960s, in most western industrialized societies. In the past three decades the state, not only in Britain but in the United States, France, Germany and other countries, has made repeated efforts to improve the probity of business by increasing legal responsibilities and criminal penalties, increasing specialized investigation and enforcement personnel, establishing special courts (though not quite yet in Britain), and sponsoring more effective efforts at self-regulation by various sectors of business. The largest recent effort in Britain is evident in the regulation of financial institutions, through the Securities and Investments Board, responsible to the Secretary of State for Trade and Industry, which supervises the newly emergent Self-Regulatory Organizations representing practitioners in the various specialized sectors of unit trusts, insurance, securities and so on, with the latter responsible for the detail of the enforcement and improvement of rules and of standards of conduct. The state-funded Office of Fair Trading also acts as a powerful stimulant to improve business practice and self-regulation, investigating sector after sector where poor standards have in the past been endemic – garage services, home improvements and double-glazing for example. The object in each case is to goad the relevant trade association into stricter policing of its membership, to improve public recognition of the trade association as a body whose membership implies reliability, and the agreement by it of minimum standards of service, a code of conduct and a complaints procedure. Sometimes particular publicized failings in a sector will have a similar result. The failure of various travel companies, leaving passengers stranded in the early 1970s for example, stimulated the Association of British Travel Agents to work collectively to ensure that in future this would not be allowed to happen.

The objective of these developments is plain: it is to ensure that the consuming public can depend upon the probity, competence, reliability and safety of goods and services supplied by business without the need for detailed prior checking. The onus has shifted markedly from the nineteenth century, when the phrase enjoining consumer caution, *caveat emptor*, predominated in trade. What is on offer in the market now is presumed in many cases to be beyond the capacities of the average citizen to check in a reasonable time for quality, reliability and so on. More widely, the mass consumer economy of the post-war world relies for its success upon the new army of affluent citizens buying goods and services –

consumer durables, off-the-peg clothes, holidays, insurance and, these days, stocks and shares – which in the past were either not available or which they could not afford. As the size of this group in the population has grown, so has its voting power, and no government today can afford to ignore it. Indeed, recognition of the vital importance, both economically and politically, of continuing efforts to protect consumers by demanding higher standards from business has become one of the few unquestioned elements of all-party consensus in British politics. While scepticism about the existence of scruples and widespread honesty in business, and a belief in the corrosive effects of the profit motive has always been characteristic of the left, the right-wing administration of the Thatcher years has displayed an active concern for the stimulation and enforcement of better standards of business conduct in the explicit recognition that socialism cannot be finally defeated until the majority of the population feel able to trust business, and the private enterprise system has shown itself to be reliably civilized.

Private Interest versus the Public Good

Underlying this concern with the control of business crime lies a tension fundamental in all societies, but particularly characteristic of modern western industrialized democracies: between private self-interest pursued through the institutions of business, and the service ethic of the public good, of fairness and distributive justice, developed in Britain by the civil service after the reforms of the latter part of the nineteenth century, and further developed and expanded by the welfare state. The danger of unfettered private enterprise is that it degenerates into greed, ruthlessness and deceit, to the oppression of the interests of those insufficiently cunning, skilled, wealthy or powerful to protect themselves, and so polarizes the haves from the have-nots. The danger of the service ethic and of distributive justice is that if applied to all institutions of society it imposes minimum standards but at an ever-increasing cost, whilst also stifling initiative with bureaucracy, restrictive practices and heavy taxation. This is not a problem that can ever be resolved. Much of political debate will continue to concern the relative balance of advantage to be given by government policy to each alternative. Whilst the demands for cost-cutting, measured efficiency and the elimination of waste constitute the assault by a business ideology upon the public sector, efforts to ensure higher standards of business conduct through regulation and public debate constitute an attempt to render business more compatible with the ideals of the service ethic.

The Problem of Typologies

The chapters which follow have been deliberately described as examples, and the point has been made that they are intended to be illustrative of business crime in different areas rather than exhaustive. It may seem tempting at this stage to set up a typology of business crime which does claim to be exhaustive and then provide illustrations of each type. Such an approach has been attempted by some writers and is useful for presentational purposes, but no typology so far suggested has proved definitive.[19]

The appeal of typologies is that they divide the field, in this case a very large and diverse one, into workable units. The difficulty is that by cutting the cake in one way, other categorizations of equal merit are precluded. Thus there are obvious differences between corporate crime and employee crime, and between crimes of large corporations committed on behalf of the corporation – price fixing, pollution, unsafe working practices and so on – and crimes committed by smaller businesses on behalf of the proprietor. There are also other categorizations that cross-cut such distinctions – computer crimes for example, or corruption, or abuse of state funds by professionals such as doctors and lawyers, or the abuse of state contracting. All of these may be important issues in business crime worthy of particular study, but they are phenomena thrown up by the development of business. It may be that when the field of business crime is more adequately theorized than it is at present, they can be included in an overarching typology, but at present this is not possible.

As things stand, the imposition of the typology may serve presentational ends, but actively vitiate heuristical ones. For the intellectual purpose of typologies is to identify categories that deepen overall understanding of the field and to isolate major components which have a long-term and substantial impact on the way in which things work. Typologies form the groundwork for the development of models. To present the issues and empirical groupings which business crime presents to the investigator in the present state of knowledge as a typology is to give them an intellectual pre-eminence which they do not merit.

There are also wider grounds for caution here which have already been referred to in chapter 1. Although business, particularly in the western industrialized world, is increasingly international and integrated, there are still substantial differences between nation states in the way in which business is conducted and in the institutions through which it is conducted. To take two examples, corruption is, for historical and structural reasons, a much more entrenched and substantial problem in the United States than in Britain; similarly, a health service financed through taxes and free at the point of delivery, as in Britain, affords fewer opportunities for abuse than a privately based system such as that in the United States. A successful typology will hence need to be based upon a reasonably adequate account of business as part of the national and international political economies, which will be able to identify why and how the phenomena which emerge as issues in business crime arise. Despite the best efforts of economists of all persuasions and of political scientists, we are still a long way from this comprehensive understanding, though not without insights at particular junctures. Where appropriate and possible in the chapters that follow those insights will be explored.

NOTES

1 I am grateful to Jack Heslop for this example. See his paper 'International Maritime Fraud' presented to the Conference on Fraud and Corruption, Liverpool University, 1987.

2 See for example B. Woodward and C. Bernstein, *All The President's Men*, Simon and Schuster, 1974.

3 A brief account is available in J. Hougan, 'The Business of Buying Friends' in J. M. Johnson and J. D. Douglas (eds), *Crime at the Top*, Lippincott, 1978.

4 For a well informed account of the Nevada gambling industry see J. Skolnick, *House of Cards*, Little, Brown, 1978.

5 See H. Edelhertz and C. Rogovin, *A National Strategy for Containing White-Collar Crime*, D. C. Heath, 1980; J. Katz, 'he Social Movement Against White-Collar Crime', *Criminology Review Yearbook*, 1980, pp. 161–84.

6 A number of these developments are described in M. J. Clarke, *Regulating the City*, Open University Press, 1986.

7 *Report of the Fraud Trials Committee* (Chairman Lord Roskill), HMSO, 1986.

8 *The Times*, 27 July and 1 August 1987.

9 These and related matters are detailed in M. Levi, *Regulating Fraud*, Tavistock Press, 1987.

10 See M. Levi, *The Phantom Capitalists*, Gower Press, 1981.

11 For further comments on this point see M. J. Clarke, *Fallen Idols: Elites and the Search for the Acceptable Face of Capitalism*, Junction Books, 1981, chapter 1.

12 The key work of the symbolic interactionists or labelling theorists of deviants is generally taken to be H. S. Becker, *Outsiders*, Free Press, 1964. A good account of the theory is to be found in N. C. Davis, *Sociological Constructions of Deviance*, W. C. Brown and Co., 1975.

13 See *The Daily Telegraph*, 18 August 1979.

14 See *The Times*, 25 July 1987.

15 See J. Wilson, *Roger Cook's Checkpoint*, Ariel Books, 1983.

16 S. Smith, *Britain's Shadow Economy*, Clarendon Press, 1986.

17 The story ran in a large number of issues *The Sunday Times* from 1 June 1983 to 27 July 1984.

18 These matters are taken up at greater length in M. J. Clarke, *Fallen Idols*.

19 Compare M. D. Ermann and R. J. Lundman, *Corporate Deviance*, Holt, Rinehart and Winston, 1982, which, as the title suggests, concentrates on misconduct by big business and subdivides this into the categories: deviance against owners, deviance against employees, deviance against customers, and deviance against the public at large. Contrast this with M. Comer, *Corporate Fraud*, McGraw-Hill, 1977, which provides a very complex categorization based on types of fraud, that is, modus operandi – useful no doubt to the security expert and to the businessman comtemplating what kind of specific frauds his business is vulnerable to. Another way of categorizing business

crime is in terms of sanctions and the routes to them. Some comments on this are made in M. J. Clarke, *Fallen Idols*.

PART II

Empirical Studies of Business Crime

4 Employee Crime and Industrial Relations: Disputed Definitions

One substantial group of business offences is those committed by employees. This chapter argues that employee offences frequently become involved in industrial relations, and that there is invariably scope for management, or the employer, to resolve matters internally, and frequently a strong case for doing so. It follows that cases processed through the courts, some of which receive media attention, are somewhat unusual, and it is these that are considered first. The employer's interest in and capacity for internal resolution of employee offences are then explored, leading to a consideration of the implications of patterns of industrial relations and the labour contract for employee crime. There is a quite substantial literature which investigates pilfering and fiddles by workers, particularly those in marginal jobs with poor contracts and working conditions. Their situation is contrasted with that of workers in modern industries where tolerance of pilfering is much less, industrial discipline tighter and wages, conditions and fringe benefits considerably better.

None the less, the importance of workplace cultures and their interaction with working-class culture is inescapable in its impact on employee acceptance of workplace theft and fiddles. This point is confirmed by a comparison with some studies in the United States, which also reinforce the importance of management sensitivity to employees' attitudes and experiences of work in stimulating or restraining abuses.

The position of the middle-class employee is clearly different in class culture, in discretion over organizational resources and in the range and size of fringe benefits available, and in senior management's efforts to promote his or her loyalty to and identification with the organization. It is hence easier for the more senior employee to get away with fiddles which might be detected and sanctioned among blue-collar employees, and many benefits can, in any case, be legitimately aspired to.

This discussion leads to a consideration of the possibilities for the control of employee crime. Here it is maintained that a practical recognition by management of the opportunities for misconduct, even among a known loyal workforce, is vital. Awareness of the vulnerable points in an organization and agreed measures to prevent their exploitation are essential to the successful prevention of employee crime, which, if it is allowed to become at all significant, can have serious consequences for efficiency and industrial relations, besides the direct losses involved. Overall, employee crime appears as a widespread potential problem which has to be negotiated within the organization.

The Public Image of Employee Crime

Take two examples of employee crime as reported in the press. In the first, 'Lovers' one million pounds computer swindle', a couple having an affair who worked for the same company stole £1,125,000 by using bogus cheques and dummy companies.[1] The man was a management accountant at the victim company. The couple then paid off the mortgages on their houses and paid £25,000 into the bank accounts of the spouses they were about to abandon. They were caught when the man's wife opened his bank statement and rang his employers after finding out the size of his balance.

In the second case a solicitor's clerk awarded himself mortgages under false names, stole from clients' accounts and speculated on the property market.[2] In two years £1.5 million was involved, the man being exposed after the solicitor's practice computerized their accounting system. The clerk in question pleaded guilty to 21 charges, including 35 properties, two property companies and 13 bank acounts; £1 million was recovered. Significantly, however, the police also expected to charge six to ten solicitors, estate agents and building society managers.

How typical of employee crime are these cases? Certainly a considerable number of similar reports could be compiled from a review of the press, and there are substantial continuities over the years. Cases are described in human-interest terms, concentrating on the circumstances and motivation of the offender, who is variously described as living in a fantasy world, living the high life, or a double life. The love theme in the first case above was clearly an added attraction of the story as news. In the second case the sheer extent of the amount involved, given the offender's lowly status as a clerk, was the headline ('Solicitor's Clerk Defrauded £1.5m . . .') together with the trailer of further cases involving more senior professional people to come. In fact this was one of the earlier reports of what became in the later 1980s a substantial crime story, mortgage fraud, of which more later. The point for the present is that cases receiving media (almost always press) publicity are in most respects unusual, first in having involved criminal prosecution, and second in being selected for a press write-up.

Crime reporters maintain close contacts with the courts and the police, on which they rely to obtain information as to the most interesting stories.[3] Most cases of employee theft that are prosecuted will have little news value: the sums involved are too small, the character of the offender too colourless, the facts of the case too bald. The first point to be recognized is hence that publicized cases are unusual, either in the relatively large amounts involved, or in the circumstances of the offenders. What is reported reflects the interest of the newspaper in running a good story, that is, one which will engage its readers' attention, rather than endeavouring to reflect the nature of the offences usually prosecuted. Just as burglaries are rarely reported unless they involve large amounts or unusual circumstances, although they are widespread, socially significant and maybe devastating for the victims, so with employee theft.

Don't Call the Cops

Secondly, however, employers may be reluctant to prosecute employees even when presented with unequivocal evidence of an offence. Only a minute proportion of offences are referred to the police, and only a proportion of these result in criminal prosecution. The reasons for this are various. On the one hand the police are in difficult territory in investigating employee crimes. Certainly in many instances the case will not have been referred to them without substantial evidence being amassed by the employer, and this may be enough to produce a confession, which makes the task of the police straightforward. The decision to go to the police may, however, provoke a quite different reaction in an employee accused of a serious offence: she/he may take legal advice, which will frequently enjoin silence. The police are then drawn into a detailed investigation of the work place, its routines and responsibilities, in an attempt to amass sufficient evidence, preferably documentary, which is admissible in court to convince an independent jury beyond reasonable doubt of the guilt of the defendant. This can be extremely difficult. The police are not trained for such inquiries except for the relatively few fraud squad officers, and even these spend only a limited period of duty in the fraud squads and acquire most of their training on the job. It is frequently said that they come to be fully efficient only by the time they leave the squad after three or four years.

The difficulty for the police is in establishing what went on in the organization prior to the alleged offence. Although their attention may be focused on a single employee, their evidence has to be developed by interviews and analysis of the workings of the organization of which the suspect was a part. Even if no other employee was in fact directly involved, it is unlikely that no other employee felt any sense of responsibility for failing to detect evidence of misconduct. Police inquiries may hence provoke defensiveness by other employees, who fear not necessarily prosecution, but disciplinary action by management subsequently, either because of their failure to detect or report evidence of misconduct, or because of suspicion of active complicity. Co-operation with the police may hence be compromised by fear of the consequences after the police inquiries are over, consequences which may involve no more than doubts, but lead to lack of promotion or demeaning transfer. Further, formal inquiries into any organization will lead to the uncovering of complex patterns of informal relationships which are quite extraneous to the object of the inquiry: this applies whether the inquiry agents are police, management consultants or the health and safety inspectorate investigating an accident. Who is having an affair with whom; who has not spoken to a colleague in years despite sharing an office; who is whose protégé; who is recognized as incompetent and carried by his colleagues: all these and other ingredients of the way organizations actually run, as opposed to the way they are supposed formally to run, make the task of extracting evidence about an offence difficult for outsiders, especially formal outsiders like the police. Reluctance to give full co-operation may be based not just on fear of being implicated in the offence, but of other matters coming to the notice of management or significant others in the organization with embarrassing or painful consequences.

These factors are often summed up by saying that a reference of the case to the police is very disruptive for the organization. That disruption may be reckoned in two ways. In the longer term the disturbance of established working patterns and relationships can reduce the effectiveness of the organization and lead to suspicions and antagonisms and to staff turnover; the extent to which this may happen is unpredictable and entirely contingent on the way in which the police inquiry impinges on organizational life. More predictably, however, whilst the inquiry is in progress a large amount of staff time in the organizational sector involved will be taken up in working with the police, and even more attention will be taken up in informal discussions among employees as to the way things are taking shape. In brief, the office or shop involved may be more or less paralysed. For this reason managements frequently attempt to localize inquiries as much as possible, and to amass evidence in detail before going to the police. Unfortunately, however, what may constitute a basis for certainty on the part of management may be quite inadequate as evidence to take to a criminal trial.

For reasons of both long-term and short-term disruption, then, the police may not be called in, even where evidence of a serious offence is unequivocal. Nor is this the only reason for dealing with the issue privately. If the organization has been seriously compromised by the theft of assets or, still worse, clients' assets – creditors not paid, client accounts looted – the primary consideration of the organization is to establish the extent of the damage in order to take remedial action. What is uncovered in routine checks or by chance may be adequate to incriminate an employee but give no indication of how widespread the offence is, whether others are involved, or how long it has been going on. Until these are established there is no way of telling what the damage is, nor the potential damage, as customers, creditors and clients realize something is amiss. If this is at all extensive, it may also be that at least some of the losses can be recouped, but whether this is possible may well depend on the co-operation of the offender. She/he may claim to have gambled it all away, spent it, as press reports have it, on high living, whilst in fact stolen goods are not even yet converted into cash and are stored in a rented garage. Even when the extent of the losses is clearly identified, it may still not be clear how the trick was pulled. For it is essential to all employee offences that an opportunity is identified that is not evident to supervisors (unless they too are involved). At times this may reflect employee collusion and/or supervisory laxness, but it may also involve a particular conjuncture of organizational functioning – the routines of the accounts department, the physical structure of stores buildings and perimeter fencing, the responsibilities of delivery drivers, the design even of particular company documents, such as invoices – that has been taken as the basis for exploitation. Until the technique by which the offence was committed is revealed there is no security against repetition. All in all, therefore, the employee who commits an offence may well have significant leverage against the organization even after she/he is detected: in respect of the extent of the offence, of the possibility of recovering losses and of identifying the technique used. The employer's interests are served by obtaining this information, which may well be bargained against a decision to forgo a reference to the police.

Finally, for some organizations there may be a reluctance to contemplate a criminal trial because of the publicity involved and the consequent damage to the organization's reputation. Businesses which depend on public trust in the handling of finance for example – banks and other financial institutions – may well be most reluctant effectively to admit in public that they have been defrauded by an employee for a considerable period. Other small businessmen may feel a sense of shame at the public demonstration of the disloyalty of an employee, especially if they pride themselves on running a happy family business. Coupled with other factors, this may constitute a powerful set of incentives not to seek criminal prosecution.

Alternative means of control are after all available within the organization. A consideration of how they are and have been used leads to the calling into question of the central assumption of the discussion so far, the offence. Criminal trial establishes that an offence has been committed. Forgoing prosecution leaves that question open to alternative categorizations. Managing the problem within the organization may reconcile economic and administrative or managerial interests with the offending conduct, but it immediately projects that conduct into the organizational arena, where right and wrong become a matter of internal politics and morality, and of industrial relations. Discussion so far has implicitly been centred upon an assumption of serious misconduct unequivocally illegitimate and involving significant amounts. Such cases, which form the basis of those which go to criminal trial, are a small proportion of all those which arise, and even they may at times be subject to negotiation as to their legitimacy, and certainly as to any sanctions they may incur.

Perks, Pilfering, Profits and Crime

It may seem outrageous to suggest that there is any substantial connection between the employees in the examples above who stole more than £1 million and the kind of petty misconduct that involves, for example, the taking home of office stationery for personal use, or the similar adoption of half-used tins of paint left behind after workplace redecoration. In one sense it is true that at any rate the two cases are at the opposite ends of the continuum, but it is not a simple continuum of right and wrong, criminal and acceptable. It appears that there is a polarity in terms of economic impact – surely you cannot object to the occasional personal telephone call, use of the photocopier or diversion of company vehicles, and, is not inflation of expenses, within limits, routine? Legally there is certainly no easy solution – all such acts are as much crime as the embezzlement of millions, albeit they would not attract equally heavy penalties. In practice, economic impact is of little help: very few employees are likely to be in a position to embezzle millions, but most, if not all, are likely to be able to pilfer persistently, with the same or even greater aggregate impact. So perhaps the picture becomes clear only in individual cases where large amounts are involved. But what then of directors voting themselves inflated fees, or, as happens increasingly, valued senior staff in competitive labour markets being given large loyalty bonuses for staying on with the company for another year? Or for that matter the habit of professionals and consultants – lawyers, doctors, accountants, public relations and management consultants – charging fees which are based not on the amount of skill, time or effort involved but on what the market will bear? These cases at least have the merit of being openly negotiated and recorded, and the organization has a chance to decide to accept or reject the costs involved; though in the case of directors' and senior management's fees, perks and other emoluments, this can involve a rather small group acting as the company, in circumstances where the confusion of their personal interests with the company's interests seems inevitable. At the extreme here lies the recent embarrassing British case in which the prosecution of a company director for effectively looting a company owned and managed by him, and spending the money on the high life, failed because the court held that in effect he was the company.[4]

Perhaps it could be said, then, that there is a continuum where cases could more or less unequivocally be regarded as criminal in which (a) the sums involved are great in relation to the employee's legitimate income from the organization, (b) the means used to extract the benefits were illegitimate according to the rules and conventions of the organization and/or accounting and law, and (c) that the offence was perpetrated by an individual or a limited group, not a large proportion of employees collectively. The obvious exceptions to this lie at the top end of large companies, where precisely what is at issue is what is in the company's interests and what in the manager's or director's private interests, and what is legitimate and illegitimate practice is hotly contended. Attention will be directed to this area during the consideration of the problems of the financial sector.

The point of this anlysis is that even if it is accepted that employee misconduct can at times be categorized as clearly criminal, the number of such cases is a small proportion of the total, and indeed their unusual characteristics are just those that lead to their coming into the public domain via the criminal courts and then the press. Reasons have already been cited why even such serious cases may at times not take this route and be dealt with privately, and there is persistent evidence that organizations perceive their interests to lie in discretion. For example, the director of a recent survey by accountants Ernst and Whinney on the incidence of frauds on companies remarked that 'many companies are reluctant to prosecute senior people because of adverse publicity'. Nearly half the frauds surveyed were perpetrated at management level.[5] What unites all cases of employee crime is, in sum, the implications of employment, that is, the participation of the offender in a profit-seeking or at least a profit-conscious organization, whose economic and financial objectives may well be best served on balance by a toleration of certain kinds and degrees of employee misconduct.

The problem is then to be characterized less as one of crime than of industrial discipline, effort/reward bargaining and employee motivation. For at the other end of the continuum lie a myriad of perks, informal rights, bonuses and traditional customs, which involve employees receiving benefits other than their wages or salaries. Some of these are formal: subsidized company canteens, bonuses for production and sales targets achieved, commissions, awards for quality of production, attendance, friendliness to clients, or anything else that the organization may deem effective in conducing to loyalty to the company and sustained effort on its behalf.

Such formal benefits tend to multiply the larger the organization and the more stable the contract of employment offered, and to increase markedly in importance the further up the company hierarchy one ascends. There are solid reasons for both these features.

In smaller organizations, where employment is less stable, the organization has less resources to develop and award perks and bonuses, but more opportunity for developing personal relations between senior and junior members of the organization as a means of sustaining loyalty. Where such means are denied by sudden fluctuations in demand for the company's products, or where for historical reasons they are not developed, the purely calculative element of the employer/employee relationship is exploited. Each side then openly attempts to extort what it can from the other: the employer attempts to hire labour at a minimum cost, and the worker, forced by the market to accept the rate without any prospect of security, reacts by taking what he can in the workplace and by exercising as much control as possible over working practices. It is here that we find classic employee cultures structured around access to illegitimate but tolerated rewards from fiddles and pilfering: traditional dock labour hired by the day, hotel workers, many of them casual, fairground workers, milk, bread and other roundsmen.

Salient features of these increasingly anachronistic groups of workers, besides their low wages and insecurity of employment, are the clear specification by employers of an acceptable output, but considerable autonomy in achieving this. Thus the Newfoundland dock workers studied by Mars, whose findings were largely confirmed by Hoekema for Rotterdam, were hired by the day in gangs to load and unload ships.[6] Although the work was done with cranes and other equipment belonging to the dock company and according to established techniques and procedures, the gang members retained considerable control over their working relationships and work rates.

A significant part of the rewards of the work came from 'working the value of the ship', which meant not, as might be supposed, the relative difficulty, danger or dirtiness of loading or unloading various cargoes, and hence the ease with which their legitimate pay was earned, but the exploitation of the possibilities of pilfering. The informal rules established to manage this were designed to ensure a significant boost in income and goods without incurring the intervention of the dock management. This was achieved by expanding on the legitimate perks of the job. The target was invariably the cargo, and the theft of personal property was regarded as unacceptable. It was normal for certain losses to occur in transit, and the dockers were aware that shippers were insured to cover this. It remained for them to take advantage of the losses, and perhaps enlarge them a little in suitable cases. Thus a good-value cargo was one which contained goods that were reasonably accessible and desirable: alcoholic drinks, radios and other durables, clothing, for example. The problem of access or 'breaking bulk' was then achieved by a skilful accident with a forklift truck in the warehouse, or a crane in the hold, in which the package of goods was damaged and broken open. When this happened the goods were put aside for insurance purposes. By convention, dockers could take such damaged goods, but the art of breaking bulk lay in damaging the package sufficiently to break it open, but not to damage too many of the items it contained, and to stage the accident in an area free from company supervision. A proportion of the sound items could then be discreetly removed and taken home for personal use or distribution among friends.

Working the value of the ship also meant, however, ensuring that losses did not exceed a certain amount which it was believed would be tolerated. Up to these levels management accepted losses, knowing that some of them constituted perks for the dockers, in return for an acceptable work rate and efficiency by the gangs. If the loss rate was exceeded management would come under pressure to improve things and would in turn increase supervision of the stevedores. This would make the exploitation of cargoes very difficult, besides impinging on the freedom of their working routines: close supervision is generally resented. Hence it was liable to lead to resentment, a deliberate slow-down in the work rate and an insistence on the meticulous observation of agreed manning levels, safety procedures, supplementary payments for certain kinds of cargoes and ships and so on. In brief, industrial relations would deteriorate and ships be delayed, at considerable cost and potential hazard to the future of the port.

The dock work example has been described in some detail because it illustrates a number of important features of employee crime. First, the conduct in question is built into the effort/reward bargain, and this is quite closely tied to the relative autonomy of workers as to working routines and supervision. The worker is not hired as pure labour power to be trained and directed to perform the precise behest of the employer. He is hired as a worker with a recognized skill who is judged by his output. In the case of the dock workers, inefficient or incompetent gangs would be less likely to be hired, and incompetent members would find it difficult to gain acceptance as members of a gang. As Ditton and others have pointed out, in the course of industrialization workers have lost a considerable degree of autonomy in their control over their skills and their work.[7] The medieval guild system was developed specifically to ensure this control and to prevent craft knowledge becoming generally available. In an economy in which production processes remained fairly stable over time and in which quality of production was dependent upon the perfection of the skill of individual workers, it was customary to judge workers by their output and not to expect to intervene to verify the use of particular techniques or rhythms of work. It was also customary for evaluation and payment to be based on an agreed item of production and an agreed provision of raw materials. Tools were usually supplied by the worker and anything left over or extraneously available could be made use of by the worker for his comfort and benefit.[8] Thus excess raw materials might be appropriated along with shavings and remnants; there were quite extensive conventions and customs as to what could be taken and what the employer was required to provide for the reasonable comfort of the worker while at his task.

Employee Crime and the Modern Labour Contract

The techniques and disciplines of industrialized mass production have very largely eroded these rights and benefits. Skills now change rapidly and are dependent upon ever-evolving machine technology owned by the employer, who trains the employees in the use of this expensive plant and exercises close supervision to see that it is used correctly and efficiently. Increasingly the worker does precisely as she/he is told, and in doing so has lost all rights to perks and incidental benefits. Even the waste she/he creates is sorted, salvaged and sold for reprocessing. Thus dock workers today, radically reduced in numbers, handle not varied packages and bales to be stowed in the hold of a ship so that they do not move, crush or contaminate at sea, but large sealed containers, moved by specialized cranes and lorries and stacked like child's bricks into specialized ships. Even the stuffers and strippers of containers at inland depots are likely to be confronted with palletized units covered in tough polythene wrappers, units designed for ease and speed of handling, and minimal losses in doing so.

Another group which used to exploit the possibilities of work has been similarly modernized. Household rubbish used to be collected from open metal bins and thrown into open-sided lorries. In the course of this noisome job it was sorted for salvage – metals, glass, paper, discarded but usable household goods. Then came modern, mobile crushers with far greater capacities and the more or less simultaneous use of plastic bags, making the processing of refuse not only a much cleaner but much faster job. In the process, sorting of the rubbish, or totting, was necessarily eliminated. As in dock work, a complex change in work was involved: numbers of employees fell, wage rates rose, work became easier, cleaner and less dangerous, and productivity was expected to rise sharply. Perks from totting were eliminated, and with them the toleration of informal negotiations with householders and traders about the clearance of large and non-domestic refuse.

As other research has shown, some occupations still retain perks and fiddles as a more or less overtly recognized feature of the wage bargain. The bread roundsmen studied by Ditton discovered that management insisted that errors in giving change to the large numbers of customers on the round, which resulted in shortages at the end of the day in relation to the number of loaves sold, were to be made good by deductions from wages.[9] The solution was twofold. On the one hand roundsmen marginally overcharged those customers they knew never checked their change; this provided a buffer again mistakes and, if used carefully, a useful supplement to wages. On the other hand, in collusion with bakery staff, extra loaves could be loaded on to the van to be sold for the benefit of the salesman. Management were aware of both practices, but were concerned with the maintenance of reasonable sales, for which they insisted on an exact cash return. If customers complained of deliberate overcharging, the salesman was of course liable to dismissal. An almost precisely similar pattern has been recorded for bread and cake roundsmen in America by Altheide et al.[10] Much the same attitude has been documented for fairground rides – though here opportunities have been reduced recently by the substitution of tickets and tokens for cash – and for hotel staff supplementing their tips by short-changing customers and stealing food.[11] Low wages, poor conditions and casual employment are characteristics of these cases also.

On the whole, however, modern production and distribution methods have developed in such a way as to eliminate the overt acceptance of perks and fiddles which are at the employee's discretion. Employees have become much more tightly bound into the organization, subject to vetting and appraisal before and during employment, and to complex employment contracts and codes of discipline. Modern production, accounting, recycling and stock control techniques have greatly enhanced the employer's capacity to reduce costs by minimizing waste and incidental losses. Perks have been transformed into explicit benefits offered to employees – canteens, sports facilities, company outings and parties, cars, mortgages. In some cases these have been explicitly negotiated in wage bargaining, particularly entitlement to leave without pay, both on an annual basis and for compassionate reasons. What is and is not acceptable has been more and more tightly defined, and both penalties and procedures for what have become offences have been developed. At the same time, however, two features have not altered: the existence of an informal economy in which goods and services taken from the workplace can be bought, sold and exchanged, and the existence of widely distributed opportunities for employee exploitation of the workplace.

Together these three features – tighter, more specific industrial discipline, the informal economy and continued opportunities for misappropriation – have combined to give an increasingly criminal character to employee offences, but without removing them entirely from the industrial relations nexus. The result has been an increasing difficulty in confronting the issues involved, since to do so involves the use of the harsh moral categories, thief, fraudster and so on.

Yet the logic of tightening industrial discipline is inexorable. Take the car industry, for example. In the early days of the horseless carriage the skills of the wheelwright, the coach builder and the upholsterer still using traditional materials were vital; it was in the engine that the new technology was concentrated and new skills were required. Things began to change with the introduction of the pneumatic tyre and the redesign of car bodies, but the critical innovation was Ford's introduction of assembly line mass production. The division of car production into two sectors, the mass production of parts and their assembly into cars, eliminated many traditional craft skills and, most significantly, imposed the discipline of the assembly track, whose speed is regulated by management to produce a designated number of cars per shift. Its modern version has come to be peopled less by workers and more by robots, who are less liable to fatigue and irritability, as a means of at least partially mitigating the notoriously acrimonious industrial relations problems of the car industry. In return for strict discipline and frequently mindless work ensuring efficient mass production of high-value products, car workers have traditionally had high wages. They have also been subject to stringent security checks, with uniformed staff on the gates able to stop and search employees and their vehicles. Car plants also have high value-stores and specialist tools stored in cages with formalized access procedures, and unauthorized possession of company goods and materials often constitutes a disciplinary offence involving dismissal. Yet opportunities to take tools, parts and materials necessarily abound; all have to be readily accessible if the track is to produce finished cars. Most employees, friends and acquaintances outside the work place have cars: there is a ready market. The outcome is persistent and well-organized theft, in some cases involving large values. Pilfering and minor perks and fiddles in such an environment may persist, but become relatively unimportant because they carry the risk of detection, criminalization and severe sanction.

The difficulty of the car industry lies in the peculiarly tight nature of the discipline occasioned by assembly and the very high value of the products. Similar problems exist elsewhere also but leave more room for negotiation. S. Henry's study of a chocolate factory – one suspects it is one of the large British companies of Quaker origin, well known for their liberal paternalism – shows that an elaborate system of semi-formal and formal internal justice has been developed.[12] The example is instructive in illustrating the great range of sanctions available to management to control errant employees. Confectionery is a far less valuable product than car parts but none the less employees were strictly forbidden from taking even as much as a bar out of the plant for their own purposes. More significantly, such behaviour was formally categorized as industrial misconduct with the agreement of the trade unions. Complex procedures and machinery were established to sanction such offenders, which involved at the higher levels a disciplinary tribunal conducting a quasi-judicial hearing, with evidence being presented by both sides and the employee able to be represented by a friend or a trade-union official. By this means guilt was determined, by reference to a written code, and sanctions up to dismissal but including fines, transfers, suspensions, demotions and formal reprimand were imposed. Beyond lay, as was recognized, the police and possible criminal prosecution on the one hand, and the industrial tribunal and a suit for wrongful dismissal on the other.

Not all cases were dealt with in this formal way. Many less important ones could be dealt with at the simplest level by reprimand and warning by the immediate supervisor, or more formally by an interview with a manager, probably with notification of the trade-union steward. This informal procedure necessarily required an admission of guilt as a precondition of summary justice without a full hearing with representation on both sides, but, as in society at large, with the prospect of a milder sentence. As Henry demonstrates, the system almost exactly replicates that of the criminal justice system at large. Its nature is, however, radically different in the sense that the control which the company, in common with most other employers in a mass production economy, was able to exercise over the employee was much more wide-ranging and detailed than that exercised by the criminal justice system proper. For the employee works in an environment she/he does not own, and may behave only as permitted and instructed by the employer. Information is constantly gathered and filed on his/her performance and progress, and duties and income will reflect regular appraisals. Sanctions may be applied for formal offences, but may well equally be imposed informally for suspicion of misconduct and amount to arguably greater penalties than those normally imposed by the courts. Transfer to another post may involve distasteful and more arduous work and loss of contact with friends; failure to be promoted amounts to an annual fine of some significance, and demotion hence the more so. Formal arraignment and acceptance of guilt as the condition of staying in employment carries a stigma that will readily be evident to colleagues. Most importantly in Henry's example, the trade unions had agreed the code of conduct, and hence if an employee was found in possession of company products outside his/her duties, the acceptance of the categorization of misconduct was difficult to avoid. Perks, pilfering and fiddles had been explicitly excised from industrial relations bargaining and remained in it only in so far as union representatives were able to obtain clemency for individuals, formal recognition of guilt being the almost invariable price of doing so.

How does this picture of the successful imposition of agreed codes of conduct fit with earlier remarks about the disruption caused by allegations of misconduct? In the first place, by no means all businesses have such agreed codes, and even fewer have disciplinary machinery as elaborate as that described by Henry. Clearly, where management reacts to a discovery by allegations of misconduct in the absence of an agreed code the disturbance may be considerable, especially if the behaviour is at all equivocal – misuse of company vehicles, for example, rather than embezzlement of company cash. In the second place, the remarks there were addressed to the issue of the relative disruption caused by bringing in the police as opposed to dealing with the matter internally. Internal solutions have the considerable benefits, first of allowing the possibility of ignoring or successfully managing the side-issues that may well arise, though skill is required to achieve this; at any rate the inevitable flat-footedness of a formal outside inquiry can be avoided, and the anxiety which the attentions of the police provoke in most citizens is absent. Secondly, the possibilities of a resolution acceptable to all parties remains open. Even in cases where serious theft is demonstrated, dismissal does not always follow and rehabilitation may be attempted; criminal stigmatization is not involved, and in some cases dismissal may be disguised and the employee may leave with a neutral or even favourable reference. There is in other words much to play for.

The disciplines of the modern workplace may constrain the possibilities for employees to appropriate goods and services by categorizing them as theft or at least as serious misconduct, by buying out traditional perks, and by improved conditions and employment contracts and other means designed to promote employee loyalty. Sadly, whilst most workers derive considerable psychological benefits from being in work and having their work status given the public recognition of a wage, most people do not work for pleasure. Many work in conditions they find variously onerous and obnoxious, for hours they find arduous, doing work they find intrinsically unrewarding. They may gain secondary satisfactions from being in work and from workplace socializing, but they do not enjoy work, and would not work if it were not financially essential. In these cases company loyalty is likely to be equivocal at most. On the other hand getting a little bit extra out of the company is a source of extra gratification: that which is gained by guile and skill has a sweetness of its own.

American Comparisons

Some American studies confirm and in some respects develop points made in the researching of a problem that has largely been undertaken in Britain. A feature of the dock workers studied by Mars and Hoekema was their quite clear and elaborate moral code in relation to pilfering. Theft of personal property was regarded as totally unacceptable and theft of company property had to be kept within reasonable limits. Excessive losses of cargo from theft and damage in transit would provoke management reaction: hence the notion of working the value of the boat.

Horning's study of a Midwest television factory revealed a similar code among employees, whereby property was divided into the categories personal, company and uncertain.[13] Personal property included not only clothing and personal effects brought into the plant by workers, but also personally modified company equipment, such as chairs which individual workers had always used. Company property comprised all substantial plant and equipment and all tools and materials subject to secure administration through a signing-out system or other means. Taking property in either of these categories was regarded as theft, as wrong, and as liable to result in severe sanctions. Property of uncertain ownership included not only, as might be expected, scrap and abandoned material and equipment which was evidently of little value to the company, albeit supplied and therefore owned by it, but also a large range of tools, materials and small parts in everyday use in the plant. Tools such as pliers and screwdrivers became transferred through regular use from the category of company ownership to that of the user; materials such as screws and bolts, and small parts used in quantity were also appropriated without qualm, whereas large ones, especially television tubes, were firmly regarded as company property. The amount of property of uncertain ownership was thus substantial.

Horning lays particular emphasis upon the fact that, once understood on its own terms, the moral code of the workers was quite strict, and little sympathy was accorded to those who took what was accepted as company property. Indeed it was only where property could be rationalized in the plant culture as of uncertain ownership that workers felt able to appropriate it: moral legitimation was essential. In much the same way Sykes and

Matza described how conventional criminals employ 'techniques of neutralization' to avoid guilt for offences committed: such rationalizations as 'the supermarket would never notice the items stolen', 'the store owner cheated his customers', 'the café proprietor had abused and harassed the offenders'; all, in other words, either did not suffer from the offences or deserved to suffer from them. The management implications are that if there is a failure to understand worker culture and values, levels and kinds of theft will be hard to comprehend and manage.[14] If company standards are at variance with worker standards, control can be achieved only by an accommodation between the two.

Altheide et al.'s wide-ranging review of employee theft makes clear the consequences of managerial incompetence in this respect.[15] In example after example they report evidence of employees who react strongly to a supportive and friendly management by greater openness and by seeking extra benefits legitimately, by asking for rises, working for bonuses, or asking for time off, or cheap purchases of unwanted stock. They react equally strongly to distant and authoritatian managements which are known to be unwilling to allow time off work, to grant rises, or to allow employees cheap purchase of redundant and damaged stock. The greater the alienation of employees from management, the greater the sense of resentment, and the more justified employees feel in deliberate theft, sometimes not for personal consumption or even resale but simply out of revenge. They cite one instance of a semi-professional thief whose technique in exploiting the workplace lay in waiting to identify a resentful employee as an accomplice in a serious theft that she/he would not otherwise have contemplated. Guilt once again has to be neutralized, but unlike Horning's television factory, Altheide et al. look at workplaces where the industrial relations situation is more volatile, and show how this may have a direct effect upon employee culture and on the extent of their willingness to contemplate theft.

So impressed with the apparent moral volatility of workers in personal responses to management behaviour are the authors that they speculate also (p. 104) whether American workers are not unusually sensitive in this respect:

> Americans are specially susceptible to resentment towards superiors, since part of the cultural myth is that one's social standing is a direct reflection of one's effort and talent. Relatedly, individuals' success is presumed to be at least partially indicated by occupational success. The major practical problem with this ideal is that it is impossible for everyone to 'succeed' by reaching the top; there are more climbers than there are rungs to climb . . . Many Americans do not like the idea of being subordinate and they resist it even more when in the day-to-day rituals of interaction they are often reminded that the words and actions of some person(s) influence their lives more than the converse.

Cressey's study of convicted and imprisoned embezzlers seems at first glance to constitute an exception to the generalizations emergent from the rest of the literature.[16] The offenders had all committed serious violations of trust, had occupied in many cases middle and senior management posts and had acted alone. Their isolation was one of their distinctive characteristics. When Cressey's evidence is examined a little more closely, however, it appears less anomalous. He develops a specific explanation for the embezzlers' behaviour, pointing out that all found themselves faced with a problem that they felt unable to share with others who might otherwise have helped, to which they came to see the theft of company property as a solution. Before they were able to take the step to commit the offence however, they had to rationalize their moral feelings and beliefs. Cressey's subjects were all guilty of acts which were incontrovertibly wrong, and which they knew to be crimes, and since they acted alone rationalization was much harder than for employees operating a pilfering system. Cressey is none the less emphatic that rationalization was essential in each case, though the moral arguments involved varied from the extensive and vehement to the non-existent. Thus one former small rural bank president converted bonds held in trust for the benefit of his bank, and defended what he did by saying that the alternative at the time (the late 1930s) was to call in numerous loans to small farmers, and so bankrupt them, without the bank being able to make any more effective use of the land than they did. At the other extreme employees might get drunk to the point where they no longer cared, ruminate on their unhappy situation, and take off with the takings of a hotel or garage. What was important here was less moral reasoning than the achievement of a state of mind in which it was obliterated and they were released to commit the offence.

Cressey's subjects were also unusual in committing serious offences, and in getting caught. In a number of cases the offences had been continuing for some time, and money borrowed had been initially returned, only to be replaced by larger illegitimate loans. Skilled and successful and petty embezzlers hence do not feature in the sample, and many of the cases involved acts of desperation and incompetence that were almost bound to lead to detection. Cressey analyses that unusual group, the serious offender who is caught and imprisoned, who, whilst interesting, should not be presumed to share too many characteristics with those who are not caught, or whose sanctions do not involve imprisonment.

Employee Theft and the Hidden Economy

Goods and services obtained illegally from the workplace can be distributed and exchanged in the irregular economy both within and beyond work. This economy provides a considerable stimulus to the continued flow. As Henry, whose study of *The Hidden Economy*[17] remains probably the most important in this field, points out, the rewards obtained are more social and psychological than economic, though a distinction should be drawn here between the irregular economy described by such writers as

South[18] and Henry's hidden economy. The irregular economy is an attempt to conceptualize the economic world of the unemployed and the marginally employed, who survive, in a society characterized by chronic mass unemployment, by means of a mixture of activities varied over time and from person to person. Welfare benefits are claimed, money may be borrowed (more or less permanently) from friends and relations, credit is obtained, casual jobs undertaken, petty theft undertaken, goods bought and sold, including goods stolen by professional thieves and goods pilfered from the workplace, drugs may be used and dealt in, sporadic prostitution may be taken up. It is a modern version of the world Marx called that of the lumpenproletariat. Here the sale and exchange of goods and services from the workplace may indeed have an economic as well as a social and psychological importance as part of the means of financial survival. For Henry's hidden economy it is social esteem which is foremost. Most of his subjects are in work or small-time business. Someone who could provide needed goods and services – bricks, coal, a stereo, the use of a van – cheap, earns the gratitude of others and their repect as a wily operator. At the same time the consumer's self-esteem is likely to be enhanced, having used the right connections to avoid being a mug and paying the full price for what was wanted. Henry is clear that most of the participants in the hidden economy, even those who may deal in goods stolen in quantity by professional thieves, do not derive much of their income from this source.[19] Those who pilfer goods from work are unlikely in most cases to obtain more than a few free drinks.

The same conclusion has incidentally been reached on the black economy. This, in Smith's meticulous recent study, overlaps the hidden and irregular economies because it includes all undeclared income.[20] The additional element for present purposes and a large proportion of the whole is income from work not decleared to the authorities. Whilst the black economy may in total amount to a considerable sum and constitute a more than derisory proportion of GDP (Smith estimates it at 3–5 per cent), it is distributed among so many people that few will get rich on it.

Middle-class Employee Theft

Writers on employee theft have largely concentrated their attention on the working class, whose respect for the laws of property has, at least on the long-term historical evidence of criminal statistics, never been quite as great as that of the middle class. The hidden economy, which provides a social and cultural support for employee theft and misconduct, has been researched as a working-class phenomenon and an aspect of traditional features of working-class culture. Does this attitude to misappropriation extend to the middle classes, and in particular are there equivalent social institutions for exchanging the illicit benefits of work? The literature here is weak, but perhaps this reflects the rather different circumstances of middle-class employees. By virtue of their managerial and professional positions they have considerably greater autonomy than working-class employees. They are also likely to have a bigger range of large perks and fringe benefits in employment, as well as being treated as part of a team rather than subject to a disciplinary code mediated by trade unions. Their opportunities for exploiting the workplace for illegitimate benefits are hence much greater than those of the average blue-collar or lower white-collar employee. Two consequences flow from this.

First, the more senior employee will be more able to disguise misconduct, not only because of lack of constant surveillance, but also because of access to the resources necessary to a cover-up, that is knowledge of organizational routines, skills and access to records, stock control systems, and so on. For this to be achieved by lower-level employees frequently requires the co-operation of a group where for more senior ones an individual may act in isolation. It is not entirely without significance that a number of instances of major reported frauds by professional and middle-class employees are uncovered after an extended period by accident, often as a result of the reorganization of work – absence of the employee because of illness, transfer to another division, computerization of records, etc. It is likely then that where offences do not cripple the organization and cease after a while they may never be detected.

This however presumes that the conduct in question is such as unavoidably to provoke sanction – large-scale systematic theft of goods or money, for example. Most employees, senior or junior, would be reluctant to engage in behaviour that their own reference groups would stigmatize in this way – hence the importance of working-class culture in the hidden economy in blue-collar and lower white-collar crime. On the other hand the possibilities for more senior employees of rationalizing their behaviour as legitimate and still serving their personal interest are considerably greater. Not for nothing is the fiddling of expenses often portrayed popularly as a major middle-class employee's perk. Like those of the working class, it must be done with skill and without greed – excessive claims will not only be questioned, they may lead to sanctions. Hence it is preferable to manipulate work to include trips and occasions involving actual legitimate indulgences and real expenditure. A claim for a real trip, enjoyable in itself, which involved large expenses, can generate a larger bonus if inflated by 10 per cent than a claim for a small item of expenditure which was never incurred, and for which there is little defence if questioned. If the object of the middle-class miscreant is the same as that of the majority of his working-class countertparts, namely a little bit extra to make life marginally easier and more indulgent, rather than an attempt to get rich at the company's expense, then much that is simply unavailable to the lower participant can often be obtained without question, and much else by careful negotiation. Use of phones, photocopiers, postal and secretarial services, vehicles, machinery and materials for limited domestic purposes can often be managed with a risk only of a sharp informal reprimand if a superior notices or is testy. The managerial and professional culture, as the dominant culture, is, in short, more able – in all senses – at achieving legitimacy, and where this cannot be achieved, more able to act alone and undetected.

In one of the few studies in the sociology of organizations to include this feature of work, Dalton described how management and supervisors in the chemical industry systematically developed additional fringe benefits.[21] Items were manufactured by plant employees for managers using company time, equipment and materials, company premises were used for personal entertaining, and funds diverted for outings without economic justification. Or rather it would be more accurate to say that managers usually justified what they did as a necessary part of management, which involved keeping everyone happy. Hence abuses of company resources for the benefit of themselves and their subordinates gave a sense of indulgence which enhanced motivation and commitment to the organization. These managerial responsibilities were also taken to include a vigorous defence of each manager's own department in relation to others in an environment of competing goals – production, sales, maintenance, research, etc. Differences in the social dominance of managers of different departments were sufficiently marked to result in an elite group who supported each other's privileges and budgetary demands, whether really justified or not, in order to avoid conflict, and simultaneously colluded in keeping their weaker colleagues in a subordinate position. Their power was sufficient to frustrate even a formal attempt to regularize the position by the introduction of a new budgetary control and evaluation system. This was subjected to such pressures by the dominant managers when implemented as to make it unworkable and to cast the weaker managers yet again in a bad light. Organizational power and politics hence play an important role in the extent of practical discretion and in the negotiation of what is seen as abuse of it and of company resources.

Opportunities for achieving additional benefits are greater for a middle-class employee both objectively, because of a greater range of autonomy, discretion and access to resources, and in terms of their capacity to avoid allegations of impropriety. Even when such allegations are made however, the more senior employee has a greater capacity to resist stigmatization. Unless exposed suddenly and comprehensively she/he may well be able to suppress and falsify evidence and to block and divert initial inquiries. She/he will have considerable latitude, unlike his blue-collar counterpart, in accounting for his/her past movements in many cases. And unless the abuses are simple and his/her conduct clearly illegitimate, she/he may be able to dispute at length the necessity for his/her actions and the responsibilities especially for the worst aspects of his/her behaviour. Did he take his secretary for a dirty weekend in Brighton at company expense? Well, yes, but she was also doing vital softening up of an important client in Hove on the Monday morning – and look at the business that generated. Did she/he channel a contract to someone who turned out to be not only a friend but a business partner? True enough, but she/he was still the best available, and there had been no problems with the performance of the contract, had there? Did she/he arrange to sell off company vehicles at a cut rate to a friend? Well she/he wasn't really a friend, the point of the cut rate was that she/he could potentially introduce some very useful new business. Senior management in an inquiry may not believe these stories, and even if they do, may not accept them, but they are bound to listen and evaluate them. They may conclude that the miscreant is a liar and a thief, but they have to do so in the light of what they propose to do, and summary dismissal is by no means always the wisest course: the employee may reach for his/her lawyer and cause no end of trouble, not least in the consumption of management time. Further, clients and colleagues are going to want to know what has happened, and the reply that she/he was dismissed for theft will not enhance the company's reputation where a senior employee is involved. Someone also has to take over his/her work, which may not be easy at short notice; and, as mentioned earlier, organizations will want to ascertain the precise extent of his/her mis-conduct and the techniques used in order to repair the damage and prevent repetition. Although senior management may on occasion go for summary dismissal, in most instances there are hence likely to be grounds for more protracted, cautious and negotiated settlement, including in some cases the rehabilitation of the employee. It is probably not irrelevant in this connection that senior employees will often be well known to those who are evaluating their case.

The opportunities available to lower-level employees are by contrast considerably more limited and variable. Many will be in positions where perks, fiddles and pilfering are all but impossible, and for many that do have opportunities their successful realization will depend on the active co-operation of some others and the tacit acquiescence of more still. Lower-level misconduct tends necessarily to be collective, and to draw on class culture and rhetoric to rationalize both the collectivism and the legitimacy of the conduct – getting a bit of your own back, sticking together to keep the supervisor/manager off our backs, preserving traditional rights and customs. It is tempting to attempt to classify these opportunities, as Mars tried to do, but difficult to achieve a satisfactory set of categories which really adds to an understanding of the issues. Opportunities are extremely varied and changeable, especially when allowance for co-operation between workers is made, though it is true that there are certain standardized ones – thefts from stores and warehouses, the latter involving collusion between warehousemen and delivery drivers, diversion of company vehicles for private business, thefts by staff in retail stores, embezzlement by those handling cash.

The two essential elements for a successful lower-employee fiddle are a valued resource to be exploited and a control system that is weak or can be circumvented. Where employees work in an environment where there is simply nothing desirable, they are thrown back on abuse of company time – dragging out work so as to get overtime, prolonged toilet breaks, even sabotage.[22] Where the risk of abuse is obviously serious, control systems will normally be in place, and supervisory staff will take some interest in seeing that they are effective. This may or may not actually be the case, and its achievement may derive from effective supervision. In retail banks, for example, that handle large quantities of cash daily, the risk is so great that effective accounting controls and daily reconciliations have long been in place, which make embezzlement very difficult. Significantly, opportunities seem to have arisen recently in the ever more complex operations of the investment divisions of banks by exploiting computerized record systems and electronic fund transfers that are rapid and anonymous, in contrast to the additional ledger entries. In supermarkets technical changes have moved in the opposite direction. The publicly exposed positions of the till in the eye of the supervisor coupled with the till roll and the daily or twice-daily collection of the take, none the less permitted various abuses involving overcharging some customers, short-changing others and undercharging friends. Where items are bar-coded and pen-wiped into the till and no prices displayed on the item any more, these opportunities are much restricted, even though the main reason for introducing the new systems was speed of processing goods and customers and less time required to alter prices. Like dockers and dustmen, other employees can find their opportunities for perks and fiddles suddenly altered.

Controls

The first principle to be recognized in respect of the control of employee crime is that the role of the police will be marginal. At most, in all but the most unusual cases, a reference to the police and potential criminal prosecution will be a sanction wielded by the organization to obtain the co-operation of the offender. There are, as has been described, a number of reasons why a recourse to the police may be more trouble than it is worth. The police, for their part, are not anxious to get involved in employee crimes, and would sooner concentrate on the maintenance of public order, conventional property crimes, and crimes of violence.

By contrast internal controls on employee crimes invariably exist, but are by no means invariably given recognition by the organization. All work groups have informal norms about acceptable and unacceptable conduct. As has been pointed out, these tend to become involved, sometimes overtly, sometimes *sub rosa*, in industrial relations and the effort/reward bargain, and may hence at times involve groups of employees having views about acceptable conduct sharply at variance with those of the employer or senior management. Essentially, however, these norms recognize gradations of misconduct, from the perk, which is to be defended, to the outrageous theft, which will elicit a tip-off to higher management even amongst the most solidary work groups.

Such norms arise from the fact that employees live and work with opportunities for misconduct daily. The opportunities require a moral structure in order to be managed as part of work, and this is generated by workplace cultures. Employees and senior management will also have views about acceptable conduct, but it is an open question whether they communicate them clearly throughout the organization or whether they confine their responses to outrage when they come across behaviour they take for granted as unacceptable. Management response may hence include at one extreme what might be called the authoritarian repressive stance, the assumption that everyone knows what is right and wrong, and that if anyone pretends otherwise they are either a liar or a fool; either way, their feet will not touch the ground if they violate standards of decent conduct and morality. At the other, as in Henry's chocolate factory study, a highly complicated set of rules has been developed, negotiated with the trade unions, and promulgated, and a hierarchy of increasingly formal control institutions established to administer offences and impose sanctions. Such an elaborate strategy was clearly designed not only to see that standards were adhered to but to avoid the process of sanctioning an offender giving rise to an industrial relations crisis.

It might of course be countered that a well-motivated and enthusiastic work force would be likely to act consciously in the interests of the organization because this is seen to be in each individual's interest also. Whilst there is no doubt some truth in the wider suggestion that misconduct of many kinds is more likely in a depressed, apathetic work force with no clear sense of purpose and direction than in a successful, well-organized and motivated one, this is clearly a counsel of perfection: most organizations are somewhere in between, and even those which are apparently successful contain their less successful sectors and individuals. For this reason the most clearly articulated general expectations about proper conduct will be vulnerable unless supported by a recognition of where opportunities for serious offences are greatest. Since employees live with the temptation of such opportunities daily, it is important both that they are clearly recognized by the organization as temptations and that effective administrative means are established to prevent offences. To fail to give public recognition to an opportunity is to leave employees open to it with the impression that nobody has noticed, and indeed that probably no one would notice if the opportunity were taken up; and if nobody notices and it does not make any apparent difference to the organization, why not go ahead? For the organization's senior management later to expostulate that the employee clearly knew that an offence was being committed is disingenuous: if an employee is to be trusted, she/he needs support to sustain that trust.

Even where temptations are not merely recognized but notorious, however, effective administrative controls are essential. Indeed the very notoriety of opportunities will attract those employees with an exploitative or criminal bent. Effective administrative controls also help to overcome the embarrassing suggestion of potential dishonesty implicit in exhortation from on high not to take what is not rightfully yours. As was argued earlier, modern organizations, which offer long-term employment, pensions, fringe benefits and promotion possibilities, and which utilize non-authoritarian inclusive techniques to encourage a sense of employee identification with and loyalty to the organization, will necessarily find it more difficult to raise questions of theft and misconduct which is so evidently disloyal. And, in addition, the greater extension of control by the organization over the employee in the modern labour contract and the withering away of employee control over the work process, together with the concern's ability to save at the margins on what used to be waste and perks, creates an environment in which what the employee may legitimately do in his/her personal interests is extremely circumscribed, and she/he is easily open to allegations of abusing his/her position if she/he is seen to act in any other way than in the organization's interests. Administrative controls on the main opportunities for offences result in the routinization, both of the recognition of the opportunities and the prevention of their realization. If these means are effective they will detect problems at an early stage if they do occur, and are likely to have a major deterrent effect, principally in gaining the acceptance by all employees that 'of course X used to be a big fiddle but there's no point in trying it now, it's impossible'.

Anyone who has visited a large self-service record shop will be aware of how dramatically effective a very simple administrative change can be. Stores that sell records in their sleeves require exit barriers, security men, closed circuit TV and other devices to control shoplifting; those that display only the sleeves and supply the records from behind a counter on payment have no such problem.[23] The reluctance of management to recognize that employees will take advantage of opportunities is demonstrated in a series of cases.

Smith and Burrows describe the persistent problems of a hospital catering department in balancing its budget (in total some quarter of a million pounds per annum).[24] Checks of stock and accounts ledgers failed to show discrepancies, and it was assumed that the budget was too small to meet demand – this despite the notoriety of large-scale catering systems for employee abuse. This assumption was confirmed when further checks were made in the light of obvious weaknesses – double deliveries of food at the weekend not checked or supervised, very many people with legitimate access to provisions, orders coming into a central supplies unit which served the whole region from all over the hospital, and no record of total orders for the hospital. Everything still appeared to balance. The problems were finally diagnosed only after a tip-off to the police of a long-standing fraud. Large differences between finance department and central stores records were revealed, and the fact that stores stock checks were never verified, and hence that the abuses were being carried out by those responsible for stock control. The introduction of centralized record-keeping and stock checks, with systematic verification by supervisors and verification of deliveries both eliminated the budget deficit and produced substantial savings.

Much the same failure to police opportunities for abuse and prevent it by administrative checks on a much grander scale is evident in the long series of prosecutions in the Property Services Agency, which manages state property, including purchasing, maintenance, repairs and extensions in Britain. It hence has a large remit, and a number of area offices with large responsibilities for the allocation of contracts for construction and repair works great and small. The patronage exercised by these civil servants is hence enormous, but the dangers of it were not recognized even after the Poulson affair, in which local councillors with similar patronage powers were corrupted by the architect and developer John Poulson on a grand scale.[25] It was recognized then that the modest means and background and unpaid positions occupied by the mainly Labour councillors left them vulnerable, and that this was made worse by entrenched control of local government by one party in some areas of the country. Although a senior central government civil servant was involved in the Poulson affair, it was generally assumed that because construction projects are approved at local level (and indeed a number of cases of abuse by local government civil servants had preceded the Poulson affair), central government was not involved.

The PSA however is exceptional in its direct responsibility for building works. Reluctance to recognize the dangers persisted even when a number of abuses in the PSA led to a government inquiry by Sir Geoffrey Wardale in 1983.[26] This pointed out that morale in the PSA was poor because of an apparent lack of concern at political level with the quality of work done and an over-concern with annual budgets and with completion times. It also concluded that the abuses were not connected and were sporadic and appeared to take comfort from the fact that there was no Poulson-like figure co-ordinating them – precisely the opposite conclusion from the correct one, namely that widespread sporadic abuse was evidence of employees faced with persistent opportunities taking advantage of them individually, as they were persuaded by particular circumstances, including the blandishments of contractors. The problem was, however, large enough to stimulate concern and further inquiries leading to improved controls, with the result that a seemingly unending series of cases large and small have been uncovered and prosecuted, all hinging on the relationship of civil servants with outside contractors and their control of substantial decentralized funds.

PSA has been a telling example of the dangers of relying on the integrity of employees and their devotion to their duties, virtues long taken for granted in respect of British central government civil servants. That nothing is beyond abuse was evidenced by the appeal of environmental health officers and coroners in 1984 for government measures to improve the administration of mortuaries to prevent abuses. Remarkably, mortuaries were outside statutory control, administered by local authorities, inspected for hygiene by the Health and Safety Commission, and with coroners and pathologists answerable variously to the Home Office and to county councils. Corruption and theft were alleged to be rampant, and a number of recent criminal trials involving mortuary attendants were cited. Tips were paid by undertakers for measuring bodies and by pathologists for preparing them for post-mortem examination; drug companies paid them for taking pituitary glands from bodies to extract growth hormones.[27]

Finally, mortgage fraud is worth returning to in the light of what has now been said. A wave of such frauds apparently swept Britain in the late 1980s, involving tens and perhaps hundreds of millions of pounds. Abuse of position by trusted employees in solicitors' offices, estate agents and building societies is essential to many of the frauds. The ingredients of this development are several, but in essence it is a reflection of the property market. The Thatcher government made it an early objective to increase home ownership, and to that end has supported the retention of tax relief on mortgages, instituted the sale of council houses to tenants at discounts, and liberalized the rules governing building societies to enable them to borrow funds on the money markets and so provide a reliable flow of cash for mortgages. At the same time the societies have been encouraged to compete vigorously, as liberalization has permitted them to diversify into banking and estate agency. The prospect is that the sector will become dominated by a limited number of very large societies. In addition, competition in the mortgage market has been provided by the entry of the large retail banks. The outcome has been an increase in home ownership, a steady rise in house prices well ahead of inflation and in some periods of boom, a consequent desire by as many in the population as possible to enter the home ownership market, and an equal desire by mortgage lenders to succeed in attracting borrowers, to finance expansion and sustain income from mortgage repayments. In particular, lenders came to compete in the ease and speed in which access to mortgages was granted despite the large sums involved. None the less some would-be borrowers remained marginal and unable to meet lenders' income requirements. This provided one half of the opportunities, and rapidly rising house prices provided the other.

One part of the exploitation then consists in buying property at prices known to be below market value and reselling them at full value, an abuse most suited to estate agents; another involves buying at real values but selling at inflated values to fictitious clients and then obtaining mortages in their names, an abuse involving solicitors and perhaps building societies; a third part involves exploiting a marginal would-be borrower and offering to arrange a mortgage, but of course at the price of various additional costs (usually disguised) as the quid pro quo for falsifying the application convincingly. At times all three abuses may be used together by the same group of people. No systematic study of the problem is presently available, but it would seem from cases being processed that these substantial and often criminal abuses are not usually the unaided effort of one or two artful employees, but the result of approaches by outsiders, some of them with experience of successful fraud. None the less the lesson is plain that a small but painful number of employees will one way or another respond to such large opportunities for major fraud as were presented by the housing market. In this case the potentiality for abuse is probably short-term, and administrative remedial action possible. In the case of insurance, as will be seen, matters are not so easily disposed of.

In the mean time the principal conclusion of this review of employee crime is that it can be controlled only if those in charge of organizations give their serious attention to the identification of the opportunities for it and to the introduction of administrative means to monitor those opportunities. Above all, trustworthy employees are not to be taken for granted as proved by years of honest work or selected by background checks: their honesty is sustained by clearly articulated recognitions by organizations of the offence opportunities, and by their involvement in effective schemes to ensure that everyone keeps in line.

The most recent evidence on this in Britain is not entirely encouraging. Although Ernst and Whinney's survey found that companies had not experienced more frauds recently, half had been victims of fraud, and a fifth believed they currently were.[28] Although 80 per cent considered their fraud control measures adequate, relatively few had issued a code of conduct to employees or established an internal audit department or audit committee. Responsibility for fraud control was part of the duties of the finance manager or managing director rather than a separate position, and fraud detection showed disturbingly haphazard features. There is clearly some way to go before British industry and commerce come to regard fraud and employee theft as an essential topic for realistic discussion within the company.

NOTES

1 *The Times*, 18 September 1987.
2 *The Times*, 26 April 1984.
3 These remarks on the making of news and on crime as news are standard in the literature. Useful sources are S. Cohen and J. Young (eds), *The Manufacture of News*, Constable, 1973; S. Chibnall, *Law and Order News*, Tavistock, 1971.
4 G. Sullivan, 'Company Controllers, Company Cheques and Theft', *Criminal Law Review*, 1984.
5 *The Times*, 30 April 1988. The Ernst and Whinney (1988) survey referred to is a regular one undertaken on several hundred British companies and is available from Ernst and Whinney.
6 G. Mars's work on dockers was published as 'Dock Pilferage' in P. Rock and M. Mackintosh (eds), *Deviance and Control*, Tavistock, 1974. His work on hotel pilferage is published in M. Warner (ed.), *The Sociology of the Work Place*, Allen and Unwin, 1973. These and other occupations are reviewed and

analysed also in G. Mars, *Cheats at Work*, Allen and Unwin, 1982. The study of Dutch dockers is A. J. Hoekema, 'Confidence in Justice and Law among Port Workers', *Sociologica Neerlandica*, 1975, pp. 128–43.

7 J. Ditton, 'Perks, Pilferage and the Fiddle: The Historical Structure of Invisible Wages', *Theory and Society*, 1973, pp. 39–71.

8 Much more rarely 'her' than today.

9 J. Ditton's work on bread roundsmen and others is published as *Part-time Crime: An Ethnography of Fiddling and Pilferage*, Macmillan, 1977.

10 D. L. Altheide et al., 'The Social Meaning of Employee Theft', in J. M. Johnson and J. D. Douglas (eds), *Crime at the Top*, Lippincott, 1978, a collection of essays that contains much other interesting material on business crime.

11 See Mars, *Cheats at Work*.

12 S. Henry, *Private Justice*, Routledge and Kegan Paul, 1983.

13 D. N. Horning, 'Blue-collar Theft: Conceptions of Property, Attitudes towards Pilfering, and Work Group Norms in a Modern Industrial Plant', in E. O. Smigel and H. L. Ross (eds), *Crimes Against Bureaucracy*, Van Nostrand Reinhold, 1970.

14 G. Sykes and D. Matza, 'Techniques of Neutralisation: A Theory of Delinquency', *American Sociological Review*, 1957.

15 D. L. Altheide et al., 'The Social Meaning of Employee Theft'.

16 D. R. Cressey, *Other People's Money: A Study in the Social Psychology of Embezzlement*, Free Press, 1953. See also R. C. Hollinger and J. P. Clark, *Theft by Employees*, D. C. Heath, 1983.

17 S. Henry, *The Hidden Economy*, Martin Robertson, 1978.

18 See e.g. P. Scraton and N. South, 'The Ideological Construction of the Hidden Economy: Private Justice and Work-related Crime', *Contemporary Crises*, 1984, pp. 1–18; and J. Auld et al., 'Irregular Work, Irregular Pleasures' in R. Matthews and J. Young (eds), *Confronting Crime*, Sage Publications, 1986. A dimension of 'private justice' which is beyond the scope of this book is the role of private security agents. See e.g. N. South, *Policing for Profit*, Sage Publications, 1988; C. Shearing and M. Stenning (eds), *Private Policing*, Sage Publications, 1987.

19 For accounts of both the less effective majority for whom the hidden economy provides a marginal addition to income and the minority for whom it is the basis of affluence as well as prestige, see D. Hobbs, *Doing the Business*, Clarendon Press, 1988.

20 S. Smith, *Britain's Shadow Economy*, Clarendon Press, 1986.

21 M. Dalton, *Men Who Manage*, John Wiley, 1959.

22 For a study of the history of this tradition in Britain see G. Brown, *Sabotage: A Study of Industrial Conflict*, Spokesman Books, 1977.

23 Shoplifting falls beyond the scope of this chapter, though there are interesting continuities with employee theft, as Altheide et al. indicate. There are also interesting parallels in respect of control measures, as is indicated in a recent study: B. Poyner and R. Woodall, *Preventing Shoplifting: A Study in Oxford Street*, Police Foundation, 1987.

24 L. J. F. Smith and J. Burrows, 'Nobbling the Fraudsters: Crime Prevention through Administrative Change', *Howard Journal*, 1986, pp. 113–24.

25 There are a number of studies of the Poulson affair. One which locates it in the

larger history of corruption in Britain is A. Doig, *Corruption and Misconduct in Contemporary British Politics*, Penguin, 1984, ch. 5.

26 The Report on the Property Services Agency by Sir Geoffrey Wardale and Anthony Herron was published by the Department of the Environment in 1983.

27 *The Times*, 21 January 1984.

28 See note 5 above.

5 Insurance Fraud: Can the Insurance Industry Control It?

In the course of the past fifteen years or so fraud by insured parties has gradually become recognized as a serious problem in a number of western industrialized nations. The response by insurance companies has varied from a reluctance to recognize that the problem has become sufficiently serious to warrant any organized reaction, to a sustained effort to set up a national system of control with the co-operation of the police and other state agencies. Examples of these national variations in response will be considered later. They can be understood only in the light of an awareness of the nature of insurance and its post-war history.[1] As will be seen, the growth and development of insurance in the industralized west have provided greatly increased opportunities for fraud which insurers have not always been concerned to control before their exploitation has become a serious problem. In order to understand the nature of the problem, however, it is necessary first to understand what insurance is.

The Bases of Insurance

The principle of insurance is a simple one, the recognition of which goes back many centuries, but insurance in its modern form, administered by companies established for the purpose, operating with increasing sophistication, dates from the eighteenth century. The principle is the spreading of the burden of a relatively unlikely catastrophe among a group of people at risk of it by getting them all to subscribe a small amount, the premium, which can be pooled to cover the cost of repairing the damage when catastrophe strikes. Early insurance was concerned with shipping, and subsequently with fire and death. The basis of the agreement, the policy, consists in setting out precisely what is insured in respect of the perils (e.g. storm and flood damage to buildings, theft of personal property), in respect of the objects insured (the buildings in question, specified personal effects), and the value of the sum assured. The insurance company then computes, on the basis of its experience and researches, what are the chances of a particular loss arising by the means specified, and then calculates at rate of premium, that is an annual charge per hundred pounds of sum insured. If the company's calculations are correct, its premium income will exceed the cost of claims and administration, and it will make a profit. Competition between insurance companies will ensure that rates are kept down and profits remain at a modest percentage of premium income, allowing for some fluctuations from year to year in the number of claims.

Putting these principles into practice, however, is less easy. The circumstances of each individual loss are unique, and although many cases may prove straightforward to administer under clear rules, there will, as every motorist who has had to submit an accident claim will know, be a substantial minority which are difficult to classify. Insurers are left with two alternative strategies to cope with this difficulty. The first is to require the insured to maintain certain strict conditions (warranties), the violation of which invalidates the cover. Sometimes this may be necessary – for example household contents policies often require the property to be kept securely locked when unoccupied, and commercial policies may require cash and valuables to be kept in a safe overnight. Warranties are however onerous if extensive and threaten to undermine the very basis of the insurance, namely the undertaking to pay out if disaster occurs. For these reasons the insurance contract is written on terms of 'the utmost good faith', that is specifically forgoing the attempt at exhaustive specification of all possible contingencies. The insurer agrees to pay out in case of accidental loss of property, for example, on the basis of what is reasonably considered an accident; likewise the insured agrees to disclose all aspects of his/her circumstances, both at the signing of the contract and in making any claims, that are relevant to the risk in question, whether or not specifically asked about them by the insurer. On this basis the insured can rest content that if the insured peril should occur she/he will be paid, and the insurer can be reasonably confident that the actuarial calculations will prove effective.

The reasons for the need for utmost good faith, however, also give rise to fraud. Insureds do not lead their lives meticulously: they forget to lock doors, to notify insurers of the purchase of new items, to return renewal premiums on time and so on. Furthermore their lives are full of complexities and unforeseen troubles: they go through divorces with attendant financial, domestic and emotional upheavals, they fall on hard times in their businesses, they share houses with friends who may be uninsured or less meticulous than they. Finally they discover situational morality: 'The burglary wasn't very serious but I did lose the ring Granny gave me that I can't replace, and if I say the TV was colour not black and white, who is to know?' 'After all some people are always claiming; some people I know have had several burglaries because they are never at home.'

Exaggerated claims are notoriously attractive, and it is only too tempting to add an item lost which was uninsured, or to falsify the date of the car accident if one has failed to renew motor insurance on time and the policy has lapsed.

Different kinds of insurance lend themselves in differing ways and degrees to fraud and misrepresentation and circumstances vary over time and from country to country – a nation with a health service financed from taxes is obviously less of a fraud risk as regards health insurance than one where health care is financed through private insurance schemes. All insurance frauds by insureds however share the characteristic that they are not self-disclosing: their essence is to appear as normal claims to be processed in a routine way. In order to detect them the insurer hence has to establish a system at least for vetting all claims for signs of fraud. Such an extension of claims verification will take time, and therefore money. It also has other implications which have made insurers reluctant to pursue fradulent claims very vigorously. The easiest solution is to pay out and hope that fradulent claims are not too complex or too frequent. One can also rely on the procedures and information required at proposal stage – insurance history, details of present status and other relevant information. Traditionally this information has been quite extensive and carefully evaluated – checks can of course be made with previous insurers and supplementary questions asked in case of doubt. The easiest route for insurers at claims stage is to evaluate the amount of the claim in a purely technical sense on the evidence presented and to pay accordingly. Fraudulent claims will then increase the total annual expenditure and be recovered by an appropriate increase in premiums the following year.

Honest insureds hence finance dishonest ones, but perhaps this is financially no less significant than that cautious and prudent insureds inevitably finance the claims of the careless and stupid. The relatedness of these two aspects of insureds and their implications in increasing the insured risk are recognized by insurers in the concept of moral hazard.[2] Insurance covers primarily material hazards, the incidence of which is reasonably public and calculable. Moral hazards, whether fradulent or imprudent, are not self-disclosing and are hence problematic to add into the insurer's calculations. Although imprudence or accident-proneness and fraud are identified under the same general category however, there is a difference between them: at least the careless and stupid insured did suffer the loss claimed for. This is the real difficulty posed by fraud to insurers. If steps are taken to detect fraud and suspicions are aroused, the insurer cannot simply refuse payment. If he does, he risks a civil suit by the insured where he will be required to prove his claim of fraud, and the level of proof required in a British court is not just the balance of probabilities, as in most civil cases, but a considerable preponderance of probability, reflecting the slur upon the insured implied by the defence of fraud. The insurer's obvious recourse is to turn the tables and require the insured to prove his claim: proof of purchase of items claimed for and their value, witnesses to an accident, or to the fulfilment of security procedures required by the policy and so on. The difficulty here is that, in the first place, such evidence simply may not be available for reasons that have nothing to do with the honesty of the insured. In the second place such a reaction comes close to breaching utmost good faith.

There are further problems too. If the insurer, without actually denouncing the claim as fraudulent, none the less insists on as much evidence as possible, which he[3] reviews with the insured several times, before contesting the amount to be paid and then offering perhaps half the claim, the insured will, if she/he is honest, but either unlucky or rather disorganized in not being able to marshal convincing evidence promptly, be irritated and upset and likely to change insurers and to recommend friends to do the same. Even more, she/he may, if she/he feels especially aggrieved, go to a consumer advice organization or to the media consumer programmes and columns, in the hope that they will campaign on his/her behalf against the large, rich, over-bureaucratic, impersonal and uncaring insurance company.

There are substantial grounds for the insurer to treat a doubtful claim with circumspection and even benevolence: legal grounds of mounting an adequate defence, fear of loss of public reputation, so giving an edge to competitors, and the costs involved in resisting a claim. The latter can easily be decisive if the claim is not large: management time, legal consultations and special investigations by forensic experts and private detectives are all very expensive and may be inconclusive. If the claim is eventually paid, the costs of the inquiry still have to be recovered from premium income. On the other side stands the preferred role of the insurance companies as bastions of defence against catastrophe, friendly agencies designed to protect and rescue their subscribers. Although taught to be alert to the signs of abuse the claims inspector's and loss adjuster's working personalities are predominantly those of the technical assessor of a claim and the helper of the unfortunate claimant – and it should not be forgotten that the circumstances of many claims may be very distressing.

Insurers' Changing Attitudes to Fraud

Why then should insurers' attitudes to fraud have shifted so markedly in recent years, if it is easier for them to pay out, and increase premiums? There are two broad circumstances in which insurers are likely to take a tougher view of fraud. In individual cases where the fraud is flagrant it provokes a sense of outrage at the abuse of utmost good faith. Where, for example, it appears than an insured did not exaggerate a real loss but fabricated or staged it by setting fire to his/her own business and claiming for worthless or non-existent stock; where she/he lies and is exposed and then lies again; where she/he insures with more than one company in order to claim double indemnity, the insurer is likely to reject the claim outright and, if the evidence is clear, refer it to the police for prosecution.

It requires an insured who is both brazen and incompetent to be so far compromised, however. Where the evidence is less decisive, the insurer may delay and prevaricate endlessly, may offer a derisory payment and/or may insist on proof of claim, thereby challenging the insurer to go to law if the claim is sound. This is usually accompanied by denial of further cover, so putting the insured at risk, since a false reply to a subsequent insurer's routine question as to whether she/he has ever had cover refused or special terms imposed will invalidate any resulting policy and result in the denial of any claim if exposed.

The insurer may, however, take other steps if he suspects that fraud is becoming widespread and persistent. Here he is in something of a quandary. If he does nothing in the face of evidence of increasing abuse he risks the message circulating among insureds that insurers are an easy mark, and may end up with people insuring in order to make bogus claims. On the other hand, if he establishes complex fraud control machinery, not only does he incur the costs of doing so, but he risks alienating the majority of honest insureds who are also subject to it. In addition, he risks losing market image advantage to his competitors if they do not follow suit. Finally he risks communicating the message that insurance fraud is possible and being quite widely practised to honest insureds to whom the idea had never occurred. For this reason initial measures to control fraud have been cautious, secretive and largely confined to the internal administration of insurance companies. More claims inspectors are hired and trained in fraud detection, greater care is given to investigating and resisting doubtful claims, proposal forms require more information, and where risks are particularly severe and control difficult the company may simply withdraw from business in that area, citing it as unprofitable. If this strategy works, honest insureds will be subject to minimum inconvenience, but dishonest ones will realize that this company is no soft touch. Such measures have been deployed periodically throughout insurance history as insurers have believed, with varying degrees of justification, that they have been the object of a wave of abuse, or of deteriorating public morality.

The Changing Market for Insurance

Such measures have been tried over the past two decades and are still being tried, but they have proved ineffective. To gain some idea of why, it is necessary to appreciate the changes in the insurance market. The postwar world has seen an unprecedented change in the socio-economic structure of the western industrialized nations. Sustained economic growth, apart from the serious recession of the late 1970s and early 1980s, has produced what J. K. Galbraith identified 25 years ago as the affluent society. Instead of 60 per cent or more of the population working in manual jobs in poor conditions, relative insecurity and with significant areas of substantial poverty, 60 per cent or more of the population is now in white-collar employment with reasonably high secure incomes, which have financed the similar spread of home and car ownership, proliferating leisure pursuits, extensive ownership of consumer durables (TVs, freezers, cameras, etc), foreign holidays and so on. Rates of theft, burglary and car accidents have also increased dramatically and persistently. There has hence been a rapidly expanding market for insuring the benefits of affluence, and insurers have profited in addition from selling life assurance as a form of saving, and from a burgeoning interest in private health insurance. Figures on the growth of insurance since 1945 on a basis that allows comparisons between countries are hard to obtain, but research by Swiss Reinsurance on the group of seven leading western industrialized nations and Switzerland showed that total premium income doubled or trebled between 1965 and 1985 in all countries except Japan, where it increased sixfold.[4] Britain and the United States, with longer-established and more mature insurance industries, grew proportionately less fast than the average, but in all countries insurance grew faster than total business and increased its share of GNP continuously. Further, insurance proved more resistant than other industries to recession: in the 1980–5 period total premium volume increased by a third.

The insurance industry has also sought to offer a much greater range of services for an increased range of risks: businesses are today usually protected not just against fire, theft, storm, flood, employer's and public liability, but against consequential loss of profits from any of these perils. Householders are offered new-for-old contents policies, health policies offer income to those prevented from working, holiday policies offer cash to those who have theirs stolen.

The source of this constant development of new and more extensive kinds of cover is competition between insurers for a greater share of the expanding market. Invent a new policy to cover a risk the public had never previously considered and you create a new market in which you are the leader. At the same time insurers recognized that, although some specialization remains necessary to success, the wider the variety of policies a company can offer the more business it can pick up through easy access to existing and hopefully satisfied policy holders. In the course of this process insurance has of course moved a considerable distance from its original basis in providing cover against catastrophe. Losing your luggage whilst on holiday may be upsetting and may even ruin your holiday, but it is hardly a disaster compared to your house being burnt down; spilling a bottle of wine over the new settee may be distressing, but it is not quite on the same scale as a burglary. The more risks that insurers encourage insureds to cover themselves for, and the smaller those risks, the greater the chance that an insured will be entitled to make a claim in any year. Whereas in the past insurance was a protection against disaster one did not expect to happen, today it is a protection also against losses that almost certainly will occur sooner or later. Rather than being a naïve claimant who is the more easily appraised by the company for the normality and legitimacy of the claim submitted, today's is more likely to be experienced, if not sophisticated, as to what gets results.

At the same time as these developments insurers have also competed with each other for the allegiance of the public by emphasizing the service they offer. Traditionally this has taken the form of competitive rates, and recently of additional forms of cover, as has been described. For the insured, however, a critical feature is the insurer's response when a claim arises. Will the claim be settled promptly and in full, or will the insurer make 'a drama out of a crisis'? Advertising and image promotion have been much used to portray a benign and supportive picture of the insurer, and this has had to be backed with some substance. Not only are staff trained to be courteous and accessible, but claims procedures need to be reasonably rapid. Detailed and repeated questioning only adds to the distress of the insured, and brokers who handle claims as well as proposals soon detect an insurer who is obstructive, dilatory or offensive, and direct business elsewhere. Competition has hence taken the form of simplified proposal forms, guarantees of cover provided a few simple questions are answered in the right way, and a stress on the settlement of claims with the minimum of fuss. The message communicated to the public by the modern mass insurers has, in brief, been: 'Don't worry, you can be covered for everything and we'll always pay out.'

This message has not been communicated just to the traditional insurance public, but to the much wider affluent public of the consumer society. The traditional insured was middle-class, male, often middle-aged and certainly white. Modern insureds include all ages, both sexes, all classes and a variety of ethnic and cultural minorities in all western industrialized nations. Many if not most of these will have had no previous familiarity with insurance, and will mostly not have experienced it in its traditional form. Some may be technically ignorant – of the fact that double insurance is illegal for example. Some may come from working-class origins where there is scant respect for niceties with large, rich, anonymous organizations and a strong tradition of 'looking after number one'. Many may simply be pragmatic: 'I have a loss, so I'll make a claim. There seems to be little control on what I can claim, so I will claim for a bit more than I lost.' Once having succeeded, the temptation is considerable to try again on a rather larger scale.

Whether the above outline is an adequate explanation of it or not, insurers in a number of countries certainly agree that fraud has become a substantially greater problem in recent years, and many express regret that insureds no longer seem to have any sense of shame and morality. Insurers seem to be identified, like the tax authorities, as fair game, except that the taxman takes money, and insurers can be made to pay out. In so far as insurers recognize this change in scope and attitude, the need for something more than a private response is evident. Not only must the message go out to the opportunist who adds a few items to a genuine claim that she/he will not succeed and will find renewed cover denied, but the amateur who has succeeded as an opportunist and next time insures with three companies to improve his/her take must be detected. Even more important, the professional fraudster who sets up a business on a shaky foundation with the object of staging a burglary followed by a fire set by a professional arsonist must be stopped. All of this requires systems for collating information, both on insureds, and on the risks and techniques of various frauds, and systems for training and organizing specialist personnel to combat fraud. This in turn requires co-operation between insurers and the breaking down of the barriers of secrecy generated by competition, and the establishment of better lines of communication with state agencies such as the police and fire services.

Both of these have been considerable barriers for insurers to cross. Industry-wide action on fraud requires the routine exchange of compromising and confidential information and admission of weaknesses. Confidence has to be sustained that commercial competitors will not abuse this information and that the fraud control systems that are established are cost-effective and do not damage the image of the industry. Co-operation with the state, especially the police, is even more sensitive, since it involves loss of control of the cases that arise, which may involve failure to reach a reasonable settlement, civil litigation arising out of unsuccessful criminal prosecution, and public vilification of insurers as maligners of honest insureds. The police too are not trusted as having much interest in insurers or fraud, and thought to be inclined to give investigation of such cases low priority in relation to public order offences and crimes involving violence. The pattern which has emerged varies considerably from country to country in the extent of the response, the tactics seen as effective and the areas and extent of the frauds involved. It is worth exploring the experience of three countries, the United States, France and Britain, before attempting to draw any conclusions.

The United States

Fraud has long been a problem recognized by American insurers but, it would seem, one that was held to be within proportions manageable mainly by individual companies until the late 1960s. At this point criminal syndicates – the Mafia and others – entrenched since prohibition in the supply of illicit commodities such as drugs and pornography, began to turn their attention to insurance fraud as a source of easy money. Professional criminals – burglars, armed robbers, conmen – also realised the potential of well-planned insurance frauds as a way to earn substantial amounts of money with a low risk of detection, and even if detected only a limited chance of criminal prosecution. The impact of planned professional fraud upon insurers was considerable. It was not a matter of a few amateurs putting in false claims for burglaries, but well organized and skilled groups engaging in arson on overvalued properties, and varieties of car fraud including theft and resale of cars, as well as false insurance claims and false claims for medical expenses. These groups were at times able to corrupt vital intermediaries in insurance such as brokers, estate agents and lawyers, which made them harder to detect and control. Further, they were capable of setting up their operations in one state and running a series of frauds until insurers detected abuse, and then moving to another state to begin again.

The penetration of business by criminal syndicates and their attempt to shift their activities from their traditional areas of drugs, pornography and prostitution (though continuing with gambling, both legally in Nevada and Atlantic City and illegally elsewhere, because it is so lucrative) to business crime was sufficiently substantial to gain Presidential recognition. President Nixon – ironically in the years immediately before he was forced to resign for abuse of office – declared a war on white-collar crime and sponsored the passage of the Racketeer-Influenced and Corrupt Organisations (RICO) Act, which facilitated the investigation of criminal syndicates' business affairs and the seizure of their assets. Federal concern with business crime continued under the stimulus of the Watergate affair and the revelations of large-scale bribery and political corruption by major American corporations such as Lockhead and ITT.

The Development of Industry-wide Fraud Control Bodies

Despite this federal political interest in business crime, the response of insurers to their problem was at this stage predominantly industry-led and run. A major initial development was the foundation of the Insurance Crime Prevention Institute in 1971 as a specialized investigatory agency intended to take on inquiries into insurance fraud anywhere in the USA. It started under a former Chief of Police with the support of a few insurers and expanded rapidly in the mid-1970s after its major success in the Baltimore cases in 1973/4. Sixteen lawyers and fourteen doctors were eventually prosecuted for insurance frauds involving injury claims.[5] Insurance rates in Baltimore, having been somewhat lower than the national average, rose in the 1970s and then fell after the arrests and accompanying publicity to 8–10 per cent below the national average.

ICPI subsequently expanded steadily to gain the support of 80 per cent of property casualty insurers by the mid-1980s and by 1984 had been involved in 11,000 fraud arrests with an 80 per cent conviction rate. Its agents are all former policemen or postal inspectors, and it confines itself to the investigation of cases referred to it by insurers. It is able to concentrate on building up specialist expertise in detection because it refers completed inquiries back to insurers for a decision on the settlement of the case, and, together with insurers, will pass the results of its inquiries on to the police for criminal prosecution in appropriate cases. Apart from the technical capacity of acquiring the size and skills necessary to combat professional and well resourced criminals, ICPI serves a number of functions for the insurance industry. Although sponsored by the industry, it is separate from insurers, who are able to concentrate on their preferred role as friends of the public, whilst at the same time protecting the interests of honest insureds. ICPI can be presented in publicity as a force to be reckoned with if you are contemplating insurance fraud, and hence as a deterrent. The fact that its agents have a law enforcement rather than an insurance background reinforces this image. The fact that ICPI is a national organization subscribed to by most insurers also conveys the message that would-be fraudsters will find it less easy to move from a tough company to an easy one. This collective public response to fraud is further reinforced by the industry association, the Association of American Insurers, which runs prominent advertisements in a number of large-circulation magazines affirming insurers' determination to stop fraud and thereby to protect the premium rates of honest insureds.

The experience of professional criminals hence forced the recognition by American insurers that fraud required a very substantial response which was not within the capacities of single companies and which could not be managed discreetly. ICPI, is however, intended to deal only with a very limited number of cases which have aroused suspicion of serious fraud in the companies. It remains for insurers to detect and control less serious cases and to deal with the growing numbers of amateur and opportunist frauds, which insurers increasingly recognized as problematic in the 1970s. The danger here has been that, on a broad scale, insurance fraud may come to be seen as a bit of fun, a game to be indulged in by many insureds, and that locally particular kinds of frauds spread rapidly and become a fad – in some areas bogus claims for whiplash injuries in car accidents, in others false claims for the theft of ancient and worthless cars. To control these and other abuses two kinds of resources were needed: fraud detection and investigation capacities by individual companies, and information exchange systems to keep track of known fraudsters, to detect multiple insurers and otherwise uncover fraudsters' deceits.

Several specialist registers and data banks have been developed for this purpose. The National Automobile Theft Bureau was founded by insurers in 1912 to assist in the recovery of stolen vehicles. In response to the increases in fraud and theft it was much expanded in the 1970s and now holds manufacturers' records on 188 million vehicles as well as theft and loss data, from which it estimates that about 15 per cent of reported vehicle thefts are fraudulent. Thanks in part to its capacities and the efforts of the insurers of 95 per cent of American cars who support it, thefts declined by the early 1980s. The percentage of stolen vehicles recovered, however, declined from 90 per cent in 1962 to 54 per cent in 1982, as professional thieves switched from reselling cars to dismantling them and selling the parts.

The growth of arson in the 1970s, peaking at 160,000 cases in 1978, stimulated the foundation of the Property Insurance Loss Register by the American Insurance Association in 1977. It now holds information on fire losses reported by 95 per cent of fire insurers, and on burglary and theft claims of over $1,000. Arson became so serious a hazard that it attracted federal attention, and the Insurance Committee for Arson Control was founded in 1978 to liaise with the federal and congressional authorities (including the Federal Arson Task Force established in the early 1980s) and the fire services to attempt to improve the investigation and control of arson. As a result various legislative and other changes have been brought about, including the requirement in many states for the fire services to determine the cause of all fires, leaving none as 'cause unknown', and to refer all suspicious cases to the police for further inquiry. By no means all arson is fraudulent – disgruntled employees, criminals covering up another offence, vandals and negligence are all important causes – but insurers have to pay out on most fire losses, and the sums insured are of course very large. By 1982, when the national rates had fallen to 129,000 cases 12–14 per cent were estimated to be fraudulent. In some cities where arson had become a major problem, the fall was even sharper – 47.5 per cent in Chicago over 1980–2 for example. In what was claimed to be the largest arson ring in US history, the leader was convicted of starting 219 fires, injuring 282 people and costing £18.3 million in the Boston area between 1982 and 1984. Some members of the ring were allegedly ex-firemen, put out of work as a result of tax cuts, attempting to get their jobs back.

In the case of arson, insurers' efforts were hence directed not merely to technical detection and control, but significantly also to increasing public and especially corporate and political awareness of arson so as to identify risk-prone property and personnel, establish as far as possible work routines and business practices that avoid arson, and to mobilize political, police and fire service support for the detection and control of arsonists. Publicity, training programmes, lectures and political lobbying hence came to be regarded as having as much importance as maintaining a comprehensive register and exchanging information on losses, techniques and the movements of known fraudsters and arsonists. To this end the Arson Information and Management Systems Programme was launched in 1984 to co-ordinate industry, government and the community to identify arson-prone neighbourhoods with a view to preventing them actually burning.

Arson has been a major problem in America in which insurers have necessarily been involved but which clearly has other important dimensions including frequently the risk of loss of life. It has hence been important in bringing American insurers to a recognition that, much as they might prefer to avoid it, public campaigns and political efforts are essential if the problem is to be contained, as arson seems to have been by the late 1980s. Insurers' interests cannot be pursued privately in such a case and co-operation with state agencies such as the police is essential. Such co-operation and mutual trust between organizations with quite different expertise, interests and habits of mind takes time to build up, but only once it is established can really useful exchanges of information take place.

Control of the other major area of fraud, health and personal accident insurance, is supported by a register of third party insurance claims, the Index System. This maintains files on 30 million individuals and holds records for five years. It aims to spot the bad risks – some of them frauds – by the simple technique of collating claims, more than one in a five-year period indicating that the claimant is unusually accident-prone. Here too the police have become more involved since the late 1970s, when congressional hearings on white-collar crime led to reorganization of federal funding agencies and specialist training in white-collar crime control for police forces. Abuses of medical insurance involving corrupt doctors, clinics and pharmacists and fraudulent exploitation of both private insurance and federal Medicaid and Medicare have been recognized as significant problems.

Internal Measures of Fraud Control by Insurers

Internal measures by insurers to complement these external ones and to decide on the disposal of detected cases as well as to improve the means of detection have had two aspects. On the one hand awareness of fraud in the insurance companies, and especially in claims divisions, has greatly increased, and more staff are given specific training in fraud control and senior management specifically designated to have this responsibility. The problem for insurers is, however, that it is both time-consuming and difficult for staff simultaneously to review claims in the light of the supportive role insurers habitually wish to adopt and to make a critical evaluation of claims as potentially fraudulent. The one involves reaching a decision on a pay-out rapidly and taking the information supplied by the insured as bona fide, the other involves looking for hard evidence of all alleged facts and querying any conflicts or anomalies in the evidence. The one is a co-operative approach, the other hostile. Though this incompatibility of attitudes can be in part overcome by office routines using standard procedures for claims verification, in which anomalies and doubts are registered as requests for supplementary information from the insured, insurers seem very widely to report that once initial doubts have arisen the only way a claim can be thoroughly reviewed is with a niggling, suspicious cast of mind; the only alternative is to put the doubts aside and treat the claim as honest.

The solution to this problem has been the development of Special Investigation Units with staff trained for fraud investigation.[6] By the mid-1980s such units had become very widespread among American insurers – 47 companies representing over half of all property casualty premium income had SIUs by 1984, and only a small minority had definitely ruled them out. An industry survey of 16 major companies showed an average saving on cases investigated of $7.39 for each dollar of the SIU's costs, besides their unquantifiable deterrent effect. By then SIUs had extended to all lines of personal insurance, but they had their origins in car insurance frauds in Massachusetts in the mid-1970s. Massachusetts state law required equal access to car insurance – insurers could not refuse bad risks, and state insurance commissioners, who regulate the industry, held rates down. This attracted drivers with poor records, including insurance fraudsters, to Massachusetts. The police were unwilling to take on the task of investigating what were individually mostly small-scale frauds, and claims staff lacked the requisite skills, so specialist staff, mostly ex-policemen, but later graduates in law and criminal justice also, were hired for the purpose. Most cases dealt with by SIUs are not referred onwards to the District Attorney for prosecution, though that possibility is made plain in the publicity which SIUs use to add to their deterrent effect. As agents of the insurers, the requirements of SIUs are to obtain evidence sufficient to negotiate a settlement of the case, preferably by the rejection of the claim and the refusal of further cover. This can usually be achieved by confronting the fraudster with inconsistencies and inadequacies in his/her evidence, and investigative techniques are fairly simple – cross-question the claimant on several occasions, ask him/her to complete questionnaires and check for inconsistencies. Neighbours can also provide useful information about car ownership and driving habits. At the same time SIU staff have been able to collate information from cases completed and to develop profiles of fraudsters and checklists to feed into claims divisions and so improve the detection of the signs of fraud.

SIUs constitute a considerable success in fraud control. They remain under the control of insurers, so securing their objectives, and have both a technical and a deterrent effect, and also form a national network for the exchange of information. In addition they form a pool of specialist expertise within companies, who can be referred to for advice and provide channels for making best use of the specialist registers and of the ICPI for major cases. Above all they are physical evidence within the company of most insurers' recognition that fraud must be taken seriously on a permanent basis. It can no longer be treated either as marginal or as a temporary crisis, and indeed may prove to be a longer-term hazard than either AIDS or asbestosis, the vast liabilities of which currently concern insurers greatly.

A Substantial Response to a Major Problem

Overall the striking features of the American response to insurance fraud are its comprehensiveness, its recognition that the political and publicity aspects are an important complement to the technical detection and control side, its national scope even though many schemes and institutions started locally, and the willingness of the industry and companies in it to build fraud awareness and control into their everyday routines. It should not be supposed, however, that insurers undertook this because of some sudden evangelical conversion. What is equally striking is the scale of the problem. In 1987 after the worst of the arson and automobile fraud waves had been controlled, the US Chamber of Commerce estimated that one in ten claims was partially or wholly fraudulent, and put the cost of insurance fraud at 15 billion dollars per annum. The impact of the depredations of professional and syndicated criminals at more or less the same time as the rise in amateur and opportunist fraud clearly concentrated the minds of American insurers. Finally, although liaison with the state has greatly improved, and co-operation is now seen as essential, there is no desire or expectation that control should be exercised primarily by the state. The industry clearly wishes to retain control of the problem in its private interests.

The state, by contrast, is increasingly taking a criminal view of insurance fraud. It is now given much more recognition by police forces and by the insurance commissioners who regulate the industry in each state. The national association called in 1987 for specialized fraud divisions, with agents having peace officer status, a position so far adopted by six states. One state is also considering a law requiring all insurance frauds to be referred to the commissioners for criminal investigation.

France

Until at least the early 1980s, the French insurance industry could fairly be said to be largely traditionalistic and conservative.[7] It was and still is very complex in structure, with about 450 companies varying in size from the four general companies comparable to the larger British or American insurers, but all nationalized, to small mutual companies specializing in particular sectors and occupations, farmers for example, and to some extent regionally based. Where collective representative bodies existed they reflected this fragmented structure, and there was only a weak industry-wide body, with greater strength lying in the three sectoral associations for general insurers, for mutuals, and for agricultural mutuals. Naturally the French industry prospered from the rapid growth of the French economy following wartime devastation and under the highly successful indicative planning of the French civil service elite. Fraud was not regarded as a problem of any significance. Cases occurred, and some sectors, such as the cloth and garment trade, were notorious for their economic instability and the tendency of small insolvent businesses to go up in flames, but such problems were localized.

In the 1970s however, and increasingly in the 1980s, the picture began to change dramatically. First, in common with insurers elsewhere, French insurers began to become aware of a more persistent problem of amateur and opportunist fraud in the car and household sectors. French car insurance is relatively expensive and hence the tendency to have only third party cover and then to manipulate a claim to cover an accident or the cost of a new car has become evident. Cars were reported stolen only to be later retrieved from rivers, lakes and ravines; accidents involving the driver alone were ingeniously claimed on by getting a friend to hire a car which was then driven into the damaged car in a superimposed second accident and a claim lodged with the hire car company's insurers. Although medical services are not free at the point of delivery as in Britain, medical insurance does not lend itself to abuse quite as easily as in the American system, but none the less fraudulent claims and corrupt medical personnel began to be identified in appreciable numbers. Household contents policies were also subject to abuse in respect of burglaries and accidental damage. French insurers bemoaned the declining morality of the insured public whilst recognizing that it was larger and more diversified than before.

Secondly arson became a serious problem, both generally and in respect of frauds. Arson rates generally rose, the causes seemingly being the same as in the United States and elsewhere in Europe – vandalism, disgruntled employees, other crimes covered up, somewhat deranged night-watchmen, combined with ever larger and more vulnerable premises such as warehouses unoccupied at night. Fraudulent arson also became a serious problem in a number of different ways. France has a professional criminal fraternity with a quite strong cultural and social identity, the *milieu*. It has also, particularly but not exclusively in the south, well-established criminal syndicates processing drugs and running prostitutes. Like their counterparts in the United States, these groups turned their attention to insurance fraud in the 1970s, in part, it is claimed, because of successes in closing off traditional sources of revenue – the breaking of a large part of the heroin processing network with American assistance and pressure (the so called French Connection); the improved security of banks making armed robbery more difficult; police purges on the organization of prostitution. Arson was one easy way to make money. Criminals were already widely in control of the nightclub industry; opening additional clubs for a few months and then burning them for the insurance was simple. Much the same could be said for a time of pizzerias. So bad did arson become that French insurers withdrew from nightclubs, leaving Lloyd's to provide cover at higher rates and impose more stringent checks on claims. Arson also became a problem as the economy developed. New sectors emerged, flourished and declined, and in the latter stages were hit by arson. Furniture retailing in large modern outlets, a clear product of affluence, is one example of rapid growth and over-capacity leading to financial difficulties and susceptibility to arson.

Finally, arson has become a serious problem for quite other reasons in the countryside. On the one hand the châteaux which ornament it have in recent years become extremely expensive to run, and have in many cases fallen into disrepair, and their relative price in the housing market has slumped. A surprising number have suffered fires as their owners attempted to deal with the problem, either by taking the indemnity and moving somewhere cheaper to run, or by gladly accepting reinstatement to a condition that in reality, though not of course in the owner's allegation, is far better than before the fire. On the other hand the modernization of agriculture and the integration of European markets in the EEC, despite the notorious protection of the Common Agricultural Policy, have hit small French farmers hard, and there has been a gradual marginalization of them as their children seek work in the town and their small plots become uneconomic to cultivate. One way of surviving is through insurance claims. French farmers are traditionally quite well protected in respect of buildings, crops and livestock. Decrepit stone buildings miraculously burned to the ground, crops were devastated by freak hail storms and cattle struck by lightning.

The most dramatic area of impact of fraud however has been the development by professional and syndicated criminals of techniques for exploiting cars and car insurance. One insurance-based technique is to stage a series of accidents using the same rather aged vehicle, which in the interim is skilfully restored to look acceptable, whilst of course being structurally very weak. The roles of driver, third party, tow-away truck driver and repair garage are specialized and played at times to perfection. Multiple insurance of the vehicle improves the take. More lucrative still is the theft of new luxury cars, which imposes a considerable burden on insurers. Many are stolen in the traditional way when parked, but insurers now insist on the fitting of alarms. A more refined technique is to follow the target car, perhaps on the way home from work in a quiet suburb. When no other vehicles are around, collide gently with the rear of the target, who will naturally stop and inspect the damage. As he does so, the passenger of the following car gets out, apparently to discuss the situation, but he brushes past the bewildered driver, jumps into his car and drives away, followed by the other car. The target car is then disguised and on its way to the lucrative Middle East or North African markets within 24 hours, where stolen cars are readily sold to avoid heavy import duties.

The Response of Insurers to Fraud

The fraud problem in France has hence been very diverse, and the diversified structure of the industry has meant that a co-ordinated response to fraud in general was not likely to take place rapidly. As has been seen, partial or total withdrawal from effective markets has been one solution. Insurers have also tightened policy conditions, notably on rural properties. A national automatic monitoring system which identifies all lightning strikes in France has also been of assistance to insurers, although not set up by them. Claims administration has been tightened, and the traditional emphasis of the Napoleonic code on the rights of property has been resorted to in order to insist on proof of possession and of the value of the property alleged to be stolen, damaged or lost.

Although such measures may help with some frauds, greater awareness of the problem and more care in claims of verification inevitably leads to the disclosing of a larger proportion of frauds. Initial efforts were hence followed by blitzes on particular regions to try to impress upon insureds that detection was likely and to deter especially the opportunist and amateur, about whom evidence of more widespread abuses and casual attitudes to honesty emerged as the 1970s ended. Staff training for fraud control was increased and internal records used to improve identification of the signs and techniques of fraud. Companies began to appoint a single manager responsible for co-ordinating efforts against fraud.

Significant progress could not be made, however, without co-operation and information exchanges between companies. As the extent and persistence of the problems became clear, companies began to establish registers, but, not surprisingly, on a sectoral basis, directed at specific problems. This made more apparent sense and made it easier to overcome the problem of establishing trust in the sharing of sensitive information. The difficulty became that such data banks and registers proliferated and failed to exchange information between each other. Sixteen were eventually identified of varying degrees of size and effectiveness. For cars alone there are still three major registers, one for luxury vehicles most at risk from professional thieves; one to trace insurance histories and so help to identify fraudsters and prevent drivers from claiming illegitimately low premiums; and a third, which has links with similar registers in Italy and Spain, to assist in the tracing of vehicles by storing identification information, so compensating for the rather insecure system of official vehicle registration. The latter hence constitutes another data source, in addition to which there are manufacturers' records of vehicle identities, and a register of vehicles with registration numbers engraved on the windows for improved security.

By the mid-1980s industry-wide co-operation had improved considerably and there was a recognition that, although fraud might have distinctive characteristics in particular sectors, a successful control system needed to be nationally co-ordinated. Information exchange and pooling of knowledge is essential to success, both in catching individual fraudsters and in staying abreast of the latest developments. To this end a working party is currently attempting to establish a national computerized system for exchanging information between insurance companies, the more important registers and the central unit. This will avoid the introduction of a vast central register, besides making compatibility with data protection law easier by leaving much of the information with individual companies and exchanging only what is relevant. Such a centralized system has the appeal of simplicity and has been adopted by Dutch insurers. Under the Dutch system all insurance claims are referred to a central point, where the details are collated. If it appears that a similar claim has been made against another company, or from the same address, or other anomalies are identified, the information is referred back to the insurers for investigation. Given the continuing diversity of the French industry and the existence of registers already, some of them substantial, it seemed likely that a central system based on information exchange, rather than a central reference register, would be more acceptable in France. Whether it will prove to be so, and whether it will be adequately supported by the extensive use that will make it effective will not be clear for several years.

Two other significant developments also took place in the 1980s. As in America, a national investigatory agency has been established co-ordinating a network of agents to inquire into cases of suspected fraud referred to it by insurers. Unlike the American ICPI, its agents remain independent and contracted case by case. All are former policemen working after retirement as private investigators, and their effectiveness in producing results that lead to prosecution or the successful denial of a claim is constantly monitored. By 1988 their numbers had reached 100 and the rate of investigations 2,000 per annum, of which nearly half were into car thefts and one-fifth into fires. Not all insurers used this system, some preferring to hire their own private investigators, but the system has clearly prospered since its foundation in 1975. It is based at APSAIRD(Assemblée Plénière des Sociétés d'Assurance contre l'Incendie et les Risques Divers), the body representing fire and general insurers which, having experienced some of the worst effects of fraud, has taken the lead in the campaign to control it. APSAIRD also houses a fraud register of cases submitted to it, a further information resource to be integrated into the eventual information exchange system.

Finally the state had taken an active interest in insurance fraud control in the 1980s. The largest of the nationalized insurers, UAP, has been an active supporter of APSAIRD and its inquiry agents and of the development of effective fraud control systems. The Ministry of the Interior has also taken an increasing interest. In particular, the problem of professional criminal fraud and car theft was recognized to require active police co-operation to achieve control. In 1988 a commissioner of police was seconded to APSAIRD to act as liaison officer with the industry and with authority to ensure that local police units give the investigation of insurance fraud their attention and do not relegate it to low priority. It remains to be seen how far French insurers will welcome police involvement. Certainly they will do so where well-organized and financed professional criminals are concerned, but for many of the less dramatic frauds a reference to the police is likely to continue to be resisted and a solution to the difficulty by denial of the claims and refusal of cover preferred as better serving the interests of insurers.

Overall the French insurance industry has accelerated in recent years to be on the point of achieving a national and quite sophisticated fraud control system. Despite the interest of the state and the concern to pursue criminal prosecution by it, the system remains in industry hands. In 1988 the only area of fraud which seemed to be still beyond the capacity of the industry to contain was professional criminal theft and fraud involving cars. For the rest, although there was still some way to go to achieve an acceptably effective system, problems had at least been recognized and in some cases contained – and with current fraud cases estimated by the industry as costing 9 billion francs per annum and involving 6 per cent of claims, that is just as well.

Britain

Britain illustrates the reluctance of insurers to recognize and respond to fraud in a co-ordinated and effective fashion without overwhelming and compelling evidence, despite the fact that if fraud is not actively sought out it will not disclose itself. The most obvious respect in which Britain differs from France and the United States as regards a salient fraud problem lies in the absence of criminal syndicates with the resources to make large numbers of fraudulent crimes and so pose a serious problem. Professional criminals have posed a threat, but their attention has not been fully engaged as elsewhere: armed robbery has continued despite the setbacks of improved security, and the smuggling and wholesaling of drugs and VAT frauds, especially in the 1970s on gold, have been the basis of project crimes offering large gains. It has mainly been the general changes in public attitudes to insurers, coupled with the very substantial growth and social spread of insurance that have been remarked on by British insurers, which has in turn implied a problem largely identified with opportunists and amateurs. As a result reaction has been slow and exceedingly cautious, and British insurers conservative in comparison to their counterparts in France and America, emphasizing the costs of introducing elaborate fraud controls and the risks of giving fraud publicity and so contributing to its spread. To be sure, there is a minority, especially among those directly concerned with claims, who are campaigning for a more substantial response, and even some large insurers take a much more hostile view of fraud today than a decade ago, but industry-wide institutions have yet to be developed in more than the most limited way.

With limited exceptions, fraud is confined to the car, travel, burglary and fire sectors of insurance, each of which poses distinctive problems, and which have elicited somewhat different responses.

In the past 30 years Britain has become a nation of travellers. Its package tour industry, based on the appeal of predictable sunshine on the Mediterranean, has become second to none. Insurance of health, luggage and cash has been profitably expanded to complement both this form of travel and a greatly expanded extent of business travel. Many companies, both specialists and divisions of large insurers, compete for the business, and their commissions aid the profitability of travel agents and tour operators. Claims are not infrequent. Foreign food and foreign bugs wreak havoc on unaccustomed digestive systems, and tourists in unfamiliar cultures and environments are poorly protected against thieves, robbers and conmen. On the whole, claims are not large, since the property taken abroad is limited and serious illness a relative rarity. Claims are hence very difficult to monitor effectively, arising as they do in a foreign country, where they are hard to verify, and where the costs of elaborate checks rapidly exceed the claims lodged. In recent years tourists appear to have realized that they can get away with an exaggerated and even a false claim, particularly if they are not improbably greedy. Careful switching of insurers from holiday to holiday may mean that a large part of its cost each year can be recovered by this means. Although many insurers have increased claims inspection and revised their policies to reduce vulnerability, and some at least have partially withdrawn from the sector, no more co-ordinated attempts at control, for example by establishing a central register of insureds, have been made. Part of the difficulty here is cost – policies are in force for only a short time, and premiums are not large.

Motor insurance has also been subject to abuse, but the prospects of control here are better. All drivers require continuous cover, and hence, even though they may change cars and insurers, a collective register of driver histories might well make economic sense to insurers. So far, however, such a radical step is seen as impossible, partly because of cost, partly because of alleged difficulties with data protection legislation, but notably because of fear of public reaction. The example of consumer credit, where credit reference agencies are routinely used and known by consumers to keep up-to-date files on their credit history, which are accessible on demand, does not seem to provide a compelling model. Frauds on car insurance are certainly held to be widespread and in certain areas epidemic, as drivers circulate information about companies and techniques locally, and spates of staged accidents and alleged thefts of elderly vehicles follow. These problems became sufficiently severe for motor insurers to agree to the first national public register of stolen and written off vehicles, which was established in 1987 at a cost of £150,000 per annum to run. The Motor Insurance Anti-Fraud and Theft Register is supported by all motor insurers and is intended to detect multiple claims and false allegations of theft where the vehicle is in fact consigned to the crusher. Although the industry is optimistic that it will make inroads on a persistent problem, it is too soon to say whether this is so, still less whether it will provide the basis for larger-scale collective registers and the overcoming of insurers' reluctance to divulge to each other information that might be commercially sensitive in a competitive market, which motor insurance notoriously is.

Household and commercial contents insurance has also been subject to quite widespread fraud, though not of epidemic proportions. Many insurers and adjusters have noted a marked deterioration in claimants' honesty and at times quite brazen attempts at exploitation, including multiple insurance and a recourse to the press and to harassment of the adjuster and claims staff to obtain payment. As in the case of travel insurance, the initial difficulty is that claims for burglary are not usually large, and the costs of extensive verification may not be justifiable. The dishonest claimant may hence often be successful in adding items to or significantly exaggerating an initial claim. There is more chance of detection in a subsequent claim, especially if the same insurer is used, but no formal system of information exchange exists to control such frauds. At times of course, burglary claims, especially on commercial properties, may be quite substantial, and scope exists for staged burglaries and robberies, which may be especially attractive if the business is in financial difficulties.

The Role of the Loss Adjuster

Here the role of the loss adjuster is critical. British insurance is distinctive in the extent to which it uses independent loss adjusters to appraise claims. Although small and routine claims are dealt with in-house, anything beyond a certain threshold, which varies from company to company, is referred to adjusters who, although retained by insurers, take a professional pride in their impartiality. Adjusting grew to the status of a chartered profession in Britain in 1962 by developing specialist expertise in evaluating claims and putting together into partnerships those with qualifications in quantity surveying, engineering, accountancy and police as well as insurance.[8] Over time they have come to be recognized by insurers as having a greater concentration of expertise and a capacity to offer a better service than the insurers' claims department itself, which concentrates on the more bureaucratic aspects of claims handling. Other countries do use adjusters also – France routinely for large claims, and American insurers employ adjusters in-house, although there are also independent adjusters. Britain is unusual, however, in the extent to which claims appraisal is dependent upon an outside adjuster's report.

Part of the adjuster's responsibility is the detection of fraud. When suspicions are aroused, the insurer is referred to in order to agree the additional expenses involved in a fraud inquiry, which may involve the hiring of private detectives and, especially in the case of arson, forensic scientists. Because adjusters act for many insurers they may well get to know of multiple claimants, and unofficial requests for information which can be circulated in the profession also aid in detection. In the last analysis, however, the adjuster relies on instinct and professional experience of similar claims to detect bad ones. Where he[9] does have doubts he will follow them through in an attempt either to resolve them or to provide insurers with enough evidence to reject the claim. He has, however, to be careful, since if his suspicions are unwarranted he may risk the wrath of the insurer for causing his insured unnecessary difficulties and potentially giving rise to a damaging civil suit against the insurer.

Adjusters can hence be of considerable benefit in detecting fraudulent claims and acquire skills in dealing with insureds who are less than honest, so enabling the claim to be reduced or denied with the minimum of fuss.

In the case of household and commercial contents claims, their experience may well prove effective against an opportunist or amateur fraudster, but their resources are limited. They have no formal training in fraud detection and control and there is only limited specialization among adjusters in it. Only one firm has a specialized fraud unit staffed by less than a dozen ex-policemen. This hence represents the total of the specialized investigatory capacity in Britain. Insurers and adjusters however regard fraud detection as part of the adjuster's remit and, since the adjusters have retained the confidence of insurers because of their expertise in other aspects of claims appraisal, they are held to be competent in this respect also. Adjusters at times complain that reports that claims are doubtful are ignored and the claims paid, whilst insurers counter-claim that adjusters' reports sometimes contain inadequate evidence to deny a claim even though the adjuster clearly believes it to be fraudulent. The specialization of adjusters in claims appraisal hence interacts with insurers' reluctance to combat dubious claims and fear of the costs, direct and indirect, of doing so. In this sense the system of extensive use of adjusters is arguably acting as a buffer preventing the development of more extensive fraud control institutions as in other countries.

Arson

Insurers' fears of the costs of resisting dubious claims and their conservatism in this respect were dramatically demonstrated in the early 1980s by the case of S, who ran a carpet and furniture business. This caught fire shortly after staff had left, and there was no evidence of forced entry. The only keys were held by the owner and the manager, the latter having no animus against the business and no means of gaining from the fire. Although initially the insurer was disposed to treat the fire as accidental, the police were later alerted and S was charged with arson and, on the evidence of the insurer's forensic expert, convicted by a jury. Alternative experts were then retained to attempt to verify S's vehement claim of innocence, which they were able to do. After a public and parliamentary campaign the case was referred by the Home Secretary back to the Court of Appeal, which quashed the conviction as unsafe and had hard words to say of the competence of the insurer's forensic expert. The publicity surrounding the case was considerable and was widely taken by insurers as indicative of the damage that could be done by a single mistake, for they were convinced that the public would conclude that insurers, and certainly those involved in the case, were mean-spirited and determined to deny claims if they could.

Even in the case of arson British insurers are hence disposed to caution in resisting and identifying fraud. Arson is not impossible to prove on a forensic basis, provided the ashes and debris are examined promptly and modern techniques are used. The difficult is to link it unequivocally to the insured in order to deny a claim. Here there may be circumstantial evidence, such as the financial difficulties of the business or individual or the dilapidated state of the property, but short of a confession and the evidence of a witness or accomplice proof is difficult. Insurers accept that arson for profit, especially in small and medium businesses, is a serious hazard, though few would be as forthright as the head of the West Midlands Fire Service who said that, in the first 10 months of 1985, 33 out of 39 fires in industrial premises in his region were arson, and that his earlier impression that there were people engaging in arson for profit was confirmed. The fire chief's results were achieved with the aid of a Fire Investigation Unit designed to determine the cause of suspicious and doubtful fires so as to eliminate the category 'cause unknown' and to pass on cases of arson for further police investigation. Such units had become more or less standard in the British fire service by the late 1980s and undoubtedly had improved the rate of detection of arson.

Like other countries, Britain has suffered from a large increase in arson, which insurers have combated by encouraging the spread of FIUs and by attempting to improve fire security and protection in business premises by improving awareness of risks amongst employees. Because most of the very large fires and a considerable minority of all arson is not for profit, but, as elsewhere, the work of thieves, vandals (schools have been a favourite target) and disgruntled employees, fraudulent arson has not been a priority. Insurers express a conviction, which is not shared by all adjusters, that arson for profit is largely an opportunistic problem caused by small and unscrupulous or unsuccessful businessmen, and that detection rates are reasonably good. What is certain however, is that specialist expertise in the collection of information nationally on fraudulent arson and the careful investigation of the possibilities of professional rings is almost entirely lacking. The only body maintaining such records is the Fire Loss Bureau, sponsored by the insurers, but with such an emphasis on discretion and fear of being accused of holding black lists that many adjusters and claims managers do not know of it or how to refer to it. Moves are afoot to bring it more into the public domain and make it a more effective organization against fraudulent arson but, as in other areas of insurance fraud, British managers perfer to err on the side of caution.

In comparison to France and the United States then, Britain has done relatively little by way of establishing a fraud control system. It remains fearful of publicity surrounding fraud, both in putting ideas into the heads of honest insureds and in the publicity attendant on resisting claims and losing the case in court. It is notable that insurers frequently follow a ringing assertion that frauds will be resisted at whatever cost and that evidence of fraud will be referred to the police with the caveat that of course a claim cannot be resisted without compelling evidence that will stand up in court and that without it the police will take no interest.

Certainly the latter point seems to be valid. The British police are under no instruction to give any sort of priority to insurance fraud, and widely take the view that insurers are rich and experienced enough to deal with these problems themselves. Police priorities lie with public order and offences involving violence. They are hence more interested in arson, especially if there is injury or loss of life. Their structure is such as to be geared to dealing with offences which either occur in public or are reported to them by the public. Fraud squads are small and many have quite often large cases to deal with. No equivalent to the American insurance commissioners exist (the role of the Department of Trade in supervising the industry is less local and interventionist). The chances of state involvement in fraud control in Britain are hence small.

It is adjusters who are in the front line of control and they have not seen it as in their professional interests to call for more substantial fraud control institutions, at least in part because that might be seen to reflect on their own limitations. Individually many adjusters regret the amount of fraud they are unable to pursue effectively, and the lack of a more substantial and co-ordinated system for monitoring it. How much more fraud such a system would expose is at present not an answerable question. It is likely, however, that pressure for the introduction of institutions similar to those in France and the United States will increase.

Conclusion

Insurance fraud illustrates clearly the preference of the industry for retaining control over the management of offences itself. Only where offences are substantial, and especially where professional and syndicated criminals are involved is the state called in aid. Normal cases, whether undertaken by a special investigation unit in the United States or a loss adjusting practice in Britain, are negotiated. The stronger the evidence of fraud, the more likely the insurer is flatly to deny the claim; the weaker the evidence, the more likely to accept some kind of pay-out, even though this may be illogical, given the nature of the claim – paying 25 per cent of the amount claimed may not be explicable except in terms of fraud, and if there is fraud in any respect, the entire claim should be considered void.

Besides illustrating the scale of what can be undertaken by an industry to deal with a particular category of offence, insurance fraud also shows the variations in the models of control – the state may be more or less involved, and the institutions of control take various forms. These in part reflect the structure of the industry itself and in part local variations in the form the problem offences take, the latter of which in particular may change with time. As in the case of employee crime, nothing is achieved until the existence of the problem is clearly recognized, and resources, financial but especially managerial, are specifically devoted to dealing with it. Also, as with employee crime, the negotiated character of most insurance fraud resolutions indicates that the offender, the insured, is not without leverage and bargaining power.

Finally, the case of insurance fraud illustrates how the development of societies, and economies and industries in them can give rise to additional opportunities for business crime. In the case of insurance, there is little doubt that the enormous growth and diversification of insurance products and their intensive marketing, and the accompanying emphasis upon ease of access by the public and speedy processing of claims, have made an important contribution to the growth of fraud, whatever the jeremiads of some insurers about declining public morality. Recent reaction by insurers in some countries indicates that a considerable amount can be achieved by way of rectification if the industry acts concertedly and with determination and, above all, if it is willing to recognize fraud as a significant long-term problem.

NOTES

1 This chapter draws on research undertaken by the author into insurance fraud and published at greater length elsewhere. See M. J. Clarke, 'Insurance Fraud', *British Journal of Criminology*, 1989, Part I, which concentrates on Britain, and M. J. Clarke, 'The Control of Insurance Fraud: A Comparative View', *British Journal of Criminology*, 1990, Part I, which reviews fraud control in a number of countries.

2 On the concept of moral hazard in insurance, see the analyses published together by the Chartered Insurance Institute as Occasional Paper No 3, London, 1988: R. A. Litton, 'Moral Hazard and Insurance Fraud'; A. E. B. Alport, 'Risk and Behaviour: Some Notes towards the Definition of Moral Hazard.'

3 Here and below the insurer is referred to in the neutral masculine: 'the insurer' means the insurance company, not an individual in it who may, of course, be female. The insured, by contrast, is frequently, though not always, a real person.

4 'Premium Growth and Structural Shifts in Leading Industrial Countries, 1965–1985', *Sigma*, Swiss Reinsurance (UK), vi, 1987, pp. 1–17.

5 There is a quite extensive literature on fraud involving the medical professions but it does not discuss the issues from an insurance viewpoint. See for example D. E. Vaughan, *Controlling Unlawful Organisational Behaviour*, University of Chicago Press, 1983, which is concerned with pharmacists; H. R. and M. E. Lewis, *The Medical Offender*, Simon and Schuster, 1970; H. N. Pontell et al., 'Policing Physicians: Practitioner Fraud and Abuse in a Government Medical Programme', *Social Problems*, 1982, pp. 117–25.

6 All Industry Research Advisory Council, *Special Investigation Units: A Survey of Insurance Companies' Use of SIUs for Fraud Investigations*, AIRAC, 1984; S. Ghezzi, 'A Private Network of Social Control: Insurance Investigation Units', *Social Problems*, 1983. See also, 'There Will Always Be a Conman – Or Will There?', *Journal of American Insurance*, 1984. Claims settlement and the role of adjusters in the United States in the 1960s is discussed in H. L. Ross, *Settled Out of Court: The Social Process of Insurance Claims Adjustment*, Aldine Press, 1970.

7 On France the best source is M. Grémont, *Fraude et anti-fraude à l'Assurance*, CAPA (Comité d'Action pour la Productivité dans l'assurance) 1986.

8 The loss adjusting profession in Britain has published the first two volumes of its

history up to 1970, which contains interesting comments on its role in fraud control in the past, see E. F. Cato-Carter, *Order out of Chaos: a History of the Loss Adjusting Profession*, Part I, Chartered Institute of Loss Adjusters, 1984; C. T. H. Sharp, *A Profession Emerges: A History of Loss Adjusting*, vol. 2, CILA, 1988.

9 There are a few female adjusters.

6   Taxation: Enforcement, Equity and Effectiveness

Tax offences may seem a distinctive and very widespread form of business crime. As offences against the state, without in any given instance an immediately evident victim, they are not infrequently portrayed as of lesser importance than those, like industrial pollution or investment fraud, where the damage is evident. This chapter takes the ambiguity of tax offences as its starting point. It looks first at the continuing political debate over rates and systems of taxation and uses this as a basis for assessing the evidence on the powers of enforcement and the use of these powers by the state in various countries. Income tax is taken as the prime example of taxation, and the institutionalization of the ambiguous and contested nature of taxation in the distinction between avoidance and evasion is explored. Valued Added Tax is then compared with income tax, leading to a conclusion that it poses in some respects even greater problems of enforcement, and certainly has created new opportunities for criminal exploitation since its introduction as the main form of indirect taxation in the EEC from 1973.

The Politics of Taxation

'In this world nothing can be said to be certain except death and taxes', said Benjamin Franklin in 1789. To the modern employee subject to deduction from income for the Revenue at source, this may evoke a wry smile, which may become sour if she/he compares the position to that of his/her self-employed counterpart. The latter's smile, however, is likely to be grim rather than joyful as she/he applies her/himself to yet another attempt to devise a credible set of accounts and bemoans the extensive powers and persistent enquiries of the Revenue. Yet Franklin was writing at a time when the certainty of taxes had only relatively recently become established, and in the very year when the basis of the kind of society in which regular and efficiently administered taxation is essential was being established in France. The United States had been an independent democracy for thirteen years, and the emphasis on equality of condition and the abolition of a formally privileged aristocracy and monarchy were as essential to its political system as to that emerging in France.

Part of this equality lies in the right of every citizen to elect representatives who decide on rates of taxation; part also lies in the obligation upon every citizen to make his contribution to the exchequer. 'No taxation without representation' had been a slogan of the American Revolution, and became part of the ideology of middle-class enfranchisement in Britain in the late eighteenth and early nineteenth centuries, to the Reform of 1832. Its history runs back at least as far as the confrontation between the nobility and King John at Runnymede in 1215, when the Magna Carta contained provisions preventing the King imposing taxes or seizing land or property without due consultation. The attempt by Charles I in the seventeenth century to impose taxes without the consent of Parliament was a prime cause of the Civil War and the establishment of constitutional monarchy.

Tax in Franklin's time had only recently made the transition to a status where it was seen to be a regular necessity to be decided upon collectively to finance the provision of those social benefits – the military, public highways and sewers, for example – that could not be effectively provided individually and privately. In earlier times taxes had been imposed irregularly by a combination of force and political persuasion. Their character as expropriation was, in the experience of many, unvarnished. For in pre-democratic societies taxes were usually farmed, that is, the right to collect them was auctioned to the highest bidder, or given to favoured individuals. The exchequer then set a figure for the take it required and empowered the collectors with executive authority to extort it from the population. Collection rights were sold on down the hierarchy of collectors to that of the front-line collection from peasants and artisans. What each collector could obtain over and above what his superior in the chain required was his: tax collection was an unpleasant and lucrative trade, clearly associated with oppression and unjust enrichment quite incompatible with democracy.

Expropriation continues to feature as one aspect of tax collection even in modern industrial societies. This theme is given continued life in part by the lack of immediate connection between the losses suffered by a citizen and the services he consumes, but more so by the continuing debate about appropriate levels of taxation. Conservatives usually argue that current levels are extortionate, and socialists that all, but especially the rich, should pay more as the only means to build the institutions of a civilized society and to achieve social justice. Taxation is hence subject to competing sets of values. One of these centres upon equity of contribution – everyone paying their fair share, whatever the detailed principles of fairness are decided to be. The realization of this set of values requires first, as has been pointed out, a democratic political system to establish rates and types of taxes, and secondly machinery for collection which is honest, efficient and effective in seeing that all pay their due.

A competing set of values which celebrates the expropriative aspect of tax is entrenched in a capitalist society in the freedom of entrepreneurs to accumulate wealth in a competitive environment. This is seen to be in the interests of all, despite the great inequalities of wealth and income which it generates. On this view in its pure form, progressive taxation of the rich is unjustifiable because they make their contribution by their necessarily great efforts to survive in competition with others, and in doing so generate jobs, incomes and goods for the benefit of society. A variant of this frequently cited in modern times is that taxation may sap the willingness to engage in entrepreneurial risks, in which case there will be less economic activity to tax, and society will be the poorer.

Finally the traditional requirement of government, be it king or parliament, for a predictable revenue upon which to organize a budget and to administer the nation constitutes another competing value. The tax collection system must be able to generate the revenue asked, a require-ment that has its political dimensions in the consent of the population to the level and distribution of taxes required, and its administrative dimensions in the system of tax collection and its effectiveness and efficiency.

It is the interaction of these competing sets of values that produces the detailed practices of tax collection in different societies, with results that sometimes appear anomalous, and public attitudes that are sometimes contradictory: many citizens dislike having to pay taxes, but at the same time complain about the inadequacy of public services. Different societies have different long-term solutions to these problems, besides of course altering their views from time to time over what are appropriate tax levels, as has happened in the 1980s in Britain and the United States.

In France, for example, the attitude of the tax authorities is simple and traditional: its efforts are directed at securing the tax take. Hence, as Lascoumes has put it in his research in the early 1980s, for the Direction Générale des Impôts, the best control system was that which produced the maximum income with a minimum number of investigations.[1] Conse-quently, a consideration of tax collection in terms of the honesty of the public was completely alien to the DGI, and they kept only the crudest figures on tax delinquency, despite holding elaborate computerized records. Investigations are expensive, prosecutions even more so. In 1982 there were only 420 prosecutions by the DGI, and special investigations fell from 43,710 in 1980 to 40,591 in 1981, but with an increase in the tax revenue resulting from them from 1,407 million francs in 1980 to 10,650 million francs in 1981. As research by the Centre d'Etudes sur les Revenus et les Coûts in 1985 showed, the outcome of this kind of stance by the DGI is a decidedly relaxed view of taxation by the French public. Income was widely and substantially understated, with taxi drivers predictably heading the list at 52 per cent of income undeclared, but including lawyers (36 per cent), vets (31 per cent), chemists (30 per cent), and tax advisers (20 per cent). Tax evasion was estimated at £7.85 billion in total. The relaxed attitude of the authorities was indicated in, for example, the requirement introduced only in 1985 for receipts for contributions to charities claimed as tax deductions. A charity representative ruefully pointed out that the revenue of the Foundation of France, which co-ordinates this field, was £3.1 million, but tax payers claimed to have donated £22.1 million. As a secretary to the budget put it, 'most Frenchmen defraud with a clear conscience.'[2]

That a relaxed view of tax collection is not incompatible with economic success whilst at the same time placating popular resentment of taxation is illustrated by Italy, where professionals routinely declare only a fraction of their income, and where the black economy is semi-officially supported. Large numbers of Italians have second, un-taxed jobs, and most small and medium-sized businesses escape taxation almost entirely, enabling them to operate at significantly lower costs and hence, it is argued, remain in the market. In 1987 Italy proudly proclaimed the 'sorpasso' the overtaking of Britain in per capita income, but only on the basis of allowing in official statistics for a contribution to GNP of 15 per cent by the black economy; and a number of informed commentators regarded this as conservative. The benefits are widespread and obvious: 100,000 additional homes built each year, 1.5 million equivalent full-time jobs. One might of course question the desirability of some of the consequences of this: of a postal service grossly overmanned with moonlighting employees, which takes more than a week to deliver letters between major cities and twice as long between rural areas, with mail lying in post boxes three days before collection. It is scarcely surprising that Italian bureaucracy is slow and civil servants hard to locate, given an official figure of 54 per cent having second jobs.[3]

The balance between an efficient and thorough tax collection system and oppressiveness, between securing adequate revenue and ensuring that all pay their due, between impartial enforcement and the stifling of economic activity, between controlling evasion and respecting citizens' liberties and privacy, between preventing avoidance, making tax-paying more or less optional, and overly burdensome and complex financial legislation, is complex and subject to constant negotiation in the light of social and economic development. An understanding of the acquisition and use of the powers of the revenue and of public attitudes to it can be achieved only in the light of these tensions. Much of the debate on taxation tends implicitly to take income taxes as its main reference point, but sales or value added taxes on goods and services and corporation taxes are also important. In what follows more detailed consideration will be given to Britain and especially to recent changes, and the reasons for them, taking income tax first.

Income Tax

Given the social and political complexities of taxation, public attitudes to it are likely to be difficult to measure. As Levi points out, most surveys fail to include any measures of seriousness when they repeatedly come up with the finding that defrauding the taxman is regarded as of much less significance than defrauding an employer or a neighbour.[4] Tax fraud of £5 may be regarded in a different light to that of £500, even though defrauding a neighbour of £5 may be regarded as totally unacceptable. These broad findings probably reflect two significant features of tax fraud. The first is its characterization as a regulatory rather than a criminal offence. Ensuring payment of every last pound of tax is unnecessary and the enforcement of such payment would be oppressive. Where amounts undeclared are substantial, however, the consequences are important for the exchequer and allow a significantly more indulgent lifestyle for the citizen. Furthermore a large proportion of the population engage at some time or another in informal economic activity – exchanging favours and sometimes bartering goods and services with others – and this can easily become extended into the black economy – accepting payment for goods and services. It may be that I can arrange to fix someone's car in return for them doing my typing, but it may be more convenient to pay cash. The point is that, as Smith shows, this kind of black activity spreads the undeclared income very thinly in the population.[5] Secondly, tax is expropriation and is felt as such. In not declaring income one is preventing that expropriation. In contrast, theft and fraud on neighbours or employers is expropriation of their assets by direct action rather than omission. It is probably for this reason that, as table 1 shows, a MORI survey in 1985 of 2,050 adults found false claims for social security benefit less acceptable than the non-declaration of taxable income.

What is not revealed by the MORI or other general surveys is the context-specific nature of many tax frauds. Thus the building industry is notorious both for income tax and VAT fraud, with employers failing to pass on money deducted through PAYE, sub-contractors avoiding both income tax and VAT, and contractors paying sub-contractors in cash to avoid VAT. In such an economy, as in the Italian black economy, market rates are likely to adjust to the expectation of paying little tax. If enforcement is successful, similar incomes could be maintained only by raising rates. On the other hand, the MORI figure that only 14 per cent had personally paid cash to someone who does not pay VAT defies belief until the figure of 70 per cent regarding it as morally acceptable to do this is compared. Part of the art of handling situations involving tax fraud lies in avoiding complicity by specific mention of tax. It may be that only 14 per cent of the population has started to write a cheque and then stopped when told, 'If you do that I'll have to add VAT and give you a receipt'. Far more than 14 per cent have probably paid cash without thinking about the

Table 1 Attitudes to the black economy

Offence	Thinking morally wrong %	Thinking generally acceptable to most people %	Knowing someone else doing %	admitting having done themselves %
Paying someone in cash who doesn't charge VAT	30	49	25	14
Accepting cash for some work in order to keep earning free of VAT or income tax	35	37	20	7
Using an employer's telephone without permission	36	35	26	20
Paying cash to someone if you suspect he or she isn't paying income tax	41	33	20	8
Taking time off when you're supposed to be at work	66	21	28	11
People on the dole earning some money without telling the social security office	67	24	32	3
Claiming expenses from an employer to which you are not entitled	70	16	18	4
Taking home things from work without paying for them	72	19	25	10
None of these	4	9	16	36
All eight of these	16	4	8	1

Source: MORI poll, conducted for *The Times*, October 1985

implications: since 70 per cent do not regard those implications as important why should they enquire about them?

Similarly, the report by the House of Commons Public Accounts Committee in 1987 that a fifth of tax relief for home improvement loans probably went on other purposes not qualifying for tax relief, at a cost to the exchequer of £100 million per annum, up from £17 million per annum in 1984, does not necessarily indicate a sudden surge of immorality in the population.[6] To a limited extent it will reflect the increasing rate of house ownership in the 1980s as a consequence of government policy, but more significantly it will reflect the increasingly strong competition between lenders to sell home loan finance. Additional loans for home improvement have become exceptionally easy to obtain, with the minimum of administrative delay. And if an improvement loan is inflated a little to finance a new boat or caravan, and the cost of the home extension turns out to be less, because the jobbing builder turned out to be so reasonable once he discovered he could be paid in cash instalments, well what harm is there? Taxation lends itself to this kind of situational morality, particularly because there is no obvious and immediate victim and the margins of applicability are blurred.

Comparisons too are important. It is not merely that most citizens regularly come into contact with the black economy, whether they close their eyes to it or not, besides being regaled by the media with tales of serious infamy about the tax havens of the rich, the ghost workers of Fleet Street (though not of Wapping apparently), the moonlighting of postmen, and the tax debts of film and popular music stars. These are excesses, the more outrageous of which largely come to public attention only when pursued and repressed – such is the secretive and deceitful nature of fraud. Besides those who have 'got away with it' to the tune of thousands, or are 'doing quite nicely' thanks to more modest evasion, there are those who benefit legitimately with the clear recognition of the annual Finance Act. Half of the new cars bought in Britain each year are purchased by companies for their employees at a cost to the exchequer, according to the Institute of Fiscal Studies, of £1.1 billion per annum.[7] This is despite the fact that for the past decade company cars have been treated as notional income for the employees, and taxed. Such notional income is not, however, charged against national insurance contributions, and cars are allowed as depreciation against corporation tax. Employees also benefit greatly from employers' group insurance schemes. Cars are the most widespread perk, but by no means the only substantial one. Employees in financial institutions usually expect heavily subsidized mortgages. Many employees, particularly from middle management upwards, are given free private health insurance. For company directors, perks including these and also share options and special bonuses amounted to an average 45 per cent addition to their salary, according to a Hay Management Consultant survey in 1987 of 325 large and medium-sized companies.[8]

Devising a system to administer and regulate taxation in these circumstances is hence not straightforward. It is tempting to argue, for example, that since opportunities for evasion are very unequally distributed, and since it is known that the amount of revenue lost is very large, though exact estimates are hard to achieve for obvious reasons, enforcement should be rigorously universal to preserve equity and public respect for the law. The experience of the various special offices and teams concerned with bringing hidden income to light shows a constant increase in take rising from £60,000 per annum per member of staff employed in 1979 to £138,00 per annum in 1983, despite an increase in staff from 1,650 to

2,495 over the same period.[9] It is tempting to say that the Revenue should go on expanding its work on evasion at least until the take per new officer per year stops rising, and even maybe until it falls to the level of the costs of employing the officer. Such a figure certainly appeals to the sense of social justice of some, particularly when long-term unemployment persists and the numbers of staff employed to combat social security frauds is constantly increased, and further claimants by this means and others are squeezed off the register. In one sense such comparisons are irrelevant: if the rich and powerful did not manage to secure such privileges against the poor and impotent they would not remain rich and powerful. Less tautologically however, a political system that has at its centre a respect for individual property rights, entrenched over many centuries, and which bases its economy upon competitive entrepreneurial capitalism, has necessarily to exercise a certain restraint as to the formulation and application of tax laws.

Avoidance

Tax avoidance is the product of progressive taxation, which is in substance, if not in essence, a twentieth-century phenomenon. Although income tax had become established in the nineteenth century as a levy on the well-off, it was only with the expanding responsibilities of the state and the provision of social services – old age pensions, education and so on – and the rise of socialism and the Labour Party at the turn of the century that it became more widely spread. Egalitarian and socialist ideology required that an increasing number of basic social institutions for the welfare of the population should be provided by the state, according to objective standards of adequate quality, and without regard for the ability of the individual to pay: housing, education, health care, pensions, unemployment benefit. These could be achieved only by the state, which needed to raise much greater revenue to do so. This was levied by a contribution from all according to ability to pay: there was no point in attempting to raise taxes from those whose poverty the new arrangements were mean to benefit most. Progressive taxation hence came to be regarded as an essential element of social justice. The threshold for payment of income tax was established at subsistence level. Higher-level rates or surtax were then imposed on incomes regarded as substantial, because they were well able to make a larger contribution without hardship. In a sense progressive taxation formalized the *noblesse oblige* of charitable work dating back to the middle ages. The difference was that, in eliminating discretion and control over such charity, it raised the spectre of the over-mighty state as expropriator, and secondly that it conflicted with a nineteenth-century principle of reward for meritorious effort: God helps those who help themselves.

Income, however, does not derive for the rich predominantly from employment, but from investment, and this provided a further moral and fiscal dilemma. Social justice ideology pointed to the fact that investment income required no effort other than that employed in making the investment decision. Income from shares, government stocks, property rents, banks and so on is still referred to as 'unearned income', and taxed on a separate basis from earned income. Social justice arguments would maintain that these sources of income could be regarded as a useful source of additional revenue in time of need. Traditionalists, or perhaps one should say conservatives, including today's neo-conservatives, point, however, to the fact that capitalist enterprise, which generates the incomes and propierty which have made industrialized society and its welfare institutions possible, depends upon continuing substantial and intelligent investment. Those investments are naturally made in the expectation of gain, both from interest and dividends and from increases in the value of the investment itself, capital gain. And of course investments can go wrong and be dissipated; normally the greater the risk of losing the investment the greater also the potential returns. Taxing successful investments takes little account of these risks, and any heavy taxation is likely to deter risk taking. Governments have traditionally managed this dilemma selectively by giving tax advantages to kinds of investments which they wish to promote – the oil and gas industry in the United States in the mid-1970s after the establishment of OPEC and high price increases, for example. Secondly they have increased rates to raise revenues in times of national emergency, most notably war.

An additional problem for conservatives was the importance, especially in Britain, of inheritance as the basis of wealth. It was one thing to argue that the successful entrepreneur should be allowed to invest accumulated wealth and enjoy the benefits. It was quite another to maintain that an aristocrat who had inherited great tracts of land which generated a huge income in rents should be so privileged. The outcome was a tax on the transmission of wealth to successors, a capital transfer tax, or death duties as it was originally called.

In the end the rich faced five kinds of taxation: higher rates of income tax, a tax on their investment income, capital transfer tax on death, a tax on capital gains if they realized assets to advantage, and a tax on the profits of any of the companies they owned. It is not surprising that the rich took the best available advice on how to minimize the impact of these taxes. As a consequence of the complexities of the schemes devised and the playing off of tax advantages in one area against disadvantages in another, the most elaborate challenges have been made to the tax authorities, which have necessitated appeal to the highest legal levels for decision. A minor industry serviced by accountants and lawyers has hence grown up to devise successful schemes, many of them eliminated in due course by governments anxious not to lose revenue, but more anxious that taxation should be seen to be equitable, and that the rich should not be able to buy specialized services to exempt themselves from it.

Avoidance Schemes: The Duke of Westminster and the Vesteys

More interestingly however, neither the political nor the legal system has shown itself capable of producing a clear and agreed set of principles of taxation. It has rather been the very fact that taxation has been fraught with uncertainty that has permitted tax advisers to flourish and produce ever more complex and varied avoidance schemes. Despite ringing rhetoric about 'soaking the rich' – Denis Healey was a good example as Chancellor of the Exchequer in the 1970s – Labour governments have been no more decisive or definitive than Conservative or Liberal ones, and no more able, in devising a Finance Bill, to avoid complex rules and myriad exemption clauses. The law lords, confronted with persistent attempts at circumvention by rich taxpayers pursued by the Inland Revenue, have been reluctant to devise rules and principles also, and have clearly felt themselves caught in the same dilemmas, sharpened by their responsibility for the legal determination of enforcement. On the one hand they have held that the taxpayer is obliged to pay taxes imposed by Parliament; on the other that he/she is not obliged to pay more than Parliament requires, and if his/her affairs are complex and Parliament does not provide clear rules of taxation in his/her circumstances, she/he may manage them to the best advantage. In the words of Lord Tomlin in pronouncing judgment on the affairs of the Duke of Westminster in 1936,

> Every man is entitled if he can to order his affairs so that the tax attaching under the appropriate Acts is less than it would otherwise be. If he succeeds in ordering them so as to secure this result, then however unappreciative the commissioners of Inland Revenue or his fellow tax payers may be of his ingenuity, he cannot be compelled to pay an increased tax. This so-called doctrine of 'substance' seems to be to be nothing more than an attempt to make a man pay, notwithstanding that he has so ordered his affairs that the amount of tax sought from him is not legally claimable.[10]

Although it was the earlier sentences here which became celebrated, it was in fact the last one concerning 'substance' that became of critical importance, expressed in the revised form of whether a court was required to wear blinkers when reviewing a tax scheme, considering each element in isolation, or whether it could consider the scheme as a whole, including its consequences and background. The Westminster case was taken as meaning that the law lords did not propose to do Parliament's work for it. Tax was to be construed as a narrow set of rules explicitly imposed on the subject. The law lords would not set about devising general principles, nor would they, as they not infrequently did with other legislation, ruminate on the intention of Parliament when attempting to construe a statute in a hard case. The status of taxation as expropriation was evidently still at the back of their lordships' minds.

This is more evident when the techniques at issue in the Westminster case are considered. The Duke proposed to reduce his liability for higher-rate tax by transferring some of his income to his servants by way of a covenant. The success of the ruse lay in the continuing right of his servants to demand wages for their employment, although in practice they declined to do so. To any layman the scheme was utterly artificial and wholly designed to avoid payment of tax which Parliament had clearly intended to levy.

The Westminster case, though it became central to the mythology of avoidance, was by no means the earliest or most radical success. Well before 1936 the Vestey family was presented with what it regarded as an intolerable tax burden. The Vesteys were entrepreneurs, not aristocrats, who had made their considerable fortunes from meat, recognizing early the immense advance offered by refrigeration.[11] They established an integrated production, freezing and processing, and shipping and distribution business based in Britain and the Argentine. Up to the introduction of industrial freezer plants, meat had been so perishable that it could be transported over long distances only by being dried, salted or canned. Freezing enabled fresh meat to be raised and slaughtered in the most profitable conditions in Argentina, frozen and then shipped to the lucrative markets of Britain, Europe and the United States. The Vesteys retained control of their businesses – production, processing, shipping and wholesaling and retailing – in the family. They were thus particularly vulnerable to the consequences of taxation introduced in the first national economic mobilization of Britain in the First World War. The effect of increases in company taxation, income tax and death duties (which the Vesteys regarded merely as deferred income tax) was that of every £100 profit from their businesses they would in the end receive only £17.10p.

William Vestey wrote to the Treasury pointing this out, in the expectation of a constructive response to such extortion. He was disappointed. The Treasury was preoccupied with ensuring adequate revenue to finance the war effort, and to entertain his claim would have been to invite a flood of others. Like many modern tax avoiders the Vesteys responded by going offshore. An American company was established which was given control of all Vestey operations: in return it paid the British company just enough to fund its costs and pay dividends. Profits from the Vestey empire hence went to the American company, so avoiding British tax. The company was, however, owned by the Vesteys themselves, who settled in Argentina, where there was no income tax.

Tax exile was not a permanently acceptable solution however. A scheme was devised which enabled the Vesteys to become British residents again by 1921, which has proved effective to the present day in all but eliminating tax liability. Like many of its successors, it was based on the establishment of a trust fund. This was based on the accumulation of funds of £960,000 per annum from a 21-year lease of most of their operations to Union Gold Storage, paid to three French residents known and trusted by the Vesteys. These funds were invested for the long-term benefit of the Vestey family. Transfer of the £960,000 annual payments for the lease avoided tax because it was not Vestey income. The money from the trust fund was then invested rather than paid as income to the Vesteys, so avoiding problems over the trust as a legal entity, which would be invalidated if those establishing it also had the power to enjoy its benefits. Investments were, however, directed in large amounts to Western United Investment in Britain, which in turn acted as philanthropic bankers to the Vesteys, neither charging nor paying interest. Technically the Vesteys received loans, but there was never any pressure to repay them. This policy by Western was imposed by the Vesteys who owned the only four voting shares.

The Revenue was in some difficulty in mounting a case against the Vesteys because of the Paris base of the trust and the fact that most records were kept in Buenos Aires. It took them until 1942 to bring matters to a head, when it imposed a heavy assessment on the estate of one of the two Vestey brothers who dominated the family, and on the income of the other still living. It also demanded more information and increased demands for back tax. The Vesteys lost at every stage up to the House of Lords. As Lord Justice Somerwell said in the Court of Appeal,

> There was a finding which was not disputed before us that the main purpose of the creation of the £960,000 rent and its transfer to the settlement was the avoidance of UK taxation. Looking at the arrangement as a whole it seems to me that the Vesteys were receiving benefit in the shape of loans without interest . . . The result is that in my view the whole income of the transfers has to be deemed the income of the Vesteys.

Clearly Lord Somerwell did not approve of tax avoidance, and was disposed to take the necessary steps to prevent it in looking at the substance rather than the form of the scheme.

The law lords took a quite different view, explicitly construing the trust deed 'without regard to the fact that (it) is part of a scheme of tax avoidance'. In their 1949 judgment they applied the provisions of section 18 of the Finance Act 1936, which was specifically directed at tax avoidance through taking money out of the UK. Under it, if a UK resident acquired the power to enjoy the income deriving from such a foreign-based trust, and if it would have been liable to tax if received in the UK, it was taxable. There had also been what was taken to be a leading case in 1948 which took this principle further. *Congreve* v. *Inland Revenue* held that even if the income of foreign trusts went to children or other relatives – passive beneficiaries – it was taxable. In finding for the Vesteys in 1949 the law lords said that neither of these two obstacles were decisive, since neither of the two Vestey brothers had an individual power to enjoy the income of the Paris trust, only a joint power. And even if the brothers had interest-free loans originating from the trust, they were loans not income, and so not taxable. 'To say of a man that if the trust income should be invested in a loan to himself he has the beneficial enjoyment of that income is a misuse of language . . . The words point to an out and out disposal of an income for the benefit of some person or persons, and are wholly inappropriate to an investment by way of a loan.' So concerned were the senior judiciary with the distortion of words that they were oblivious of the gross distortion of reality that was the outcome of the Vestey trust. Even in the face of the substance of the intention to end such schemes in the 1936 Finance Act and the lavish untaxed lifestyle enjoyed by the Vestey family, the law lords stuck to the form of the words of the law.

The language of Lord Normand in 1949 was reminiscent of that in the Duke of Westminster's case in 1936:

> Parliament in its attempts to keep pace with the ingenuity devoted to tax avoidance may fall short of its purpose. That is a misfortune for tax payers who do nothing to avoid their share of the burden, and it is disappointing to the Inland Revenue, but the court will not stretch the terms of the taxing acts in order to improve on the efforts of Parliament, or stop gaps which are left open by the Statute.
>
> Tax avoidance is an evil, but it would be the beginnings of much greater evils if the courts were to overstretch the language of the Statute to subject to taxation people of whom they disapproved.

It took the Revenue until the 1970s to mount a further case against the Vesteys, in part because of great difficulties in obtaining the necessary information. The accounts of the Paris trust were kept in Uruguay, and produced only after the imposition of a legal notice under the 1970 Taxes Act. The Revenue assessed the Vesteys for income tax on £4.3 million and surtax on £7.3 million in a period of four years in the 1960s, and the case reached the House of Lords in 1979. The Lords decided again as they had in 1949, and for good measure overturned the Congreve case as bad law and held that passive beneficiaries are not liable for tax. They did, however, identify the problem as a loophole that urgently required legislation. Although the Revenue's assessment was rejected as 'arbitrary, unjust and fundamentally unconstitutional' the law lords were by 1979 concerned to shift the burden on to Parliament, not in the passive sense of 1949 that it was not the law lords' problem, but in the active sense that a remedy was required which only Parliament could provide. In 1981 action was finally taken to strengthen the 'power to enjoy' provisions of the law on the beneficiaries of overseas trusts. The Treasury was also reported to be examining anti-avoidance laws in West Germany and the United States with a view to similar legislation requiring the inclusion of consideration of the intent behind a scheme in judgments on tax avoidance. In the meantime the Vestey case had been extensively researched and serialized in *The Sunday Times*, to the embarrassment of the government.

Rossminster and Beyond

In the event the Government did not attempt such general legislation. It was able to avoid doing so as the result of the law lords' seeming finally to have decided what the limit of their tolerance of artifical tax avoidance was in 1981. In March they decided unanimously in favour of the Revenue in *W. T. Ramsay* v. *IRC*, and *Inspector of Taxes* v. *Rawling*.[12] The crucial difference of *Ramsay* is that the court explicitly broke with strict constructionism, the blinkers of seeing each step in a scheme in isolation. In this case the scheme was stated by its devisers, Rossminster, to be 'a pure tax avoidance scheme' achieved by a complex series of transactions, including a loss allowable for tax purposes and a matching gain that was not chargeable for tax.[13] What the court decided was important in this case was at last the substantial result – neither losses nor gains, save fees to Rossminster – rather than the formal result – exemption from liability for tax. Lord Wilberforce said that the series of transactions needed to achieve this must be seen as a whole, and for what they were as a whole. 'While the techniques of tax avoidance progress and are technically improved, the courts are not obliged to stand still.' He went further and cited two American cases 'not as authority, but as examples which are expressed in vigorous and apt language of the process of thought which seems to me not inappropriate for the courts in this country to follow.' As a result of a US Supreme Court decision, American courts can look beyond the form of a business arrangement affecting tax liability to its substance and, if no purpose other than tax avoidance can be identified, ignore it. In the United States it was accepted that the courts would consider the intention of Congress in legislating, whereas in Britain strict constructionism was based on the principle that there is no equity in tax. This means that, in hard cases where statutory provisions do not apply easily, judges cannot have recourse to their own sense of justice and fairness, as they can in many other areas of law.

The principle that tax avoidance schemes could be considered for their substance not their legal form was taken a step further in 1984 in *Furniss* v. *Dawson*.[14] In this case the taxpayer Dawson tried to defer capital gains tax when selling shares in two family companies by transferring them to another company, taking advantage of a provision of the 1965 Tax Act. Tax then becomes payable when the shares of the second company are sold or the company liquidated. Although Dawson won in the appeal court, the House of Lords dismissed his case on the *Ramsay* principle that the transaction had no business purpose and was therefore void for fiscal purposes.

One might wonder why, having so often refused to take such an apparently obvious step, the House of Lords was persuaded to do so in the early 1980s. The Vestey case, in which they evidently felt bound to affirm the traditional position which privileged the wealthy, was certainly a stimulus, but the main source of pressure came from Rossminster.

Accountants Roy Tucker and Ronald Plummer formed Rossminster in 1973 after acquiring experience in tax avoidance on behalf of clients. Tucker and Plummer thought they perceived an opportunity to provide a needed service to a new category of taxpayer and thereby earn themselves a good deal of money. The years of Labour administration from 1964 to 1970 had introduced a series of rather more stringent and progressive forms of taxation. Whether one perceives the problem in terms of these taxes reaching further down among the clearly affluent but not indisputably wealthy, or whether one emphasizes the numbers of those with significant but not vast new wealth emerging after the years of prosperity in the late 1950s and 1960s, Tucker and Plummer were accurate in their perception of a market for tax avoidance. The difference that Rossminster was to bring was that its schemes were mass-marketed to the affluent, rather than tailor-made for the wealthy as in the past.

Rossminster's strategy was to devise a scheme that might be applicable to a significant number of clients: eventually 13 schemes were produced for 2,000 clients. Once a scheme was devised by Tucker and Plummer, the advice of leading counsel was sought as to whether it would hold up in court and, if the opinion was favourable, the scheme was marketed. In addition, Rossminster offered to set aside up to £50,000 to fight any case the Revenue brought against a client using the scheme. The advantage to clients was access to ingenious schemes with top-level legal advice at relatively modest rates. The advantage to Rossminster was up to 20 per cent of the tax saved. All the schemes were complex and involved a series of transactions through companies onshore and offshore (but by no means always involving tax havens) which were bought or set up for the purpose. The sum of these transactions amounted to balancing losses and gains, which involved little or no business changes in clients' affairs, but did achieve a significant loss of tax liability. In each case close reading of the statutes and precedents was involved, resulting in the setting up of a series of transactions each legally watertight, but with the magical end-result of defeating the Revenue – or so it was thought.

The Revenue was naturally not happy as it gradually became aware of the extent and sophistication of the Rossminster enterprise. Neither Rossminster nor its clients revealed more than they had to about the schemes, and, as always, the Revenue was hampered by its ignorance: it could acquire information only if it knew at least approximately what it was looking for. The Revenue's recourse was to ask for more and more information and adopt a combative stance to Rossminster, adhering strictly to correct procedures, and so consuming a great amount of time and effort.

A more dramatic turn of events however was provided by a *Sunday Times* analysis of one of the schemes, Commodity Carry, in 1977. This highlighted the deliberate and artificial character of the scheme, along with the involvement of a Tory MP. Tom Benyon owned 2½ per cent of Rossminster. Peter Rees QC, who became the Treasury Minister responsible for personal taxation in the Conservative government from 1979, was the tax silk whose opinion on the scheme was sought. John Knott, later Secretary of State for Defence, was a paid consultant to one of the companies involved in the scheme, although he later said he had no idea that transactions taking place were part of the tax avoidance scheme. The reaction of the Labour Government to the 1977 analysis of Commodity Carry was to ban it in the next Finance Act.

By the time the Tories took office in 1979 it was apparent that Rossminster was not merely an embarrassment because of its Tory connections. It represented a new stage in tax avoidance which was making it available to a much wider group in the population. By the time the *Ramsay* judgment put an end to it, Rossminster stood to have avoided £1 billion in tax. How much has since been recovered is not clear, but Tucker and Plummer certainly became rich men, having got out in 1979 and secured their personal fortunes.

It was just as well for them that they did, for in July 1979 the Revenue, acting on a search warrant under the 1976 Taxes Management Act, raided the homes of Benyon, Tucker and Plummer at 7 a.m., and then went on to Rossminster's offices. They took away twelve van loads of documents. Tucker and Plummer protested that they had taken much that was irrelevant and that their behaviour was oppressive, but the High Court to which they took their suit did not agree. On appeal however they were heard at a special sitting out of term by Lord Denning, whose idiosyncratic reputation in the defence of the rights of the individual against large and oppressive institutions was by then legendary. Denning pronounced that there had been nothing like it since 1763 when the King's messengers arrested John Wilkes, a prominent radical politician, and seized his papers. The Revenue should have given adequate information as to what their charges were: a suspected person has a right to know what she/he is suspected of. Denning also referred to the fact that the 1976 Act empowering the Revenue to obtain a warrant for such a fishing expedition had been passed by a Parliament (with a Labour government) with a narrow majority, and opposed at the time as a threat to the rights of the citizen: 'Once great power is granted there is a danger of it being abused.'[15]

Nonsense, said the House of Lords, when the Revenue appealed. The courts

> were the guardian of the citizen's right to privacy. But they must do that in the context of the times, i.e. of increasing parliamentary intervention and of the modern power of judicial review. Appeals to 18th century precedents of arbitrary action by Secretaries of State and references to general warrants did nothing to throw light on the issue. Furthermore, while the courts might look critically at legislation that impaired the rights of citizens and should resolve any doubt on interpretation in their favour, it was not part of their duty or power to restrict or impede the working of legislation, even

unpopular legislation; to do so would be to weaken rather than advance the democratic process.[16]

The powers of the Revenue and their use will be further considered below. In the present context it suffices to say that even the quite extensive and general powers permitting forcible search for evidence where fraud was suspected on reasonable grounds by the Commissioners under the 1976 Act (strictly an amendment to the Taxes Management Act, 1970) was held by the law lords to be necessary to deal with Rossminster. Their lordships showed their determination to crush grossly artificial avoidance schemes in the *Ramsay* decision of 1981 and subsequent cases. Rossminster was indeed crushed, and the involvement of the Director of Public Prosecutions as well as the Revenue in the 1979 raid raised the possibility of criminal charges of fraud being brought against at least some of those involved. In 1983, however, it was decided that no charges would be brought – apart from the embarrassment of Benyon and Rees being potential witnesses, a criminal case would be long and expensive, and the DPP will not sanction charges unless he believes he has a greater than even chance of success.

The determination of the Government to control tax avoidance was underlined by the Chancellor's firm action on bond washing in 1985. This involved the rapid sale and repurchase of Government bonds to convert liability by higher-rate income tax payers into capital gains tax, charged at 30 rather than at 60 per cent. Action was also taken against offshore roll-up funds, which had become widely used in a similar way by higher-rate taxpayers to convert income into capital. The main purveyor of these services admitted defeat by the Chancellor, but simultaneously a new scheme was advertised by a rising group of investment advisers, which, it was claimed, would achieve the same object: Barlow Clowes, of whom more in the next chapter. More strategically, the government sought to eliminate the need for tax avoidance by reducing tax rates, especially the higher ones, which came down from 60 to 40 per cent. At a certain point the effort and expense involved in avoidance is no longer justified by the amount of tax saved.

Ramsay and the demise of Rossminster were widely taken to have ended aggressive tax avoidance, that is, elaborate schemes devised to defy the law, as opposed to a simple procedure in taking advantage of tax privileges plainly offered by the Chancellor as an incentive for particular kinds of investment, for example those of the Business Expansion Scheme in the late 1980s, designed to further investment in small businesses. Tax advisers and their clients did not, however, go out of business, or entirely abandon their objectives. The new target was to see just how comprehensive the opposition to artificial schemes had become. For their part the Revenue sought to interpret the law in its favour, and to rule inadmissable many transactions which had only a tax avoidance rather than a business purpose, and to review a series of transactions in the light of their impact on avoidance in retrospect.

Things came to a head in 1988, when a series of cases were considered jointly by the House of Lords, which, surprisingly to many, found predominantly in favour of the taxpayers.[17] The arrangements under review were much less elaborate than the Rossminster schemes, and some of them involved traditional avoidance techniques: others appeared to reflect changing business circumstances - deals falling through - and reactions to them. The essence of the law lords' decision was that artificial schemes were to be ruled void only where they involved a series of pre-ordained steps which had no business purpose. Schemes could be considered as wholes, rather than in terms of the legal effect of each individual step. If, however, there was a significant break in time between one transaction and the next, and if each stage did not require the next, that is a series of seperate decisions was involved, then the Revenue was bound to consider each stage on its merits, and to acknowledge that businessmen have a right to respond to their circumstances as they develop and to include mitigation of tax liability in that response. As Lord Oliver put it:

> A critical feature was that the intermediate steps had to serve no purpose other than that of saving tax. Further, all stages had to be pre-ordained with a degree of certainty, with the tax payer having control over the end result at the time when the intermediate steps were taken. Last, there should be no disruption between the intermediate transaction and the disposal to the ultimate purchasers.

The decision was a close one, however, of three to two. Lord Templeman in particular was most unhappy with it, saying that the speeches of the majority

> accepted the extreme argument of the tax payers that Furniss was limited to its own facts or to a transaction which had reached an advanced stage of negotiation - whatever that expression meant - before the preceding tax avoidance transaction was carried out.
>
> Those limitations would distort the effect of Furniss, were not based on principle, were not to be derived from the speeches in Furniss, and if followed would revive a surprised tax avoidance industry and cost the body of tax payers hundreds of millions of pounds.

He added that 'of course two transactions separated in time might be independent and not part of a scheme. It was for the commissioners to ask themselves whether on the evidence two transactions were part of a scheme. In most cases where there was a scheme there would be evidence of arrangements.'

The law lords hence upheld the principle established in the Duke of Westminster's case of the right of the taxpayer to arrange his affairs so as to minimize liability for tax, and added the rider that this meant also a right of changing arrangements in the light of changing circumstances. Lord Templeman's comment as to the evidence of an artificial scheme does seem to be critical here, for it is only on such evidence that in many cases it will be clear whether what purported to be a series of reasonable responses to a developing situation was in fact a pre-planned scheme of avoidance. The Institute of Taxation Conference in the autumn of 1988 reached a consensus that the Revenue's advance had been checked and that there was still substantial scope for the prudent and cautious in tax avoidance.

The situation as regards liability for tax hence remains unresolved and the tensions described at the beginning of this chapter between the interests of society at large and those of government in a predictable and honestly accepted tax revenue system, and the rights of the individual, and of the wealthy in particular, are unresolved. Furthermore, they are plainly evident in decisions about tax liability at the highest level, both in government and in the judiciary. Pressure in either direction continues, and no magic formula has been devised to reconcile them. It is against this background that the practice of the Revenue in dealing with evasion, that is, the deliberate non-declaration of income which is indisputably taxable, should be seen. It is often maintained that the Revenue acts in a way that privileges the rich against the poor, or at any rate the non-rich, and that the penalties for non-conformity in tax matters are disproportionately lenient. The point of the foregoing exposition is to suggest that, whilst this is so, the reasons for it have to do with the unresolved and equivocal status of taxation.

Evasion

When the former champion jockey, Lester Piggott, was prosecuted and convicted for tax evasion in 1987 and sentenced to three years' imprisonment he was reported as being bitter at being singled out for such attention.[18] He was convicted of supressing a total income of £3,118,788 over a period of ten years, a substantial part of it the proceeds of bets placed for him by owners for whom he had ridden. This is also an offence against Jockey Club rules since there is an obvious danger that a jockey allowed to place bets would be tempted to modify his ride in order to bring off the bet. Piggott also obtained various substantial revenues from the shares which he was given by grateful owners in the stud fees of horses he had ridden. Since a stallion is divided into forty shares and can earn £100,000 for each of the 70 mares it may service in a year, and can keep this up for ten years, a share is one fortieth of £70 million – or £1.75 million. Piggott was exposed as a result of a dispute between a leading trainer, Henry Cecil, and a bloodstock agent, Melvyn Walters. At the sale of a colt imported by Walters, bidding reached £420,000 but the winning bidder disappeared and the underbidder refused to take the horse. At a second auction, less than half the original price was reached. Walters asked Cecil to intercede to obtain more money, and when he failed to do so leaked a letter to the press. This contained details of Piggott's retainer for the 1982 season of £10,000 officially registered with the racing authorities. Additional cash payments of £45,000 were also to be made, however, as well as 7½ per cent of winners' and 10 per cent of placed horses' prize money, and one share in every winning colt ridden by him that went to stud. This letter was sent to the owners of all 140 horses in the Cecil stable, which included Walters among them.

This was just the kind of information the Inland Revenue rarely obtains and it provided a vital lever to being an inquiry which did not prove straightforward. Even when confronted with evidence of suppressed income, Piggott continued to hold out on three separate occasions. Eventually the Revenue discovered 17 bank accounts in Britain, Ireland and various tax havens. It also widened its inquiries to include possible tax offences by others in the horse-racing world.

Would Piggott have been justified, if, as reported, he felt victimized? Not, perhaps, had he known of the four-year sentence on an accountant convicted only a month earlier. But he might have cited the 1984 case of a hotel owner fined £40,000 and ordered to pay £20,000 in costs after a three-year Revenue inquiry. The six hotels he controlled were also fined £230,000 besides the tax required, resulting in the forced sale of one of them. The judge concluded that 'at each of the hotels you directed and instructed the manager in the manner of carrying out these frauds. This was a matter of settled policy.'[19] Staff wages were kept low and their income supplemented with undeclared tips and service charges. The principal offender – others were also convicted – ordered bespoke shirts from London and passed them off to the Revenue as staff uniforms. He charged the window-cleaning bills on his house and his nanny's television to one of the hotels; clearly the fraud was long-term and comprehensive, and few opportunities were missed to exploit his position in respect of tax, yet there was no custodial sentence.

In its evidence to the Royal Commission on Criminal Procedure in 1979, the Inland Revenue set outs its criteria for prosecution. These are basically two. On the one hand the Revenue will prosecute for serious cases: where for example the offender is a tax adviser or accountant, where the fraud is sophisticated and especially if it includes forgery, or where the fraud has been concerted with others. On the other hand, the recalcitrant are also prosecuted, those who either deny irregularities or who pretend to reveal all, but in fact withold information on significant other irregularities. Piggott seems clearly to fall under the latter head. Deane, in a study of actual prosecutions, concluded that over the period 1950–74 prosecutions seemed to be prompted by conspiracy, incomplete disclosure, forgery, the occupation of the defendant as a professional adviser, perjury, and the extended time period over which the evasion took place.[20] Conviction rates on prosecution were very high and sentences for principal offenders typically a fine (30 per cent) or a year's imprisonment (24 per cent). There were only 13 sentences of three years in his sample of 121 cases, and only one sentence in excess of that. Piggott may hence have had some grounds for feeling aggrieved at the length of his sentence.

Clearly the Revenue does not resort to prosecution very often. How then does it organize its enforcement work and what are its objectives? Two major features are of importance. First the overall strategy seems similar to that of Theodore Roosevelt's foreign policy: talk softly and carry a big stick. The Revenue has very wide powers but abuses them sparingly. Thus its powers of forcible search and seizure under the 1976 amendment to the 1970 Taxes Management Act, which was used against Rossminster, was used, according to Levi, only 15 times between 1976 and October 1982, and according to the Chairman of the Board of Inland Revenue in March 1988, only 11 times in the preceding three years.[21] Further, the Board's legal power to require the production of documents was used only 25 times over this latter period. It was the experience of defendants defying the Revenue by destroying evidence rather than producing it that was the basis of the granting of the power of forcible entry, search and seizure in 1976.

Much more widely used are the administrative powers of the Revenue to request detailed information about a taxpayer's affairs, going back as far as the Revenue wish. Inquiries begin very gently with a vague letter asking for an assurance that all taxable income has been declared. Such letters are invariably inspired by information on undisclosed income that has come into the Revenue's hands. A game of cat and mouse ensues, with the Revenue insisting on the obligation of the taxpayer to make a complete declaration of all sources of taxable income. Sanctions ascend in a measured scale. Initially the taxpayer has to respond to the Revenue's detailed enquiries, and if recalcitrance is suspected the Revenue may, as in the Rossminster case, require proof of everything. Secondly, the taxpayer may become aware that if he persists in suppressing income, he risks the continued attentions of the Revenue in future years, even after the settlement of the current issues. Further, if he fails to disclose taxable income, he risks the imposition of an administrative penalty on top of the tax due of 100 per cent of the tax due if the failure to disclose is negligent, or 200 per cent if it is deliberate. And at the end of the day, continued defiance can lead to prosecution. Most taxpayers probably live in greatest dread that once the Revenue has them down as suspects they will be subject to detailed inquiries every year. Certainly this can be the case if the Revenue's suspicions are not resolved, but normally it is not so, as their experience is that businesses and individuals subject to detailed investigation once tend to be honest in the future. The strategy of the Revenue hence appears to be that of convincing the taxpayer that honesty and co-operation are the easiest way out of trouble.

Such methods save time and money on criminal proceedings, but they are themselves time-consuming in concentrating efforts on getting the co-operation of targeted individuals or companies. They also risk the accusation that tax offenders are dealt with much more leniently that burglars and pickpockets. Inasmuch as lenience is equated with administrative penalties and fines rather than loss of liberty and the public stigma of a criminal conviction, this is clearly true. The question is, why?

Part of the answer to this lies in the unresolved ambiguity of taxation and tax offences discussed in relation to tax avoidance: they do not have the same moral simplicity as offences such as burglary, however cynically some of the rationalizations of the self-employed evader may be regarded by the employee who is honest perforce. Part of the answer also lies in the difficulties of discovery and enforcement which tax offences share with other business crimes. Unless the Revenue is supplied with draconian powers of investigation and vastly increased personnel it will remain simply unable to extract the whole truth from all taxpayers.

Alarm has been expressed at a number of points in recent years on both sides of the debate. The House of Commons Public Accounts Committee was concerned in 1981, for example, at the extent of tax evasion and at the proportion of cases examined in which understatement of taxable income was discovered: up from 73 per cent in 1977 to 85 per cent in 1980, with serious irregularities up from 6 to 17 per cent. The black economy and its growth during the recession of the early 1980s and the attendant rise in long-term unemployment also gave rise to considerable concern in 1984, when the Revenue was authorized to take on 850 additional staff for special inquiries. The Rossminster affair gave rise to public debate about the Revenue's powers, and this and concern at VAT cases (see below) led to the establishment of the Keith Committee on the Enforcement Powers of the Revenue Departments. This reported in 1983 with a variety of detailed recommendations, but expressed itself generally satisfied that the approach of the Revenue was reasonable and appropriate, and their powers necessary to deal with the recalcitrant minority.[22]

The approach of the Revenue in these circumstances has been to concentrate its efforts upon major offenders: targeting. Its efforts have hence been directed at identifying occupations where abuse is rife – the construction industry has been subject to repeated investigations because of the subcontracting system, which is frequently managed on a cash basis; Fleet Street print workers were shown in a purge in the mid-1980s to have been extensively engaged in abuses; taxi drivers have been similarly targeted. Besides this, the Revenue compiles extensive statistics on the profitability and income of different kinds of business and their sources of revenue. When scrutinizing the tax returns of a particular travel agent, say, the inspector can then note that 54.5 per cent of typical business for travel agents come from inclusive tours, on which average commission is 7.9 per cent. If the agent in question varies significantly from these figures there are grounds for further inquiries to verify the position. A continual reduction in the percentage of individuals investigated has hence produced a radical increase in the tax recovered as targeting has become more successful. The take increased by 500 per cent in real terms over the decade to 1984–5 to reach £550 million. At that point the Revenue was investigating 1.7 per cent of company accounts and 3 per cent of individual's, mainly the self-employed. In 1981 the Chairman of the Board of Inland Revenue cited a figure of 2 per cent of self-employed businesses and 1 per cent of companies investigated, with a take of £750 million.

Clearly there remains a large area which the Revenue finds it difficult to attack. The Chairman, in evidence to the House of Commons Expenditure Committee in 1979, estimated that one in eight taxpayers might have undeclared income of £1,000 a year, and one in four of £500 a year. Most of these are unlikely to be subject to detailed investigation unless the income comes from an occupation that is targeted for inquiry. The existence of a modest black economy is hence tolerated administratively, and the Revenue may be disposed to look kindly upon the offender who forgets to declare limited amounts, provided he co-operates if detected. In evasion, as in avoidance, the Revenue is aware that it must not be seen to be acting oppressively, and whatever the law and regulations are as to tax liability, popular sentiment as to what is reasonable is not to be ignored. The taxman may not be accorded much respect or overwhelming support by individuals in respect of their own earnings, but that is quite different from a potential situation in which heavy-handedness leads to his being heartily loathed, and every citizen's hand turning against him.

Tax Compliance: Avoidance and Evasion

Avoidance and evasion derive from the desire to pay less tax, and Britain is somewhat unusual in having permitted the development of a formal avoidance sector with a distinct life of its own which has powerfully reflected the British class system. The position finally reached in Britain in the *Ramsay* and *Dawson* cases in the 1980s was articulated in the United States by Judge Learned Hand in 1934.[23] In *Helvering* v. *Gregory* he said, 'Every tax payer is entitled to arrange his affairs so that his taxes shall be as low as possible; he is not bound to choose that pattern which will best pay the Treasury', but in another case in the same year, *Commission of Internal Revenue* v. *Ickelheimer*, he said,

> No doubt the most important single factor in ascertaining the Statute's meaning is the words its employs. But the colloquial words of the Statute have not the fixed and artificial content of scientific symbols . . . Here we can have no doubt of the purpose at which Congress was aiming. We truncate if we do not include transactions by which, in accordance with a pre-ordained design, property passes, by whatever combination of moves, from one member to another of specified categories.

As American tax practitioners sum up the approach: 'Tax is an intensely practical subject', that is, one in which the detailed business context is of the greatest relevance. Whilst this pragmatic view has prevented the growth of a legalistic tax avoidance industry in America in the same form as in Britain, it has not, however, eliminated tax avoidance. As the theoretical economist Stiglitz points out in analysing the implications of avoidance techniques, fundamental features of the taxation system necessarily leave it open to manipulative avoidance.[24] So long as taxation is progressive and so long as capital gains, capital transfers and unearned income are taxed separately and at varying rates, there will be tax advantages to be gained by judicious switching of assets. Indeed he concludes (p. 335),

> In a perfect capital market these principles of tax avoidance are so powerful as to enable the astute player to eliminate all taxation on capital income and possibly all taxation on wage income as well. The fact that the tax system raises revenue is thus a tribute to the lack of astuteness of the tax payer and/ or the lack of perfection of the capital market.

Here it should be noted that most of the standard techniques discussed by Stiglitz bear a marked similarity to those of which Rossminster's schemes took advantage.

The issue, then, is whether it is worth the trouble required of the tax payer to mitigate tax, and which is the best route to achieve this. Around these questions a quite substantial economic literature has developed, attempting to model the behaviour of taxpayers and largely relying on an implicit background of the US economy and taxation system. Although the Internal Revenue Service (IRS) is one of the largest Federal agencies, with a staff of some 85,000 and a budget of some $3 billion, it has to monitor 170 million returns a year, 135 million for income tax, of which 95 million are individuals. Not all who should do file a tax return – a 1979 General Accounting Office study estimated that 5 million people earning $30 billion and owing $2 billion in tax failed to file a return.[25] Total revenue lost from non-compliance was estimated by the IRS in 1983 to be $90 billion in 1981 and to have been increasing at an average rate of 14 per cent per annum since 1973.

Unlike the Inland Revenue, the IRS lacks the administrative capacity to undertake the detailed monitoring of individual returns that is necessary in order fully to verify compliance. In the circumstances of the tax revolt of the later 1970s and early 1980s, beginning the with Proposition Thirteen referendum reducing property taxes in California and carried through into the tax-cutting Reagan presidency, it is remarkable that a statute was passed in 1982, the Tax Equity and Financial Responsibility Act, which increased penalties for non-compliance and envisaged the expansion of third party information to the IRS. Empirical work by Witte and Woodbury suggests that the Act was likely to achieve some of its objectives if the administrative reviews of the IRS became more extensive.[26] Their research showed that individual taxpayers responded to IRS enquiries and requests to submit information on, for example, unearned income, rather than leaving it to taxpayers to request the forms themselves, and that small businesses were, like British ones, responsive to audit by the Revenue.

A picture hence emerges from the American literature which in some respects rectifies the artificially great gulf in Britain between avoidance and evasion. The taxpayer will not go to the time, trouble and expense of avoidance unless the sums to be saved are substantial and the marginal rates of tax involved significant. Whether she/he adopts the alternative route of evading tax by a deliberately misleading declaration of income will depend upon expectations of the vigilance and effectiveness of the tax authorities. What is implicit in the research in both countries is an underlying willingness by citizens to pay tax despite continuing debates on rates and systems, using at times rhetoric from the past which questions the very legitimacy of taxation itself. One route by which this latter question might again become a real issue is a progressive breakdown in the capacity of the Revenue collection agencies to obtain compliance by diligent effort. At that point taxpayers would become reluctant to comply on the grounds that others were not being made to do so, a position characteristic of many third world countries, and to which Italy probably comes closest in Europe.

Value Added Tax

VAT was introduced in Britain to replace Purchase Tax as a consequence of Britain's entrance into the EEC in 1973, where it forms a substantial part of the tax base for community budgets. It was first adopted by France in the 1950s and was fraught in its early years with substantial abuses. As a tax on all transactions involving transfer of added value rather than a simple tax either on business turnover or on retail sales it was bound to be complicated to administer. Given variations in rates for different commodities and businesses and the inapplicability of the tax to exports there was obvious scope for criminal exploitation. In the event a variety of lucrative tax frauds were operated in France until exposed by the police and a very persistent and able Judge, Jean Gosson, who later wrote up the material for publication.[27] The outcome was eventual modification of the administration of VAT, making it harder to defraud, but the problem has by no means disappeared.

Italy had even worse problems with VAT after it was introduced in 1973, which illustrates the problems of achieving compliance in tax matters. By 1980 the Finance Ministry estimated that businesses and the self-employed were reporting only half of their true income, at a cost in lost VAT of $10 billion, a figure revised in 1981 to $18.5 billion. Attempts to enforce by requiring the use of numbered state-issued receipts and then tamper-proof electronic tills provoked a strike by three-quarters of the country's bars and nearly all the restaurants in the 1980s, and continued widespread evasion. The underlying reason for this widespread refusal to comply lies in the extent of the adaptation of Italy to dependence upon the 'submerged economy'. As Mattera puts it, 'There has been a growing sense in Italy that regular and legitimate economic pursuits are not the best financial route to security. The basic economic structure remains somewhat shaky, and it is only by people operating informally in and around institutions that things somehow stay together.'[28]

Unlike income tax, VAT also attracts professional fraudsters because of the possibility of either a secure and easy income, or of gaining something for nothing. Thus Britain suffered to the estimated extent of £120 million per annum in lost revenue in the early 1980s through frauds involving gold smuggling. Initially these exploited the fact that gold coins were exempt from VAT whereas gold bullion was not. Coins were melted down into ingots and with VAT at 15 per cent there was an easy profit to be made. Cases continued to flow through the courts into the late 1980s involving millions of pounds each, such was the length of inquiries necessary to expose them. Once coins had been subjected to VAT, attention switched to smuggling the gold in from a source where there was either no tax or a much lower one and then selling the bullion on and including a VAT charge. As a result of sustained efforts, the Customs and Excise were able to conclude that by 1987 gold frauds had been significantly curtailed.[29]

Other frauds of a clearly criminal nature included the setting up of dummy businesses against which VAT returns were made and rebates claimed, the smuggling of other goods on which VAT is due, and the failure to pay VAT on goods legally imported on which the tax is legitimately deferred at the point of importation. In all cases of this sort the object of the enterprise has been fraud and the financial and organizational backing of established criminals is often necessary for the larger cases.

Failure to pay VAT is, however, a feature of the black economy and a temptation to many otherwise honest businessmen. The difficulty in obtaining full compliance with the tax is hence very great. Businesses below a certain threshold turnover, which is regularly raised (currently £22,000 a year), do not have to register for or pay VAT. Many small-scale operators in the black economy are hence free of the VAT man's attentions. Like the Inland Revenue, Customs and Excise keep information on the likely turnover of different kinds of businesses, and this will be supplemented by the knowledge of local offices. The more or less conventional business has little alternative but to register for VAT since trade cannot be continued publicly without coming to the attention of the inspector. The question at issue is normally whether VAT is being administered competently and proper accounts kept, on which matters advice can be offered and whether and how much turnover is undeclared. Here the value of cash transactions is paramount, and it may be hard for the inspector to make a significant impact in personal service businesses, such as garages and plumbers.

The powers of Customs and Excise which also has responsibility for collecting excise duty on tobacco and alcohol, betting duty, and customs controls on smuggling, are more substantial than those of the Inland Revenue. They have had a general power of entry to business premises to assess VAT at any reasonable time since 1972. Since 1985 they have had a power of arrest in relation to certain offences, including the use of documents to deceive, and under the same Act they can obtain a search warrant by recourse to a magistrate, a power similar to that of the police, when they believe a VAT offence has been committed. Between 1976 and 1980 they used these powers 702 times, in comparison with the Inland Revenue, who have to obtain their warrant from a judge, using their power 13 times over the same period. None the less they appear to be cautious since they achieved success in 94 per cent of searches in finding evidence of fraud. The Keith Committee noted that only three out of 14 complaints deriving from 834 searches were found to be of any substance.

The enforcement structure of Customs and Excise reflects their concern with serious criminal offences involving drug smuggling, the increased incidence of which has led to a sharp increase in the specialist staff dealing with the problem. At local level all VAT offices have since 1985 had a two-person inquiry team. These staff are non-specialists with only a week's fraud training. Besides investigation and dealing with smaller local cases and liasing with enforcement staff at regional and national level by exchanging intelligence and referring larger cases upwards, the function of the local teams is to sensitize all staff at local level to the problem of fraud. As can be seen from table 2, the work of local teams has expanded considerably in the 1980s.

Cases too large for local resolution are referred up to the 21 regional offices or collections for investigation by the Collections Investigation Units. These had a total staff of about 400 in 1987. Far more of these staff are trained specialists, and inquiries take much longer. Revenue collected in non-drugs cases in 1985/6 was £26.7 million, an average of £37,225 per case. In the half-year to the end of September 1985, there were 171 VAT cases involving more than £10,000, 55 between £1,000 and £10,000, and two below £1,000. No specific national thresholds for the larger-scale CIU inquiries are set and the value of VAT involved varies from £20,000 to £75,000 where regional offices had formulated their own thresholds. Given that VAT is charged at 15 per cent, the size of business involved was clearly not negligible.

At national level enforcement is managed by the Investigation Division, whose numbers have risen to 474, including 121 drug investigators in 1988. ID completed 62 cases in 1985/6 as against 458 by the CIUs. The average revenue of ID non-drugs cases was £167,921, very substantial and hence requiring considerable time to complete inquiries. Of the 1,101 cases completed by ID in 1985/6 including 271 drugs cases, which would almost all involve prosecution, 539 were prosecuted, 450 compounded and 112 dealt with otherwise, mainly by seizure alone. Even for large-scale

Table 2 Local VAT offices : cases completed

	1981-2		1985-6	
	No. of cases	Revenue gained (£)	No. of cases	Revenue gained (£)
Settled by assessment	388	1,582,974	410	4,860,898
Settled locally by compounding	8	42,192	175	1,438,175
Settled by local court penalty	0	–	19	50,743
Accepted for regional/national investigation	423	–	387	–
Reported upwards for prosecution/compounding	349	–	277	–
No fraud	210	–	267	–
TOTALS	1,378	1,625,166	1,535	6,349,816
Average revenue for locally settled case		4,104		10,513
Man-years spent on fraud investigation	104		116	

Source: National Audit Office, *Customs and Excise Department Investigations of Fraud and Smuggling*, HMSO, 1980, Appendix 6.

cases involving substantial sums in revenue, Customs and Excise widely use their power to compound, that is to settle cases without prosecution by administrative penalties in the same way as the Inland Revenue. In part but not exclusively because of the Department's involvement in drugs control, the national office has a substantial Intelligence Division, with 135 staff in 1987, and since 1985 it has been integrated into a single organization covering drugs, VAT and other inquiries. Since 1983 information has been computerized in the Customs and Excise Departmental Reference and Information Computer (CEDRIC), which is linked to terminals in the CIUs, and whose scope and access is to be further widened, including access to the main VAT records computer.

The enforcement of VAT is hence organized on a model much closer to that of the police, and would apparently support the view that ordinary offences involving incompetence and relatively small-scale deliberate non-declaration are dealt with locally by administrative means. Larger cases are dealt with regionally and nationally and have a much greater chance of prosecution. Clearly prosecution does feature substantially in the larger cases, but compounding is also employed, even where the case is apparently of a plainly criminal character. Thus in 1981 a prosecution was withdrawn after agreement to pay £2.7 in arrears and penalties, and in 1984 £400,000 was paid to settle a gold coin VAT fraud by a well-known professional criminal. The claim was made in 1989 that a series of recent failures in criminal trials had overstretched the Department's budget but it seems undeniably the case that its prime target is revenue collection and the closing down of opportunities for fraud, with criminal prosecution only a secondary objective, to be undertaken if the chances of success merit it.[30] Nor does the level of fines and imprisonment for VAT cases give grounds for believing that conviction is treated seriously. As the Keith Committee pointed out in this connection, referring to three cases involving three-quarters of a million pounds in VAT, which attracted sentences of nine months, 21 months and 2 years, such penalties are scarcely likely to deter, especially since a large proportion of arrears, particularly in larger cases, is never recovered. One is driven to the conclusion that serious and plainly criminal frauds on VAT have stimulated the investigatory manpower to control them, but not the appropriate level or kinds of sanctions. To a significant extent the model of negotiation and the objective of revenue collection appropriately employed for lower-level VAT offences pervades the upper level also and hence this least respected of taxes is treated not merely with contempt but with criminally exploitative contempt.

Conclusion

This chapter has sought to show that tax offences share the characteristics of other business crimes. They obviously benefit from the cloak of legitimacy and hence have the non-self-disclosing feature of other business crimes: taxpayers are presumed to be honest until evidence arises to suggest otherwise. Some space has been devoted to attempting to establish also the ambiguity and negotiability of taxation, a necessary exercise in the light of the typical British taxpayer's sense of helplessness in relation to the demands of the Revenue. For the self-employed and for those with significant additional incomes this sense of foreboding is alleviated by the support and advice of their accountant, who has both the professional standing to maintain credibly to the Revenue that its demands are mistakenly excessive, and experience of successful negotiation. Behind these practicalities in the life of the individual taxpayer lie more powerful reasons for asserting the negotiability of tax liability: the continuing political debate about taxation, both as regards its extent and its administration. Behind this lies an age-old resentment of taxation as expropriation.

Taxation has hence a politically charged character which feeds into the workings of the institutions which administer it.

Like other business crimes, individual liability is further protected by privacy. Although the taxation bodies have acquired extensive powers to violate this privacy, they exercise them with a caution that borders on trepidation. For, at the end of the day, the success of a taxation system relies, employee salary deductions apart, upon a substantial degree of willing compliance. In default of that, payment can rapidly become an optional matter. Notwithstanding their investigatory powers, taxation bodies would become grotesquely expensive if they were to have the resources for comprehensive rather than selective enforcement.[31] It is one function of public political debate about taxation to act as a substitute for the internal regulatory efforts of businesses in managing employee crime. There it was seen that the problem tended to become part of industrial relations, and that successful control initiatives required the negotiation of acceptable standards with the work force. Taxpayers cannot similarly debate the regulations with the tax authorities, but the issues are regularly debated as part of the macro-political process, which gives rise both to changes in rates of taxation and to selective changes in enforcement procedures and regulations.

The political and negotiated character of taxation can perhaps be finally highlighted by a brief comparison of Income and Value Added Tax with Corporation Tax.[32] The value-added principle is a straightforward one, and businesses are unable to avoid some liability to it. Individuals are, as discussed above, not capable of entering into political debate as taxpayers with the Revenue about the system, but only as citizens in the wider political process. Corporations are, however, when sufficiently large and powerful, capable of negotiating with the state what tax they will pay, if any. To put it simply, for large corporations the payment of Corporation Tax is optional. This may seem an over-dramatic way of putting the point, but it has to been seen in the light of the fact that, for example, true corporate taxation, as opposed to advanced Corporation Tax, which is really a tax on dividends and hence on personal incomes of shareholders, amounts only to about 3 per cent of total tax revenue in Britain. Corporations can be divided roughly into a third who regularly pay tax, a third who move in and out of liability, and a third who never pay. This last group, it should be added, are not unprofitable by any normal commercial criteria. For the medium-size corporation the careful management of accounting and company results can appreciably affect taxable profits. In addition, the judicious management of tax allowances, for example for investment in plant and machinery, can result in the carrying of extensive allowances against corporation tax from year to year: a Green Paper on Corporation Tax in 1982 put such unused tax allowances at £30 billion.

For the larger corporation with multi-national operations, political clout is greater and even more public. The threat of removal of operations to a country which is cheaper to produce in is ever-present, and governments openly compete with each other to offer the greatest inducements for major multi-nationals to establish new plants. It is for this reason that major corporations not infrequently advertise the apparently vast sums in tax which they pay to the government each year and emphasize their contribution to national revenue, besides acting as sponsors of sport and the arts. Nobody supposes, none the less, that they are philanthropic bodies. The decision to locate in a particular country carries its obligations in terms of the payment of taxes, though these can be mitigated to a large extent by allowances, accounting practices and transfer pricing. The decision to locate, however, carries expectations of good citizenship which will be reflected in a sizeable tax donation to the state in question. The compensations for it are access to an important market without tariff barriers; access to a skilled and reliable work force at reasonable costs; and the political stability of the society, and a low risk of terrorism, wild changes in government policy, and, at worst, expropriation.

NOTES

1 Pierre Lascoumes's extensive research on business crime, including some comments on tax, are to be found in *Les Affaires ou l'art de l'ombre*, le Centurion, 1986.
2 *The Sunday Times*, 14 April 1985.
3 Philip Mattera has an interesting chapter on Italy in his book on the underground economy, which he analyses from a Marxist position, emphasizing its consequences in terms of increased worker exploitation, lower wage rates, lack of safety, etc: *Off the Books*, Pluto Press, 1985. For details of the *Sorpasso*, see *The Times*, 5 August 1987.
4 Michael Levi's *Regulating Fraud*, Tavistock, 1987, contains a useful review of tax law and enforcement in Britain. See also his 'The Powers of the Revenue Agencies', *British Tax Review*, 1982, pp. 36–51.
5 S. Smith, *Britain's Shadow Economy*, Clarendon Press, 1986.
6 House of Commons Committee of Public Accounts, *Matters Relating to the Inland Revenue Department*, HMSO, 1987.
7 *Fiscal Studies*, November 1987.
8 *Boardroom Remuneration Guide*, Hay Management Consultants, London, 1987.
9 *The Times*, 3 April 1984.
10 The Rossminster and Duke of Westminster cases are reviewed in H. H. Monroe, 'Fiscal Finesse: Tax Avoidance and the Duke of Westminster', *British Tax Review*, 1982, pp. 200–12.
11 David Knightley's investigation of the Vesteys was serialized in *The Sunday Times* in 1980 and published separately as *The Vestey Affair*, Macdonald, 1981. A brief account of the Vestey and Rossminster cases is to be found in M. J. Clarke, *Regulating the City*, pp. 129–40. Quotations from legal judgments in the affair are taken from Knightley.
12 *The Times*, Law Report, 17 March 1981.
13 The Rossminster tax avoidance enterprise is described at length in M. Gillard,

In the Name of Charity: The Rossminster Affair, André Deutsch, 1986; and in N. Tutt, *The Tax Raiders: The Rossminster Affair*, Blackstone Press, 1985.

14 *Furniss v. Dawson, Selected Tax Cases*, 1982, p. 267.
15 *All England Law Reports*, 1977, vol. III, p. 384.
16 *The Times*, Law Report, 14 December 1979.
17 *The Times*, Law Report, 22 July 1988.
18 *The Times*, 24 October 1987.
19 *The Times*, 11 January 1984.
20 K. D. Deane, 'Tax Evasion, Criminality and Sentencing the Tax Offender', *British Journal of Criminology*, 1981, pp. 47–57.
21 *The Times*, 11 March 1988; Levi, *Regulating Fraud*, p. 168.
22 The Report of the Keith Committee was published by HMSO in 1983, entitled *Committee on the Enforcement Powers of the Revenue Departments*.
23 American and British approaches to tax avoidance are compared in P. Millett, 'Artificial Tax Avoidance', *British Tax Review*, 1986, pp. 327–37.
24 J. Stiglitz's economic model of tax avoidance is to be found in 'The General Theory of Tax Avoidance', *National Tax Journal*, 1985, pp. 325–37.
25 See Mattera, *Off the Books*, p. 68.
26 A. D. Witte and F. Woodbury, 'The Effect of Tax Laws and Tax Administration on Tax Compliance: The Case of US Individual Income Tax', *National Tax Journal*, 1985, pp. 1–13.
27 J. Cosson in *Les Industriels de la fraude fiscale*, Editions du Seuil, 1971 (revised edition 1978). See also his *Les Grande Escrocs en affaires*, Editions du Seuil, 1979.
28 Mattera, *Off the Books*, p. 97.
29 A considerable amount of information on VAT administration is available in *Customs and Excise Department: Investigations of Fraud and Smuggling*, Report by the Comptroller and Auditor General, National Audit Office, 1988. See also Levi, *Regulating Fraud*.
30 *The Sunday Times*, 15 April 1984.
31 For a review of the systems used in seventeen countries to achieve compliance in tax matters see N. Boidman, 'Tax Evasion: The Present State of Non-compliance', *Bulletin of International Fiscal Documentation*, 1983, pp. 451–79.
32 Corporation Tax is a subject too complex to be documented properly here, but for an illustration of the complexities of company structure in this connection, see T. Hadden, *The Control of Corporate Groups*, Institute of Advanced Legal Studies, University of London, 1983; and for a brief review of the field, see G. Edwards and C. Mayer, 'What are the Options for Corporation Tax?' *British Tax Review*, 1982, pp. 65–8.

7 Liquidations and Receiverships: The Battle for Control

Sally Wheeler

The Insolvency Problem

This chapter looks at the struggle between administrative receivers, liquidators and creditors of insolvent companies for control of remaining assets. It concentrates on inter-business disputes and struggles, not on struggles between the business community and the public for recompense. The data used in this chapter were gathered by interviewing insolvency practitioners, lawyers and businessmen, by examining files of creditor disputes, and by participant observation of the actual day-to-day running of insolvencies.[1]

Little attention has been paid to the large number of business insolvencies which occur each year and the resulting consequences for other businesses. Attention which has been paid has come either in the form of government reports (e.g. the Cork Report)[2] which, while recommending sweeping changes in the insolvency legislation, carried out little empirical research, or in the form of investigative journalism (e.g. Stephen Aris, *Going Bust*). This at least looks at empirical material but its standpoint is necessarily unrepresentative and selective.

The size of the insolvency problem can be seen from table 3.

Insolvency Procedures

When a company has an overdraft or has borrowed money in the form of a loan, it often has to grant a floating charge over some or all of its property as security for the overdraft or loan facility. A floating charge is a security

Table 3   Administrative receivership and liquidations

Type of proceeding	Year			
	1985	*1986*	*1987*	*1988 (7 mths)*
Administrative receivership	1,944	1,905	1,265	691*
Voluntary liquidation	13,160	13,734	10,528	5,372
Compulsory liquidation	6,149	6,291	4,742	2,833

* There have been 126 Administration orders in 1988, which may well have reduced the number of receiverships. However it is clearly too low a figure to account completely for the drop in the number of receiverships.
Source: Figures from Department of Trade and Industry

which, instead of attaching to a specific piece of property (a fixed charge), floats over the whole or part of a company's assets. The property which is caught by a floating charge is not ascertained until the charge is crystallized (i.e. 'called in') by the floating charge holder. This type of arrangement is peculiar to company law. The reason for its use is that it leaves the company raising the finance able to deal with the property in the ordinary course of business while the arrangement subsists. A conventional type of security arrangement (e.g. fixed charge) does not afford this flexibility and can interfere with effective company management.

This type of financial arrangement is usually funded by an institutional lender such as a bank or perhaps by another company in the business of providing financial assistance, such as Investors in Industry. The entering of this type of financial arrangement does not necessarily mean that the company seeking finance is in financial difficulties: finance may be required for expansion and business development.

If the lender of the money becomes unhappy at the company's financial state and feels that either now or in the near future the assets of the company will not cover the value of the security he holds, he can act to remedy this situation. The normal course of action is to appoint an administrative receiver (power to make this appointment and the timing of the appointment are granted to the lender as one of the terms of the security agreement). An institutional lender will not normally want to become the owner of the company assets by means of the remedy of foreclosure, because this will entail problems of personally disposing of and realizing the assets; hence the attractiveness of appointing an administrative receiver. The administrative receiver acts on behalf of the floating charge holder and realizes the assets for him.

This realization can be achieved in several ways. The business, or parts of it, can be sold, or the administrative receiver can continue to run the business of the company, so that the profits from trading can be used to repay the lender. Often a combination of both these methods is used. In many cases a better price can be obtained if the business is sold as a going concern, rather than broken up and sold piece by piece. If the business can continue to trade and so complete work in progress, and possibly start on new contracts in the order book, then this gives the administrative receiver more time to market the business and find a purchaser. The business will also look more attractive to a prospective purchaser as a thriving entity with goodwill.

A popular method employed to realize assets is a device called 'hiving down'. It involves the administrative receiver forming a subsidiary of the company in receivership and transferring all or some of the assets of that company to the new subsidiary. When a purchaser is found for the company, he purchases shares in the subsidiary from the company in receivership. In practice this is a complicated, time-consuming device to set up, and during trading it will involve the administrative receiver in keeping two sets of books and records. However, it does have certain advantages which can be weighed against this: the tax losses of the insolvent business are preserved, the administrative receiver can trade through a limited company and so protect himself against personal liability, and the most attractive parts of the business are presented as a going-concern package for a purchaser.

Hiving down has a bad reputation amongst creditors. It is not hard to see why: it is a complex legal device which is not easily understood, and to the layman appears a way of stripping out the asset part of the business for the benefit of the institutional creditor at the expense of other creditors. This is not the case. However, the feelings generated by this type of operation reflect those which pervade insolvency proceedings generally: the ordinary unsecured trade creditors approach the problem of the insolvency of trading partners with the attitude that they will do badly out of the insolvency because of the illegal devices employed by insolvency practitioners to exploit the situation.

A company does not actually end life and cease to exist under an administrative receiver. Even if the company is left an empty, debt-ridden shell by the administrative receiver, a further process is required to end its life: liquidation. A company does not have to go through administrative receivership to go into liquidation, nor does every administrative receivership end with liquidation. A liquidator's function in relation to the insolvent company is different from that of the administrative receiver. A liquidator owes a duty to all creditors; his primary function is to collect in all the company's assets, discharge the company's debts to its creditors, and distribute any surplus to the shareholders. In reality, frequently insufficient is realized to pay the debts, let alone distribute to shareholders.

As table 3 indicates, there are two types of liquidation: compulsory liquidation and voluntary liquidation. Compulsory liquidation occurs when the court orders it by reason of section 122 of the Insolvency Act 1986. One of the most common reasons for this order is that a creditor has brought a petition alleging that the company cannot pay its debts. This creditor is often an ordinary unsecured creditor rather than a large institutional lender. Voluntary liquidation occurs when the company itself votes for liquidation. When looking at the figures in table 3, it must be remembered that there are other grounds under the Insolvency Act 1986, section 122, for a court-ordered compulsory liquidation than inability to pay debts, and that there are other reasons why a company may decide to vote for liquidation than financial difficulties. The figures in table 3 do not cover just companies in financial difficulties, although they account for the overwhelming majority. Insolvent liquidations tend to be far distant from the 'big business' image of administrative receiverships. Often they concern smaller businesses, where the financial situation is such that there is no question of continuing trading or selling the business as a going concern. The only option for the liquidator is to sell the assets and hope that the revenue generated meets the debts of the company; often this is a forlorn hope.

Classes of Creditors

Business failure is a problem which touches all sections of the business community, from the large institutional lenders and investors to the suppliers of food to the staff canteen. These creditors are ranked by the law into priority groupings for payment out of the insolvent company's assets. The groupings are: (1) fixed charge holders; (2) costs of the office-holder; (3) preferential creditors; (4) floating charge holders; (5) unsecured creditors.

1   A fixed charge is similar to a floating charge in that is is security taken over property of the company, in exchange for finance provided. However, unlike a floating charge, it is taken over a specific, identifiable piece of property. This property then cannot be dealt with without the consent of the fixed charge holder. The fixed charge lends itself to items of property like buildings, whereas the floating charge is used to take security over items which change frequently and over which the company needs unrestricted powers of disposal if it is to be able to carry on business. Stock and work in progress are good examples of assets which are frequently secured by a floating charge.
2   The costs of the office-holder are the costs of realizing the assets.
3   The list of preferential creditors is found in the Insolvency Act 1986, schedule 6. A glance at the list reveals that the majority of secured creditors are central and local government departments, such as the DHSS, Customs and Excise, and the Inland Revenue. Certain limited claims by employees are given preferential status, such as salary arrears of up to four months, provided that the claim does not exceed £800 per person.
4   The floating charge has already been explained.
5   Unsecured creditors are creditors whose claims do not fall into any of the

categories listed above. Generally creditors in this category are suppliers of goods and services.

6 In addition, the members (shareholders) of the company may, on the liquidation of the company, be entitled to receive a return of capital.

The battle between creditors usually occurs in groups 4 and 5. The insolvency practitioner appointed as office-holder (this is a generic term covering every type of appointment that can be made in relation to an insolvent company) is appointed by the floating charge holder, and acts as his agent. Unsecured creditors are unlikely to receive much, if anything at all, from the insolvency. This is recognized even by the judiciary; Templeman L J observed in *Borden* v. *STP*,[3] 'Unsecured creditors rank after preferential creditors, mortgagees and holders of floating charges, and they receive a raw deal.'

A typical account of a failed company is provided by *Business Computers* v. *Anglo-African Leasing Ltd*.[4] Business Computers Ltd were in financial difficulties, and the institutional lender involved appointed a receiver under their floating charge. (The appointment was made prior to the Insolvency Act 1986; the office-holder would now be termed an administrative receiver, although their function, i.e. realizing the floating charge would be exactly the same.) The company had assets of about £1 million. The preferential creditors were owed about £300,000, which they took from the £1 million asset value. The remaining £700,000 went to the floating charge holder. Unsecured creditors, for example the suppliers of raw materials, who had extended credit to Business Computers Ltd and so were in part responsible for it continuing in business, were owed collectively £3 million. They received nothing.

Since 1976 supliers of goods to companies have begun to use a device called 'reservation of title clauses'. The date 1976 was significant not because of any legislative change but because a case involving a Dutch company came to the notice of English lawyers.[5] The idea is a very simple one: ownership of the goods is retained until they have been paid for, regardless of delivery.[6] The significance of this becomes clearer by looking at the situation on the insolvency of the buyer company: title to goods normally passes on delivery, whether they have been paid for or not; hence when the company falls into insolvency the goods become the property of the floating charge holder who uses them or sells them for his/her own benefit. A reservation of title clause prevents this from occurring by reserving ownership beyond the point of delivery. The effect of a reservation of title clause can be seen from the following revised hierarchy of priorities to the realizable assets of an insolvent company:

1 Reservation of title claimants take their goods back.
2 Fixed charges.
3 Costs of the office-holder.
4 Preferential creditors.

5 Floating charge holder.
6 Unsecured creditors, i.e. those unsecured creditors who either did not use a reservation of title clause over goods, or supplied a commodity like services where the clause is inapplicable.
7 Members.

The Position of Insolvency Practitioners

The return of goods held on reservation of title will affect the pool of assets left for the floating charge holder to realize. The presence of goods held on reservation of title terms makes it more difficult to carry on running the insolvent company (this is often necessary to get the best possible realization of assets for the floating charge holder). In the context of a liquidation, reservation of title claims increase the costs of the liquidation, so leaving less from which the liquidator can take his costs. The focus of this chapter is the battle between the insolvency practitioner and the reservation of title claimant for the remaining assets, and the form of this battle. For the insolvency practitioner there is little room to push members of categories other than this one down to the level of unsecured creditor. The fixed charge will be legally documented, and the list of creditors who must be regarded as preferential is laid down by statute (mainly the Inland Revenue and other Government departments).

From the beginning of the recovery process the claimant encounters an adversarial stance from the office-holder. This is often an attitude which the claimant is unprepared for. This is for two reasons. The claimant may have heard about reservation of title clauses from a fellow supplier of goods, or may simply have taken the clause from another manufacturer's sales documentation. If this is the case, then he is unlikely to be aware of the procedures which are necessary to enforce the clause. Secondly, if a lawyer is consulted by a claimant to set up a reservation of title basis for the supply of his goods, then the clause the supplier is given may be one taken from a decided case[7] or one used on a previous occasion by the lawyer. The point being made is that consultation with a lawyer at the planning stage will not necessarily ensure that the supplier knows what will occur at the enforcement stage. Only a lawyer familiar with the process of recovery would be able to impart this information.

The adversarial stance of the office-holder is exhibited in several ways and may differ, depending on whether the office held is that of liquidator or administrative receiver. In administrative receiverships the office-holder himself declines to see the claimant when he visits the premises to see if any of his goods are there. The claimant is shown round by a junior member of staff, who is unable to give him any information about how soon claims will be processed. The claimant is often one of several claimants being shown round, and each claimant is taken into a side office to agree the inventory of goods found. The attitude of the staff member involved is one of indifference; the decision will be made by someone else, who is very busy doing other things at the moment. The visit to the insolvent company's premises takes place at the outset of the claimant's enforcement career. It is only at that point that he realizes that enforcement is going to be much more difficult than he thought and that the administrative receiver, rather than simply returning his goods, requires evidence, and regards individual claims as being of little importance within the context of the insolvency as a whole. Claimants interviewed complained of military-style operations at the premises of the insolvent company – car numbers being taken for example. The fact that potential claimants are accompanied by an employee of the administrative receiver for the entire time that they are on the premises creates an atmosphere of hostility and distrust, as the obvious inference is that they are going to take something. The whole inspection process is stage-managed to create, in the mind of the claimant, the idea that whatever he believes the legal status of his claim to be, he will have to fight for recovery, and that he and his claim are regarded as a small and insignificant part of a much larger operation.

The liquidator is often not in a position to manipulate the dramaturgical setting of the insolvency in this way. His position in the context of the insolvency is different from that of the administrative receiver, in that time to the liquidator can be of the utmost importance: it can make the difference between a profitable and non-profitable liquidation. Liquidators do not normally carry on the business of the insolvent company, and the liquidator often wants to be able to move the site of the liquidation away from the insolvent company's premises and back to his own office. This saves on rent (if the premises are rented or leasehold) and time, if the liquidation can be worked on at his own office, and other jobs can be run alongside it. To relocate the liquidation requires stock disposal or the finding and renting of expensive storage premises. The liquidator wants to dispose of stock *en masse*, as this will realize more than piecemeal disposal, and he does not want to risk a suit for conversion, at worst, or a publicly damaging dispute over ownership, by selling goods which are the subject of a contested claim. He introduces his adversarial stance by pointing out to the claimant from the beginning of his enforcement career that as liquidator he owes a legal duty to all creditors and so must check carefully the validity of all claims.

The entire claims process is characterized by the power of the insolvency practitioner. Possession is very much 'nine-tenths of the law'. The fact that the goods which form the subject matter of the claim are on the premises of the insolvent company and are under the control of the insolvency practitioner places the onus of proof of the claim very much on the claimant. In terms of litigation experience the situation resembles the classic repeat-player/one-shotter differential. This terminology was first adopted by an American, Marc Galanter, who uses it to describe the experience that some sections of the community had in using the legal system, compared with their probable opponents. A good example of this is professional landlords and letting agencies, who, while not lawyers, will have much more experience of landlord and tenant law than the tenants, who are likely to be the parties opposing them in any litigation. The insolvency practitioner is experienced at dealing with reservation of title claims. The market for administrative receivership and liquidation appointments has to a great extent been cornered by different sectors of the accountancy profession. The majority of administrative receivership appointments go to accounts from 'the big ten'; the largest accountancy firms nationwide, if not worldwide (see Appendix to this chapter, table 5). These insolvency practitioners are backed up by large technical director-ates within their own firms. The majority of liquidation appointments go to accountants in much smaller units, often within the locality of the insolvent company. Obviously they do not have the same level of technical input in terms of the latest developments in the law, etc. as their colleagues from national or multinational firms. However, whatever his background, the insolvency practitioner has a standard process for dealing with claims, and his experience places him in a position to realize when good-quality legal advice, for which he is able to pay, is necessary, and where to find it. An administrative receiver who wishes to carry on the business of the insolvent company for a period after appointment, knows what goods he needs to complete which contract, and this may influence the way in which he treats claimants. Insolvency practitioners have access to the records of the insolvent company and are able to examine its procedures for the ordering and stocking of goods (two important elements in constructing a claim). They also have ready access to employees and former employees of the insolvent company, who may have valuable information about the terms on which goods were supplied and alternative sources of supply.

The Position of Claimants

Lined up against this picture of strength, there is the claimant. As a manufacturer of goods, the position of the claimant in society is such that he will often have had experience of the law and lawyers before he makes his claim, even if it is only in non-contentious matters like domestic or commercial conveyancing. He is unlikely to be in the position that some personal injury victims find themselves in: that their first exposure to the legal system comes in the form of a contentious claim, on the merits and value of which they have no developed expectation.[8] A manufacturer making a reservation of title claim will have an expectation of the value of his claim: the invoice value of goods he found on the premises of the insolvent company. Insolvency situations exhibit the classic elements necessary for business crime: they are essentially private and shadowy events; one side is able on a purely physical basis to shut the other side out of the dispute; the administration of the insolvency takes place behind closed doors; and there is little consultation with creditors.[9] What is happening here is that legal means are being used as resources in the struggle over the assets of the insolvent company. Unsecured creditors, including the suppliers of goods, having for long been the major losers in insolvencies, have discovered retention of title clauses and employed them to protect their interests. At face value, this has the dramatic effect of putting their interests ahead of the institutional financiers, whose interests are represented by the administrative receiver or the liquidator. As matters stood prior to 1976, the ascendancy of the office-holder was complete, both legally and practically. The use of retention of title clauses upsets that ascendancy of the office-holder by creating a potential division between his continuing practical dominance and the partial erosion of his legal position. The question which arises is whether the practical position will supersede the legal position of the supplier and render his recently found legal support a nullity.

An answer to these issues of inequality of bargaining power and litigation experience at a theoretical level would be the recruitment of a lawyer by the claimant, whose knowledge of the law would balance the natural advantages of the insolvency practitioner. The situation in reality is much more complex. Previous empirical research projects have established that businessmen do not see the law and lawyers as an attractive or effective means of dispute resolution.[10] Although these studies concentrated on inter-business disputes and emphasized the presence of club rules amongst businessmen as a bar to the use of the law, the study on which this chapter is based found the same dislike of the law. The refusal of many claimants (76 per cent of the sample) to seek legal advice meant that they lost the opportunity to negotiate at the level of the insolvency practitioner. However, claimants who did seek legal advice found themselves victims of the problem of strata within the legal profession. As table 4 shows, claimants who used a lawyer formed 61 per cent of the recovery group. A larger differential emerges however when the type of lawyer used was examined; of the general practitioner lawyers used, only 24 per cent were successful, but 85 per cent of specialized commercial lawyers used were successful. It is clear that many general practice lawyers instructed, while accepting the instructions, do not have either the legal knowledge or the negotiating skill to defuse the advantages of the insolvency practitioner and secure recovery for the claimant.

The Legal Rules

The legal rules surrounding reservation of title claims are similar to the legal rules in many other areas, e.g. personal injury. They provide only a framework or structure within which disputing parties can settle their differences. The idea is very much one of private ordering within the law. In the context of reservation of title claims, the law demands that the claimant shows firstly that he supplied his goods on that basis, secondly that the goods he is claiming were produced by him, and thirdly that the goods have not been paid for.[11] The law does not provide any guidance on

Table 4   Type of representation

Recovery or not	Specialized commercial lawyers		General practice lawyer		No lawyer		Total
Successful	11	(85%)	12	(24%)	15	(8%)	38
Unsuccessful	2	(15%)	37	(76%)	183	(92%)	221
Total	13		49		197		259

Note: Column percentages in brackets

what is required for these three points to be established; that is a matter for negotiation between the parties. Legal validity is only one of the planks involved in this private ordering or inter-party negotiation. Whether a claim is legally valid or not, however, is not the prime concern of the insolvency practitioner. He is looking for evidence of legal validity plus the ability of the claimant or his lawyer to recognize and assert that validity; in other words, is the claimant or his lawyer capable of realizing that the claim is strong on one point and weak on another and then able to negotiate around this base to secure recovery? If the insolvency practitioner is not convinced of this then the claim will not be settled, regardless of its legal validity.

> . . . The relationship between the degree of doubt and evaluation is not a simple one to one correspondence . . . On the one hand, a claim can support some degree of doubtful liability without serious diminution in value and, on the other, even a large degree of doubtful liability may not extinguish a claim completely. The black-and-white, liability-or-not model of the law means very little in the world of the claims man. Most . . . claims are of the grey shade of questionable liability.[12]

What the insolvency practitioner requires before he will consider settlement of the claim is evidence that the claimant or his lawyer is able to capitalize on the grey area of his claim. The following extract from the correspondence between a liquidator and his legal adviser in one of the liquidations examined indicates the 'grey' nature of many claims: 'Notwithstanding my advice to reject these claims, most of them do have some merit and for commercial as well as legal reasons I would not wish to see litigation arising out of them.'

The Establishment of Defence Strategies

Traditional analyses of negotiation situations assume a bi-party dialogue which moves slowly towards some sort of agreed settlement.[13] The nature of claims in insolvency situations is that they are zero-sum; if the claim is admitted as belonging to a particular group, then in the overwhelming majority of cases the claim must be satisfied in full and there is no room for settlement at some point between the stances of the two parties. We have already seen how the insolvency practioner is very much the dominant actor; he has possession of the goods, repeat-player experience, and access to the records and employees of the insolvent company. As a result, negotiation between the parties takes the form of the establishment of defence strategies by the insolvency practitioner. These defence strategies are imposed on the claims process by the insolvency practitioner. Any claimant wishing to recover has to overcome the strategies to the satisfaction of the insolvency practitioner. The insolvency practitioner forms his particular defence strategies by looking at several factors. One of these is the circumstances of the insolvency in question. The purpose of this was neatly summarized by one of the lawyers interviewed:

> If you know that they [i.e. the now insolvent company] stored their goods with the packaging removed in large bins, all mixed together, or that their stock records were hopelessly inadequate, or that they did initial work on some material as soon as it arrived, you can state with much more conviction that they [i.e. the claimant company] have not adequately identified their goods etc., and that they can't reply with two sheets of paper that will solve the problem. What I'm saying is that knowing the company and the claimant greatly increases the chance of successfully defending the claim.

Another factor looked at is the status of the claim itself within the insolvency. A claimant supplying specialist goods which are difficult to obtain elsewhere, or a large important supplier of goods in an adminis-trative receivership continuing to trade, may be treated differently from other claimants. The claimant has no control at all over these strategies, they are examples of the insolvency practitioner capitalizing on his advantages, and there is nothing that the claimant can do to redress the power imbalance. These two factors dictate the type of defence that it is possible to put forward within the context of the particular insolvency. The only factor over which the claimant has any control is the way in which he presents himself to the insolvency practitioner and his lawyer. This is important, as it dictates the level of technicality of defence that will be raised against him. This was described by a lawyer experienced at defending claims on behalf of insolvency practitioners thus:

> You can put some sort of defence to nearly all claims, but you have to be careful about the points you raise. A good, experienced lawyer will spot a spurious defence a mile off and then you lose credibility. Even the good points you have will be ruined. I look very carefully at who replies to rejection letters. It's fair to say that I would raise points against a non-

specialist or a claimant acting for himself that I know wouldn't be worthwhile raising against someone who had more idea of what they were doing.

Defence Strategies in Practice

Many of the defence strategies put forward by insolvency practitioners contain loopholes which claimants could exploit to bargain for recovery, or indeed could effectively counter. However very few do so: only 15 per cent of the sample recovered. This is not because insolvency practioners exploit the strength of their position by using illegal defence strategies. The problem for claimants is that there is a clear incompatibility between the insolvency practitioners' requirements for proof and their understanding of the situation. This leads to anger and frustration on the part of the claimant, who believes that the defence strategies put forward by the insolvency practioner must be illegal. Quite frequently the claimant has, from an objective standard, a good claim, but is unable to present his evidence in the required form. The insolvency practitioner is not required by the law to go through evidence presented and draw his own conclusions. An illustration of this incompatibility problem can be seen from the claim described below:

> The claim was worth £374. The lawyer representing the insolvency practitioner wrote to his client and said that the claim 'may have to be admitted, but I think it is worth trying to evade it on the grounds that they can't link the stuff to unpaid invoices.' The lawyer wrote to the claimant asking for this evidence. The claimant replied that the packaging on the goods had been removed, which made their identification more difficult, but as the claimant was the sole distributor of goods of that type in the UK, the goods must belong to him. The claim was then rejected by the insolvency practitioner and his lawyer on the grounds of lack of evidence that the goods had not been previously paid for. This drew an angry response from the claimant. 'We have given all the facts and supported them where we can with written proof in an effort to legitimately claim back what is ours. Quite honestly, do you think we would be doing this if the goods were not ours in the first place?' The claim would probably have been successful if the supplier had understood initially what was being asked of him.

At times the defence strategy may be to require information which, from a commercial perspective, is either impossible for the claimant to produce, or difficult for him to locate. For example, the insolvency practitioner may ask the claimant to produce documentary evidence of his entire trading history with the insolvent company, or to show that the goods he produced and supplied were individually numbered so as to distinguish them from goods supplied on other occasions, which may have been paid for, prior to insolvency. The claimant in these instances feels that the law could not possibly require him to prove something which is so alien to the commercial culture to which he belongs, and therefore that the insolvency practitioner must be acting illegally. This further fuels the feelings of mistrust and animosity which underlie their relationship.

Often defence strategies are based on bluff. It is not unusual for insolvency practitioners to present a general bluff to all the claimants in a particular insolvency, in the hope of convincing them that there is a hurdle in the way of recovery which they will find impossible to overcome.[14] A typical example of this occurs in the context of identification. A letter will be sent to all claimants saying that, in the experience of the insolvency practitioner, goods of that type are not identifiable in terms of pinning down a sole source of supply. This is not illegal conduct on behalf of the insolvency practitioner; he is simply saying that this is a problem that many industries face, and unless a particular claimant operates practices which depart from the norm, then his claim will be liable to fail. It has the effect of creating doubt in the mind of the claimant about the likelihood of the success of his claim.

Delay is a third defence strategy. The rationale behind the use of delay is that 'it takes the heat out of the claim'. As time passes the claim fades into insignificance in the claimant's mind. Added to this there is also the psychological factor that a delay in time means that the insolvency practitioner and his lawyer are not treating the claim as important, and consequently settlement prospects are diminishing. Delay is used as a tactic at all stages of the enforcement process. Some claims analysed contained file notes to the effect that there was to be no communication with the claimant until absolutely necessary. This has the effect of taking the immediate heat out of the situation and giving the insolvency practitioner time to compose a defence strategy for rejection. Delay can also be used to counter what would otherwise become a potential blackmail situation. Some suppliers know that they are supplying custom-made goods to a trading administrative receivership, so that if their claims were to be rejected outright, they would then use the supply of future goods as a bargaining counter for success in the recovery process. A holding letter saying that the claim is being looked at, followed by a period of non-communication, even if it has already been decided that the claim is totally invalid, ensures the necessary supplies and leaves the insolvency practitioner free to reject the claim at a later date.

Compliance with Ineffective Laws?

These appear from the sample to be the most commonly used strategies. There are of course others, and variations on those described. However the descriptions are sufficient to illustrate the fact that insolvency practitioners deal with creditors' claims in an essentially legalistic way. This method is time-consuming and so must also be expensive. The average length of the process of an individual claim in the sample was nine months. The number of letters involved in correspondence exchanges ranged from two to twenty. The point of interest here is why this lengthy method of processing is chosen. The result of the claims process is that large numbers of claims (85 per cent in the sample) are unsuccessful. We have already illustrated that the insolvency practitioner holds all the cards in terms of these claims, so the claims process is something for him to design and then impose on the claimants.

There must be cheaper, quicker methods of achieving a rejection of the majority of claims. What is there to prevent, for example, the office-holder and his staff from simply moving stock out of the insolvent company's warehouses, and then inviting potential claimants to come and see if any of their goods are still there? That would dispose of claims quickly and cheaply. Although the insolvency practitioner's method of disposal is based on manipulation of the facts of the insolvency and the law involved, it is not extra-legal, and yet it is perceived in that way by claimants. If the purpose of this elaborate disposal process is to convince claimants that their claims are being rejected by legal methods, it is a failure. Also, the attitude of the insolvency practitioner to claimants during the insolvency is one of hostility or indifference, so it seems unlikely that this process is designed just to impress them.

A few insolvency practitioners interviewed did describe their method of claims disposal as 'selling all the stock and telling them it's all gone', which would certainly be an illegal method of disposal. However, when their claims disposal methods were examined by means of documentary analysis and participant observation, it became clear that this was an instance of a two-story tradition. The first story was the way in which they would like to behave in relation to claims, but in practice a second story was revealed: there was something constraining them to act in a more legalistic way, to achieve the same end-result. We must now attempt to find the source of the constraints on their behaviour.

The claims process is honed out of the structure offered by the civil law. What must be examined now is whether there are sanctions contained in either civil law or criminal law which force the insolvency practitioner to behave in this way. The only civil action open to a claimant who feels his goods have been 'misappropriated' is an action for conversion.[15] Conversion is a tort which requires an intentional dealing by a person with a chattel belonging to another in such a way as to deny the owner possession. Disposal of goods claimed by a claimant before that claimant has a chance to put his case, or while the case is being argued, would be sufficient to amount to conversion if the goods turned out to belong to the claimant. At common law there is no defence to an action for conversion: an insolvency practitioner cannot evade liability by asserting that he did not realize the goods were not his to dispose of. This sounds very attractive in terms of explaining why insolvency practitioners compose this elaborate process and defence strategies: it is to prevent large numbers of conversion actions, which would occur if all goods were simply used or sold without claims being argued through and rejected as being unproved.

However the reality of the situation is quite different. Conversion is something which a claimant would find difficult to prove against an insolvency practitioner. The situation for the claimant is a circular one. Although disposal of his goods would be conversion, he will not be in a position to allege conversion unles he knew and could prove that there were goods of his on the insolvent company's premises which subsequently disappeared. It is also more difficult to prove a reservation of title claim in terms of showing that the goods have been identified and have not been paid for if they are no longer available to look at. Given the large number of claimants in the sample who did not instruct lawyers and yet felt that the structure for recovery being imposed on them was illegal, it would seem that few claimants would take action over a potential conversion action. It is interesting that the Insolvency Act 1986[16] encourages office-holders to use goods which may belong to others by moderating the tort of conversion and allowing the office-holder to escape liability if he can show that he reasonably believed the goods to belong to the insolvent company. The legal implications of this are adequately discussed in other literature,[17] but the policy implication is that the formal law recognizes and encourages the private ordering of disputes within its basis framework. It also shows that the legislature, rather than reflecting the empirical view of insolvencies and accepting that there is no need to offer protection against conversion actions as they very rarely occur, chooses to protect and bolster the interests of the already dominant actor.

The only criminal offence that can be committed during this battle for control is theft. There are two interwoven problems for the claimant here. One is that there are the same problems of proof with an allegation of theft as with an allegation of conversion, and the second is the attitude of the police to allegations of theft in these types of situation. A typical example of the attitude towards alleged criminal activity in these circumstances came from one of the interviewed sample of businessmen:

> This incident occurred immediately prior to insolvency. The directors of the company that was within hours of being declared insolvent decided to salvage some money from the business by selling goods of which they were only the lessees, passing themselves off as the owners. The real owner [the businessman interviewed] found out about the proposed sale and also found where his goods had been removed to, prior to their illegal sale. The goods had been placed in storage, and could only be released from that storage by the signature of one of the recalcitrant directors. The owner turned to the police for assistance believing that he was the victim of theft. The police, however, were very reluctant to confirm that this was a case of theft, or indeed a case which merited the involvement of the criminal law at all. Their attitude was that the businessman had courted this type of incident through his own conduct in entering into a business relationship of this type.

The situation in this case was resolved obstensibly through use of the civil courts. However, it was clear that there had been a certain amount of private ordering behind the veil of the civil court action which was certainly extra-legal. Insolvency practitioners do not resort to extra-legal tactics to help them win their battle for the assets, but the point is that the enforcement agents of the criminal law do not ensure that they or anybody else operating in the business arena keeps within the confines of acceptable conduct under the criminal law. They actively encourage the parties to pursue private ordering by their refusal to see this type of incident as within their remit. It seems that any dispute which involves parties who are in a private business relationship with each other, and questions of ownership of material which forms part of the subject matter of that business relationship, will attract from the police the label of 'a civil dispute', or 'a matter for your solicitor'.

The legislature appears to be unaware of this attitude, as can be seen from its policy of criminalizing certain business offences. The idea is clearly that the possibility of incurring criminal sanctions will in some cases be a more effective deterrent. Insider dealing[18] is perhaps the best example; another is involvement with a company while being an undischarged bankrupt.[19] Leaving aside questions of the difficulties involved in the proof necessary for criminal offences and how this fits with business crimes, a more basic problem seems to be the disdain of the police in actually investigating crimes of this type. The businessman in the example above was informed by the police that one of the directors of the company with whom he was dealing was an undischarged bankrupt. They also informed him that they did not see it as their role to take action against him. This certainly raises questions of the value of criminalizing this type of conduct if it is not to be an empty label.

Insolvency practitioners do not feel constrained to act in the way they do by the fear of criminal sanctions. Many of those interviewed felt that the shadow of illegality fell unfairly upon them and their conduct, and that the inactivity of the police in the sphere of commerce was a much greater hindrance to them than to their opponents in the asset battle. A typical viewpoint is the one given below, put forward by a liquidator in the sample:

> Security is often a real problem in liquidation work. As we're not trading, we're not on the premises for most of the time. It's not unusual for someone to try to break in, or actually get in and take stuff . . . Often you can tell by what's gone who the likely candidates are. If they've taken stuff that other people were also claiming, then it's a real problem. You can ask for it to be brought back, but in the absence of strong evidence you're on a loser. The police are never interested unless you are lucky enough to get them out while the theft is actually taking place. Then they will intervene not to make arrests for theft, but because they think a breach of the peace may take place, they'll only preserve the status quo, they don't actually want to do anything in cases like this. They would much rather sit at a discreet distance and leave you to get on with it, getting out of their cars only if there's about to be a punch-up.

The threat of immediate civil or criminal action is clearly not a potent enough threat, on its own, to act as the force which constrains the actions of insolvency practitioners. The desire to comply with the ethical standards and disciplinary rules of their own profession is unlikely to be the sole force either, as once again the proof that there has been a breach of these restraints would be very difficult to obtain for the group that suffered as a result. Added to this, in a practical context few claimants, given their dismissive view of law and the legal system, would see allegations of breaches of professional ethics and regulations as a viable option.

Conformity with the requirements of the law seemed to arise from a combination of the pliability of the law, the actions of claimants themselves, and potential damage to professional reputations. The underlying view was that the room for manoeuvre the law offered was in the insolvency practitioners' favour. Added to this were advantages they enjoyed as repeat-players and the failure of most claimants to grasp what the claims process was all about; many of them had good claims, and yet they and their lawyers could not translate this into recovery. Given this strong position it seemed the best course was to use it rather than risk damaging allegations. As one insolvency practitioner explained:

> It's all a game. Every so often they [i.e. the courts] may change the rules, but there is always a way of getting round it. That's what law is all about isn't it? Granted there's plenty of opportunity to do stupid things and sometimes it's very tempting, but what's the point? The chances of getting found out are very small, but there is always that chance. The guy in the unit opposite may see you throwing the packaging away, or busing the stuff out. The insolvency game is a highly competitive market, we could lose future appointments if the banks thought we sailed too close to the wind. They want their money, but shutting down businesses is not that good for their public image. The last thing they want is an administrative receiver with a dodgy reputation.

The law is used to achieve what could be achieved by illegal action more quickly and cheaply. It may be encouraging that members of a large, respected profession are prepared to use legal methods even when they are well aware that the law is largely ineffective to make them do so. The main detraction from this is that they do so not because of any overwhelming desire to be law-abiding citizens *per se*, but because it is in their best business interests to be seen to be complying with the law.

Claimant Behaviour

The use of reservation of title clauses at the planning stage costs little. At its most basic level it simply involves the insertion of a clause into sales documentation. Often this does not require the services of a lawyer, as a clause can be copied from a fellow manufacturer. The effect of this is that when the clause fails at the enforcement stage the supplier has lost little in terms of the start-up cost of the device. However the device has not achieved what he thought it would, and, given the view of many claimants that they have been the victims of illegal activity, does this provoke them into resorting to illegal activity?

There are two basic ways in which claimants can attract legal liability: one is by forcibly removing their goods from the premises of the insolvent company, and the second is by falsifying evidence asked for during the disposal process. During interviews and participant observation it became clear that stories abounded amongst claimants of goods being taken back as a result of extra-legal action including threats of physical violence against the insolvency practitioner and his staff. However this picture was not a true reflection of events. Only one attempted removal was witnessed during participant observation, and only one actual removal was found in the documentary analysis of claims. From evidence gathered, it seems that perhaps only one or two incidents underlie all the stories, and that they have been magnified by rumour. Both these incidents occurred in liquidations, where there is often no significant on-site presence by the office-holder and his staff. Demands for the return of goods made at the outset of the insolvency were deflected by the claimant being given assurances that his claim was not being rejected at that stage but merely being examined.

It is standard practice for office-holders to return, on a 'without prejudice' basis, goods which are both the subject of a small claim and not required for continued trading. The idea is that this costs the office-holder less than spending time constructing rejection grounds. Obviously what attracts the label 'small' depends on the profitability of the insolvency. The goods are returned on the grounds that the claim is not legally valid, but a commercial solution for both parties would be the return of the goods. The caveat on the return of the goods is often forgotten by claimants describing their success to business colleagues, and so the return becomes turned into an incident where pressure and threats were successful.

The interviews with suppliers revealed that there was general awareness that forcibly removing goods was illegal conduct, and should not be attempted.[20] There was a general view that goods obtained on this basis would not be chased by insolvency practitioners, but it was, in spite of this, not conduct to be embarked upon. The necessarily public nature of this type of action is thought to underlie the diffidence of claimants to use it as a recovery method, rather than any underlying desire to act in conformity with the law. This would account for the championing of those who had supposedly used it, and the reluctance of those who had not to dirty their hands.

The same view was not taken of supplying forged evidence. This was thought to be exactly what the insolvency practioner deserved in asking for the sort of information he did. Only four examples of the use of forged evidence were found in the documentary analysis. The probable reason for this reflects the practical ascendancy of the insolvency practitioner and his model for the disposal of claims: claimants did not understand why particular evidence was requested or how it could be effectively fabricated to improve their claim.

It appears that the overwhelming majority of claimants do little actively to pursue their goods; they follow the defence strategies set up by the insolvency practitioner, and they drop their claims as and when their resistance is overcome by the dominance of the insolvency practitioner. Reservation of title clauses have to be placed in a wider context in order to explain the actions of claimants. The perspective of manufacturing companies tends to be forward-looking: although a bad debt has occurred and steps must be taken to try and recover something from the situation, of greater importance is the pursuit of new customers to replace the business lost. This is not always true; there are cases in which the principle of 'these are my goods and I want them back' fuels the claimant's actions for many months. However, often when recovery shows itself to be much more difficult to obtain than the claimant first envisaged, the exchange of letters becomes more spasmodic as interest declines. A problem encountered by liquidators was that they needed to dispose of claims quickly but could not contact the claimant to find out whether it was intended to pursue the claim further.

Reservation of title clauses are just one component part of credit control. This control encompasses both legal devices, such as factoring of invoices and debt insurance, and administrative devices, such as the imposition of credit limits. Within this package, reservation of title clauses are the last line of defence, an indication that everything else has failed. Many claimants adopt the view that lengthy pursuit of recovery is throwing more money away, that the law has failed commerce once again, and that effective protection systems are the ones that they themselves control in direct dealings with other manufacturers. There is a recognition that the way to protect business interests is largely through business planning and internally administered mechanisms of control, not by using legal devices and lawyers.

NOTES

1 The actual sample was an analysis of 259 claims spread over eight liquidations and eight receiverships. 15 lawyers were interviewed and 18 insolvency practitioners.
2 Cmnd 8558 of 1982.
3 (1981) ch. 25.
4 (1977) 1 WLR 578.

5 *AIV* v. *Romalpa Aluminium* (1976) 1 WLR 676.
6 Sale of Goods Act 1979, s. 19 (1) allows parties to a contract of sale to decide when title to goods passes.
7 S. Macaulay (1979) 14 *Law and Society Review* 162, terms this type of lawyering the 'trickle down' effect.
8 See H. Genn, *Hard Bargaining*, Clarendon Press, 1987.
9 There are sections in the Insolvency Act 1986 which demand creditor consultation. However, their effect in practice is negligible.
10 S. Macaulay (1963), 28 *American Sociological Review* 45; H. Beale and T. Dugdale (1975), *British Journal of Law and Society*; A. Taeusch (1934), 83 *University of Pennsylvania Law Review* 147.
11 A guide to the complex legal position can be found in G. Stewart, *Administrative Receivers and Administrators*, CCH Editions, 1987, pp. 55–65.
12 H. Ross, *Settled Out of Court*, Aldine Press, 1970, pp. 159ff.
13 For a useful review of the literature, see R. Tomasic, *The Sociology of Law*, Sage Publications, 1985, pp. 58–66.
14 An interesting discussion of the relationship between law and bluff can be found in K. Hawkins, *Environment and Enforcement*, Clarendon Press, 1984.
15 Torts (Interference with Goods) Act 1977, s. 1.
16 Insolvency Act 1986, s. 234.
17 S. Wheeler (1987), 8 *Company Lawyer* 170
18 Company Securities (Insider Dealing) Act 1985, s. 8.
19 Company Directors Disqualification Act 1986, s. 11.
20 Beale and Dugdale, *British Journal of Law Society*, found that businessmen had knowledge of the law in certain areas, and law and lawyers were used to a larger extent than that found by Macaulay, ibid. The findings here support that contention.

Table 5 The distribution of receiverships between the major accountancy firms in the first part of 1986 and 1987. The majority of receiverships are concentrated in the hands of these firms, as can be seen from a comparison between the subtotal figures and the total figures

Position 1st half 1987	Position 1st half 1986		Number of appointments	
			1st half 1987	1st half 1986
1	(1)	Peat Marwick	66	(104)
2	(6)	Ernst & Whinney	59	(49)
3	(8)	Deloitte Haskins	58	(41)
4	(2)	Coopers & Lybrand/ Cork Gully	56	(99)
5	(3)	Grant Thornton	49	(71)
6	(7)	Arthur Andersen	40	(45)
7	(11)	Arthur Young	32	(22)
8	(12)	Stoy Hayward	30	(22)
9	(5)	Price Waterhouse	25	(53)
10	(4)	Touche Ross	24	(62)
11	(9)	Spicer & Pegler	21	(31)
12	(15)	Levy Gee	18	(16)
13	(17)	Binder Hamlyn	17	(12)
13	(10)	Robson Rhodes	17	(28)
14	(13)	Leonard Curtis	16	(18)
		SUBTOTAL	528	(673)
		Other firms	160	(203)
		TOTAL	688	(876)

Source: All figures obtained from the *London Gazette*

Table 6 The distribution of receivership between accountancy firms in July 1988

Name	Industry	Firm
Barber-Greene England Ltd	Asphalt plant manufacturers	Binder Hamlyn
Semtex	Flooring contractors	Touche Ross
Kammac Trucking Ltd	Haulage and warehousing	Latham Crossley & Davis
MF O'Malley Formwork Ltd	Subcontractors	Touche Ross
Hydromech Ltd	Hydraulic manufacturers	Grant Thornton
Martin Sudborough Ltd	Shoe manufacturers	Touche Ross
Stradford Shopfitters Ltd	Interior design	Touche Ross
Legra Electronics Ltd	Manufactuers of components	Leonard Curtis
Millmixes Ltd	Dried food preparation	Spicer & Oppenheim
MG Fire Protection Ltd	Fire prevention	Spicer & Oppenheim
Paul Press Ltd	Packaging house	Leonard Curtis
The Harley Group Ltd	Medical consultancy	Leonard Curtis
Yale Construction Co. Ltd	Construction	Grant Thorton
Arnold and Warden Ltd	Steel blasting	Spicer & Oppenheim
Basetest Ltd	Truck and trailer parts	Grant Thornton
Rigg and Remington Ltd	Industrial cleaning	Leonard Curtis
Crawford Precision Castings Ltd	Precision castings	Peat Marwick McLintock
Euromet Engineering Co. Ltd	Sheet metal engineers	Touche Ross
AD Metal Design Ltd	Shopfitting and display	Touche Ross
Level Air Conditioning	Air conditioning	Binder Hamlyn

8 Financial Institutions:
Securities and Investments

Although this chapter is concerned with the financial sector as a whole, the institutions involved and their regulation are so complex and diverse that it is necessary to select in order to be able to provide a meaningful account of issues and developments. For reasons cited below, securities and investments have been chosen as illustrative of the great difficulties involved in adequate regulation. The first part of the chapter takes up the question of the general regulatory issues posed and the solutions adopted and the changes over time in Britain and the United States. The latter part focuses more narrowly on the problems associated with takeover bids, in part because these have been a major recent concern in the securities industry in both countries. In addition, however, they illustrate vividly the tendency of offences in this area to politicization and the centrality of the problem of obtaining agreement on acceptable standards in a complex and dynamic market. The implications of this are that whilst the law, including the criminal law, has its place, it is clearly a marginal one.

Maintaining Confidence in an Expanding Market

There are a number of reasons for expecting that controls upon offences involving financial institutions should be stringent and punitive. Financial institutions are particularly difficult for the layman to assess as to competence and quality of service. Whilst every customer of a retail bank will have a fair idea of the basic terms for lending and borrowing, very few will have an informed idea of the stability of the bank as a whole. In the recent round of concern about sovereign risk for example, how many customers were aware of the exposure of their bank to major Latin American debtor countries that looked at one point as if they might default? Nor were they in a position to evaluate what would happen if their bank were to become financially unstable. Would the government secure them and it, as the American government did when Continental Illinois bank crashed, at a cost of some $4 billion? Would their savings be secure? Would their overdrafts be called in at short notice, or their personal loans, or their mortgages? Similarly, few customers are able to make more than a rudimentary judgement on the quality of the advice offered by a bank or other financial adviser. Is an inheritance of £10,000 best invested in a single-premium life insurance policy, or in unit trusts, or in a building society, and in each case is the advice which is offered really the best, or does it reflect limited knowledge, or even the commissions earned by the advisory institution? And in any case is there not a far better rate of return offered by commodities futures?

Implicit in the above illustrations is a recognition that a far greater proportion of the population of western industrialized nations is now involved with financial institutions. Mortgages, bank loans and savings, life insurance, unit trusts and pension schemes are widespread. Some of these arrangements are long-term, and any significant failure in the institutions involved to deliver a return at the end of the period may constitute a devastating blow to individuals' financial security. In the meantime the stability, prudence and probity of the institutions is not likely to be subject to regular informed appraisal by the long-term client.

Nor are relations with financial institutions confined these days to stable organizations with highly diversified risks and long experience. Not that even these are necessarily secure. Even the largest and oldest British and American banks put themselves at risk to the extent of thousands of millions of dollars on the false assumption that nation states cannot go bankrupt. They assumed that even third world countries, highly vulnerable to fluctuations in commodity prices, upon which their export income depends, and to interest rates, none the less will always repay loans on the terms agreed. In Britain two very well-established and respected life assurance companies, National Provident and London Life, got into such difficulties in the late 1980s that they agreed to mergers with other insurance companies. If such substantial organizations can go to the edge of financial security, what are the prospects for the increasing host of much smaller investment advisers, securities dealers, commodities and futures brokers and others? Over a quarter of Americans hold stock and, as a result of the government's privatization programme, rapidly rising numbers of Britons do also, although there is doubt about how long many retain the shares that they buy, and how many will repeat the exercise after privatizations end. It is government policy in both countries to encourage wide participation in the full range of financial services now on offer, and major and minor organizations have competed over the past decade to establish new and better services and products for potential customers. The British government in particular has been keen to promote a major change of habits in the more affluent half of the population towards a much wider-ranging participation in financial services. How are the customers to appraise this bewildering array? How much reliance are they entitled to place on the claims made? How much security is there in the schemes and organizations in the medium and long term over which investments and loans frequently take place?

All these features of financial institutions bespeak their central requirement: trust. Clients trust in the competence and honesty of the organization and have no alternative. They trust that an investment scheme can operate on the stated terms and is so run, and hence that the risks and returns specified are just those they are subjected to. They hence trust that at the end of a year the organization does not tell them that it regrets that it is in liquidation and their assets have disappeared; they also trust that they do not read in the papers that the principal has been arrested for embezzling the funds.

For there are plenty of criminals who foster and abuse trust in financial institutions. The amount of money at risk being investigated by the Metropolitan Police fraud squad rose from £36 million in 1970 to £1,349 million in 1985 and showed no signs of abating. Crimes involving financial services have vastly greater rewards than burglaries and robberies, for in many cases there are multiple victims. Shapiro reports that the average robbery nets 338 dollars in the United States, where the average white-collar criminal federally convicted took 300,000 dollars.[1] Burglary, robbery and theft in the London Metropolitan Police District in 1985 involved only 40 per cent of the amount at risk in cases investigated by the fraud squad, and these were much limited by lack of manpower to the most serious.

Clearly criminal sanctions are visited upon offenders in the financial sector, as the fate of Levine and Boesky among others in the United States, and of the Guinness affair in Britain have so publicly illustrated. It is when the range and complexities of offences involving financial services are considered however, that the reasons for the lack of a stringently criminal approach to control emerge. For the requirement implied by the points made above is not criminal prosecution of offenders, but the protection of customers and clients from incompetence and dishonesty, that is, the achievement of reliability.

At one end of the scale there are simple rogues, those who purport to be offering a financial service, but in fact are offering theft and extortion. Thus there are boiler-room operators who tout hot shares on which you are guaranteed to make a killing, but which in fact are worthless; the fraudulent loan fixers who offer businessmen loans on preferential terms from wealthy foreign concerns, but demand an up-front arrangement fee and disappear; the time-share salesmen who claim to be offering luxurious fully appointed apartments but in fact are selling an undeveloped site or even less; the advertiser of lucrative employment abroad, who collects fees from those who reply via an accommodation address and then disappears. At the other end of the scale are technical offences which may or may not be significant in covering more substantial deviance: failure to lodge annual accounts in time for public inspection with the relevant authorities, failure to specify the directors of the company or its registered office on company notepaper, failure to abide by all the compliance rules of a regulatory body. In between are those offences which clearly compromise client interests but do not amount to unequivocal theft: the classic example is the investment of clients' funds in much higher-risk ventures than was agreed, but with the chance of a higher return.

Because diligence and competence are in practice probably more important to clients' security in the financial sector than honesty, control systems directed at the overall objective of reliability are structured to recognize both that criminality is by no means the only hazard, and that the products, services and organizations to be policed are highly complex and subject to constant innovation. Furthermore, changes in public expectations may take place at the same time as changes in products and services. Building societies in Britain now offer insurance, estate agency and share dealing schemes as well as mortgages, as do banks. In the past, bank and building society managers often gave insurance advice to customers as part of their service, but did not expect to have to divulge the commission they earn from policies sold, nor whether they had a particular relationship with one or two insurers, or indeed whether their recommended insurers were affiliates of the bank or building society. They are now required to disclose this and also to be able to prove that, within their terms of reference, they have given the client the best advice the market has to offer. Precisely what this form of client protection consists in at any given time will of course change according to the needs of the client and the development of the insurance market.

Very rapid changes in financial services have been taking place in the past decade or so worldwide but particularly, because of their international prominence, in Britain and the United States. These can be summed up as internationalization. Financial institutions, led by the banks in the late 1960s and 1970s, began to expand their trade significantly beyond their national boundaries, developing new products and services as they did so to circumvent exchange controls and other regulations imposed by national treasuries traditionally keen to ensure that important financial institutions did not expose themselves to extra unpredictable risks abroad and continued to constitute a reliable pillar of the domestic economy. This coincided with and was in part a product of the disintegration of the international monetary system founded upon the dollar and sterling as reserve currencies, agreed to shortly after World War II at Bretton Woods. With no substitute still even in prospect (the European Monetary System is a local embryo attempt) sterling and the dollar had fixed parities withdrawn in the 1970s, and the international transfer of capital and financial services was greatly facilitated.

Increasing international trade in financial instruments led also to the demand for easier access to international trade in other financial services – securities, commodities, even mortgages. In addition new powerful players appeared in the market as a result of the much wider participation of the mass public in some of the financial services referred to above:

pension funds, unit trust funds, life assurance, investment funds. In time these vast new concentrations of wealth came to take a decisive part in the ownership of blue-chip shares and in government and company bonds, and to demand bigger and better investment services.

The consequences of these immense pressures and opportunities – internationalization, the rise of the big institutions as investors, the much wider diversification of investment amongst the mass public – contributed to a sharp intensification of competition. There was also a recognition that a global market was coming rapidly closer, with improvements in communications technology and information storage and retrieval making 24-hour operations worldwide possible, which implied that the survivors in this market would not be small and medium-size specialist organizations servicing particular nations, but vast international financial conglomerates with huge capitalization and a large range of products and services on offer. Regulatory problems of an increasingly international scale are hence being posed and have to some extent been recognized, especially by the heads of the national banks of the industrialized western nations in respect of banking supervision.

Enough has already been said to indicate that whilst there is ample scope within the financial sector for very serious outright frauds that require criminal sanctions, the requirements of managing increasingly large and complex institutions to standards of reliability adequate to sustain the public confidence that is essential for their survival, and in turn for the economic stability of nations, are for a system of management and regulation that relies on the expertise of insiders and the co-operation of the staff of the institutions in question. Hence although policing powers are to some extent formally exercised by specialized bodies, such as the Department of Trade and the Securities and Exchange Commission, who co-operate with the police and prosecutorial agencies in preferring criminal charges where this is possible and appropriate, much of the regulatory task is undertaken by the various arms of the financial services industry constituted as self-regulatory bodies. Whether this is deliberately acknowledged, as in Britain, or whether public precedence is given to an enforcement and surveillance agency such as the SEC in America, it will be argued below that self-regulation has been an inescapable necessity.

Before proceeding to the comparison of the British and American systems to demonstrate this point, the necessarily selective character of this chapter must be specified. What follows will concentrate on the securities sector of finance. Banking could equally well have been chosen as a sector of equal or greater importance, which has played a leading part in recent developments, and even the inclusion of both would leave out a number of other interesting and important areas. Space permits of only one to be given even limited consideration. The reasons for the choice of securities are that, in the first place, the changes in the regulatory regimes have been well-defined and serve illustrative purposes well, as does the fact that, whilst the services surrounding securities are by no means lacking in complexity, they are not quite as esoteric to the layman as those, particularly, of modern international banking. Secondly, securities are of two broad kinds, government and industrial. Trading of the latter is closely bound up with important issues in industrial policy which recent events have raised in dramatic form. Should those who trade in the shares of a publicly quoted company be required to have a closer regard for the implications of their actions for employment and production, as well as their immediate interest in making a profit from the buying and selling of shares? The specific form in which this age-old problem has been presented is that of takeovers and corporate raids. The securities sector hence also illustrates a feature of business crime that is frequently to the fore in the financial sector: its political character. As will be shown, the distinctions between offences currently designated as criminal and behaviour which is regarded as of the very essence of the functioning of securities markets are by no means easy to sustain.

The United States

Up to the great crash of 1929 American financial institutions were almost entirely dependent upon explicit self-regulation.[2] As in Britain, membership of the various trading bodies such as the stock exchanges, dominated by the New York Stock Exchange (NYSE), was akin to membership of a club: there were rules governing proper conduct, and membership could not be attained without some indication of appropriate capacities. It was accepted that there would be breaches of procedure and good conduct, and that there would be failures of firms and banks, just as these problems arose in the industrial sector. What was not anticipated was that the speculative fever of the 1920s would collapse in on itself, bringing down the entire financial system, including a large number of banks and brokerage firms. Nor was it appreciated what devastation this financial cataclysm would wreak upon the industrial and agricultural economy, ushering in the great depression.

The severity of the 1929 crash and the ensuing depression through the 1930s is important to emphasize because it threw seriously into question for the first time the way in which the American economy was run, and in particular the role of the state in regulating business.[3] Up to this point the American economy had, with some ups and down, expanded at an extraordinary pace, fuelled by vast natural resources, the huge national territory to be settled and exploited, and successive waves of immigrants, many of them young adults, constantly swelling the work force. The pioneering spirit of individualism and independence had derived much support from this long period of expansion and success, though in the early decades of the twentieth century the development of vast industrial and financial conglomerates and the harsh working conditions in the new industries such as steel and motor cars had given rise to significant working-class opposition and a populist socialist movement.

The election of Franklin Roosevelt and his espousal of the New Deal constituted a marked shift towards state intervention. One side of the New Deal strategy was to use state funding to regenerate the economy on an enormous scale; the other was to introduce regulatory and structural changes, to ensure as far as possible that the great crash would not be repeated. For, as public hearings on the banking, investment and securities markets began, it became plain that self-regulation had failed. Evidence was produced of incompetence, irregularity and fraud on a vast scale, with very little attempt at remedial action by those responsible.

Three major pieces of legislation were introduced as the focus of the new financial order. The Banking Act of 1933 (the Glass Steagall Act) separated commercial from investment banking, hoping thereby to protect the general public who relied on the former from the hazards of imprudence and of stock market cycles which beset the latter. The Securities Act of 1933 imposed upon the issuers and distributors of securities requirements to disclose substantial information about what was offered to allow the purchasers to make as informed a judgement as possible of the risks they were running in investment. Finally the Securities Exchange Act of 1934 established the Securities and Exchange Commission (SEC) as a federal agency to regulate the securities industry. Stock exchanges were required to register with the Commission (there are 10 at present), and in doing so to show that they had effective internal regulation against dishonesty, acted to promote fair trading, and were capable of discipling offenders. Detailed regulation was however left to the exchanges themselves, which became accredited self-regulatory organizations under the SEC, responsible for establishing and administering membership qualifications, rules of business conduct, ensuring compliance with these rules and the identificatin of members who broke them. The SEC was given ultimate powers to require rule changes and to revoke or suspend accreditation. In the following thirty years it used its powers to suspend an exchange only once, and only twice imposed rules on exchanges. Despite the recognized failure of self-regulation in 1929, therefore, the remedy was seen to lie in a new system explicitly based on self-regulation. William Douglas, the Chairman of the SEC in 1938, described the powers of the 1934 Act as being like a shotgun kept behind the door ready for use in an emergency, but in the hope that it never would be used.

Before considering why this apparently strange conclusion was reached, the picture of the regulation of the securities industry should be completed. Not all securities are or were traded on exchanges: those are merely convenient for trading, but they do not suit everyone or all securities. Securities were also traded by brokers and dealers direct to the public, the so-called over-the-counter (OTC) market. This too required regulation, which was initially provided by a committee of members of leading firms, backed by delegated powers under Roosevelt's National Industrial Recovery Act. In 1935 the Supreme Court ruled that the Act was unconstitutional, and enforcement hence became impossible. The new and more durable regime was incorporated into the Moloney Act of 1938, after negotiations with the SEC and leading industry figures. Under the 1938 Act the OTC market was regulated directly by securities associations, which would in turn be registered with the SEC. In practice there was only one such association. In 1939 the National Association of Securities Dealers registered and, as an approved SRO, was enabled to engage in restrictive practices, including the imposition of minimum rates of commission on deals in the interests of regulatory order and probity, which would otherwise have been illegal under anti-trust (restraint of trade) legislation. Membership of the NASD, although in theory voluntary to OTC practitioners, hence conferred sufficient market advantages to be essential. Between them, the NASD and the exchanges have become responsible for the effective regulation of the securities industry, subject to oversight by the SEC. In addition, full responsibility for setting standards in financial reporting was devolved to the accounting profession in 1938. When the SEC did seek rule changes, it almost invariably negotiated informally with the SROs and the accounting and legal professions before going through the formal public procedures.

The Persistence of Self-regulation

Why then was a failed self-regulatory system, which after all had boasted as far back as the 1870s that it had laws and regulations that bore upon its members as strongly as the laws of the land, been superseded by another self-regulatory system? The answers are partly ideological and partly practical. Ideologically, it was extremely difficult, even in the atmosphere of the great crash, to escape the hegemony of business freedom and American individualism. Regulation was easily portrayed as bureacratic, which was taken to be synonymous with slow, cumbersom, inefficient, inflexible, and incapable of measuring up to the needs especially of the securities industry, whose workings were said to be complex, swift and rapidly developing. Regulatory bureaucracy would act as a drag on the dynamism of the industry and in any case probably would not address the vital issues appropriately or fast enough. Practically there was also the question of who was to constitute the new regulatory personnel. The industry itself, because of its self-regulatory past, had an inevitable monopoly of expertise. Even if a large staff could be obtained from this source how could it be funded? Competent practitioners would not suspend lucrative careers for a spell as regulators without handsome compensation. Hiring outsiders or lower-grade staff would be cheaper, but would play directly into the hands of those who claimed that a big bureaucracy would be bumbling and ineffective. A substantial measure of co-operation with the industry was hence inescapable, and it was in the event deemed more profitable to maximize that co-operation and hold a watching brief; after all, the enormity of the 1929 catastrophe should also act as a stimulus upon practitioners to strive for genuine improvements, and the SEC did establish extensive rights of access and monitoring of progress for the state.

The outcome of this arrangement has, not surprisingly, been a regime in which misconduct is very largely dealt with by the self-regulatory bodies, and indeed often at a lower level than that, within securities dealers, firms and investment houses. All the same considerations apply to the financial sector as apply to industrial and commercial businesses but the more so because of the vital importance of public trust in the firm as a competent and honest manager of clients' money. The pressure for employee misconduct and client complaints to be handled internally and without undue fuss is thus very substantial. Likewise when firms cut corners and become deviant, it is in the industry's interests, either, if they are small and relatively new, to distance themselves from them by referral to the SEC, or, if they are more established and larger, to seek to rectify the situation without public scandal.

Recent Developments in Regulation

Before looking at whether this conjecture is confirmed by detailed research on the working of the SEC, however, the development of the regulatory regime in recent years needs to be described. The SEC may have begun life at a considerable disadvantage, but in the course of the next thirty years it built up considerable expertise. By the time of the next major crisis in the securities industry it was hence in a rather different position. That crisis once again politicized securities regulation. It consisted of two elements.

By the late 1960s the big institutions – banks, pension funds, unit trusts and others – were becoming conscious of their investing powers and of the marked difference in the scale of their operations, dealing daily in investments of millions of dollars, from those of private investors. All investors were non the less still subject to the minimum commission rates laid down by the exchanges and the NASD as a buffer against cut-throat competition, which might lead to the cutting of corners to stay in business. The institutions' view was that minimum rates meant unduly rich pickings for securities firms dealing in very large blocks of shares. Since securities firms were naturally reluctant to cede their privilege, the institutions began to lobby politicians to seek legislative change to abolish fixed commissions. This they eventually succeeded in doing, after a series of Senate hearings on securities regulation in 1971/2, with the 1975 Securities Acts.

Regulation became a wider political issue at this point because of the so-called back-office scandals of the late 1960s. The NYSE was subject to a speculative boom after 1966, and such was the rush to take on new business that the back offices of a number of firms, which had the job of registering deals made on the floor of the exchange, became overwhelmed. Not only were there long delays in registration, but also serious breaches of trading rules. In a business based on verbal deals rapidly transacted and often involving large sums, and with prices constantly changing, the orderly and rapid registration of deals was always recognized as an essential function of broker/dealers' business, and one which exchanges were supposed to monitor strictly. In the aftermath of the back-office scandal, 160 firms went out of business in 1969 and 1970, and the exchange's compensation fund was unable to meet all the claims of clients. The NYSE was forced to draw on funds earmarked for a new building, and legislation was passed in 1970 to establish the Securities and Investment Corporation to provide adequate funding against any future failures. The SEC undertook a detailed study of the episode, which was highly critical of the conduct of self-regulation. As a result, the 1975 regulation not only abolished fixed commissions, but also considerably tightened SEC control. SRO internal rule-making was made subject to more detailed SEC control. SRO governing bodies became more closely regulated, and the legal powers of the SEC to intervene in the SRO rule-making process was increased. In brief, the ascendancy of the SEC was recognized and reinforced.

Once again however, the abolition of self-regulation remained inconceivable. Even though the SEC had by this point a staff of around 2,000 and had clearly demonstrated its capacities in its reports and testimony at public hearings, the move to ending self-regulation would still have required its enormous expansion. Ideologically also there was a recognized danger that transferring all or most regulatory responsibility to the SEC would have taken internal pressure off the industry itself and fostered a game-playing, 'catch-me-if-you-can' antagonism between regulator and regulated.

In recent years, with Reaganism's emphasis upon deregulation, self-regulation has been further boosted. Between 1981 and 1986 SEC staff numbers fell by 300, whilst the number of securities registered almost doubled. None the less the crisis of the early 1970s did contribute to three qualitative changes in regulatory style, which have become increasingly important, and form vital elements in the current problems in the securities industry that are the topic of the concluding section of this chapter.

The SEC was granted enhanced legal powers in 1975, but not enhanced administrative capacity. As a consequence of this and the continuing rapid growth of the securities industry, self-regulation may have endured, but it has become less formal and more legalistic. The SROs have expanded into substantial bureaucracies, with their own more formalized regulatory system, and the SEC has used its powers to promulgate formal regulation. As formal powers and distance between individual practitioners and member firms have increased, there has been a growing demand for clear regulatory rules and due process for those accused of infractions. Increasing size and complexity in the securities industry, coupled with increased legal authority but lack of regulatory reach have hence both led in the direction of formalism. This has interacted in a potent way with the other development since the 1970s, the politicization of the securities industry. From the recovery from the oil price rises after the formation of OPEC in 1973, stock markets have experienced a long period of sustained rise until the limited crash of October 1987. In the 1980s the conjunction of this long bull market, with its attendant possibilities for speculative gain, and Reaganism's successful deregulatory campaign has led to innovations beyond the capacity of self-regulatory systems to cope with: junk-bonds, corporate raids, arbitraging, for example. These currently constitute a new regulatory crisis and one considerably more intractable than those of the past. The point for the moment however is that self-regulation has survived and flourished despite its acknowledged periodic failures, and that the cumulative consequence of these failures has been the politicization of securities regulation, and the projection of figures such as Levine and Boesky as folk devils.

The SEC as Policeman

Before considering the current situation in full, however, the evidence of a study of the work of the SEC in the post-war period up to the early 1980s is worthy of examination for the light it sheds on the argument that the policing capacities of the SEC are limited, and liable to be directed principally at a fringe of smaller operators, leaving the major established businesses to be managed through the self-regulatory procedures that, among other things, have, until the recent heightened media and political interest in them, kept matters relatively informal and private. Shapiro studied the SEC in the early 1980s, at which point it carried an average annual case load of just over 300, with the average offence involving $400,000, but in some cases sums exceeding the entire SEC budget. She analysed 526 cases investigated by the SEC between 1948 and 1972.[4]

Shapiro's research focuses on the intelligence – gathering aspects of the SEC's work, arguing that different kinds of tactics might be expected to yield results for different sorts of cases. In terms of the sources of information leading to the opening of a case file by the SEC, 64 per cent were information supplied, rather than SEC activity, which generated nearly half the inquiries (the total exceeding 100 per cent because 12 per cent of cases had pro- and reactive intelligence sources). Other control agencies referred 130 cases to the SEC (federal agencies 25, state agencies 59 and self-regulatory agencies 52), but these were often late and mainly trivial. SEC surveillance of the market and the press generated 12 per cent of cases, registration procedures 22 per cent, inspectors 8 per cent, and previous inquiries 9 per cent. SEC surveillance tended to detect cases affecting larger organizations, the smaller ones being less visible. All but

12 per cent of cases concerned stock issuers and brokers. Half the individuals involved and one-third of the organizations were repeat offenders, and these figures are under-recorded; two-thirds of the sample of cases contained at least one party who was a repeat offender. Companies (80 per cent of organizational offenders) were mainly small, and half were less than three years old.

A picture emerges of the SEC as a highly offence-oriented body, whose catch is mainly of small and medium-size offenders, and whose detection techniques are by no means effective at getting at the major offenders at an early stage. Many smaller and medium offenders may disclose themselves as a result of generating complaints from clients or trading partners, or as a consequence of insolvency. Larger ones and some of the more serious offences may well continue for some time undetected. This was the case with one of the most spectacular frauds in American history, which took place during the period of study, the Equity Funding Corporation.[5]

This insurance and investment business expanded at a phenomenal rate in the 1960s as a result of claims to be generating enormous profits. It inflated its reported income by $85 million of non-existent commission income and created bogus insurance to the value of $2 billion, which it sold to reinsurers to generate more cash. Fictitious insureds were then killed off in order to claim the insurance pay-off and generate more income. 10,000 investors, some of them major institutions, held stock worth $228 million before the operation finally crashed after a run of 10 years. Investors were paid 12 cents in the dollar. Although the SEC's Washington DC headquarters was transformed over the decade 1965–75 from a 'small reactive caretaker office to a large, specialised, pro-active, self-initiating office, constantly expanding the boundairies of enforcement policy and serving as a leadeer and model for the activities of the regions' (Shapiro, p. 140), it did not detect Equity Funding in time.

Shapiro concludes that 'the evidence suggests that SEC intelligence is passive, haphazard and fortuitous' (p. 172), and that a preoccupation with enforcement has led to a neglect of detection. She comments as follows (pp. 165–6) on the ways in which intelligence gathering works:

> Because the acts of wayward capitalists are often subtle and complex, and are made even more so by the diverse strategies of cover up and deception, the offences that victimised investors disclosed to the SEC are often obvious, amateurish, small-scale, trivial crimes that rarely warrant formal legal action. The often self-serving reasons that disaffected insiders have to 'squeal' (to save their own skins, seek revenge against former co-conspirators or increase their leverage in a power struggle) often generate tainted intelligence (exaggerated or distorted allegations or non-credible witnesses) and offences for which prosecution is inappropriate or problematic.
>
> Inferential intelligence strategies – like surveillance – pose different problems. Activities detected in this way often do not merit prosecution, because investigation proves the inference to be false or trivial. Many investigations derive from the enquiries of wary investors solicited to

participate in investment opportunities [*sic*] are not prosecuted because the schemes turn out to be wholly legal, or if illegal, are nipped in the bud before significant damage is done. The offences often do not merit legal action because their impact is insignificant and the activities have ceased.

The weaknesses of intelligence affected not just the size and seriousness of cases detected therefore, but also their susceptibility to criminal sanctions, which of course require a high degree of proof and require reference to the public prosecutorial authorities. The SEC does, however, have substantial administrative powers, which can be exercised in a hearing before a judge specializing in SEC law, who then recommends a disposal to the commissioners. At its most severe this can mean deregistration for the offender and hence an end to his participation in the securities business. The SEC makes much wider use of this essentially licensing power and of its capacity to file a civil suit, typically seeking an injunction not to repeat an alleged offence, than it does of criminal proceedings. Of the cases studied by Shapiro, 15 per cent involved no violation, and 40 per cent resulted in no legal action despite a violation. In a third of the latter cases, informal remedies were achieved and cases referred to other agencies, including SROs. Of the remaining two-thirds, prosecution was not pursued because of informal settlements, or legal action elsewhere, because the offence was stale, the offenders dead or old, the victims also to blame, the evidence weak, or the case not serious. Table 7 shows the distribution of the different kinds of sanctions.

Table 7   Sanctioning of securities offenders by the SEC

Route	% of offenders proceeded against	% of all violators
Civil	48	25
Administrative	43	22
Criminal	21	11

Source: Shapiro, *Wayward Capitalists*, table 6.2, p. 154

Regulation of the Securities Industry: Policing or Self-regulation?

In conjunction with the discussion of the development of securities regulations, Shapiro's work completes a tolerably clear picture of the regulation of the American securities industry. Despite the very serious nature of some offences, involving large sums at risk, and the substantial investigatory and legal powers increasingly vested in the SEC, the control system is quite clearly based on self-regulation. Although the SEC has a substantial policing function and may be said to be biased in this direction, it lacks a really substantial detective capacity, and is reliant upon cases coming to light by one means or another. The majority of these are of limited significance and the major cases tend to be identified, if at all, only when it is too late.

This however is to look at the system negatively. Viewed in a positive light, it can be seen as a licensing system, with the SEC as the licensing authority, and with the SROs administering practitioners day to day and drawing up more detailed codes of practice. The SEC acts as a watchdog over the SROs to ensure that they maintain standards, and the SROs refer difficulties and serious deviance up to the SEC for sanction. That is how it is supposed to work, and the recent tightening of the SEC's powers over SROs suggests increased efforts to make it do so. A genuinely informed judgement on such a system is difficult. It is one thing to say that it does not detect serious cases early enough. It is another to specify a system that would. Serious offences are perpetrated by people in established positions who are experienced and intelligent. They are not easily detected, precisely because, as Shapiro points out, such operators know just how to cover them up. Increasing the resources of the SEC would yield some benefit, though this is scarcely a panacea. The alternatives, however, do not look attractive: relying entirely on self-regulation without the (unquantifiable) deterrent and stimulant effect of the SEC, or the transfer of all responsibility to the SEC, which would risk inordinately high policing costs and practitioner antagonism.

There is a further reason for the difficulties of regulation of securities: a lack of practical agreement on standards. Shapiro notes that most of the SEC's work is undertaken by its 15 regional offices, many of which specialize, because of the distinctive nature of local securities business. Standards of practice in different areas vary significantly. Aggressive practices in pushing the sales of shares which are standard in Los Angeles would evoke horror in Boston. Trading in penny mining stocks in the north-west, which is regarded as normal speculation there, would be regarded as market manipulation elsewhere. These are not trivial examples, but offences that can carry severe penalties. In the securities field in particular, as in the financial sector in general, good practice, acceptable practice, unacceptable practice and dishonesty form a continuum, and there is a vigorous argument about where certain practices should fall, and about whether individual conduct on a given occasion constitutes such a practice. Whilst there are clear cases of illegality at one end of the continuum, there is a very vigorously contested centre ground. The role of the regulatory system here is not that of catching criminals or imposing sanctions, but of stimulating debate and developing clear standards which are widely and effectively communicated in the industry. Only when that is achieved in respect of a particular practice can administrative and legal powers be deployed to sanction and exclude deviance. As will be seen later, achieving such agreement may be a politically fraught business.

Britain

Informal Regulation by an Established Elite

In Britain self-regulation was not seen to fail, and continued to operate on an informal basis until the reregulation of 1985–7 under the Securities and Investment Board (SIB).[6] Just as American securities were dominated by New York, Britain has been dominated by the London Stock Exchange. Although there have long been small exchanges elsewhere, they never became as substantial as the regional competitors that grew up in the United States. The Stock Exchange managed to retain more or less absolute control over the trading of shares until the 1980s without competition from the OTC market. In 1980 the Unlisted Securities Market (USM) was launched by the Stock Exchange to provide smaller companies with a shorter trading history with an opportunity to raise capital. Although referred to as 'unlisted', there are listing requirements, but they are considerably less extensive than those for a full Stock Exchange quotation. The OTC market has begun to become established only in the 1980s and was deliberately marginalized by the Stock Exchange launching the USM. It remains very much a fringe activity with attendant risks, as will be discussed later.

The relatively centralized control exercised by a quite small group (the Stock Exchange had only 4,200 members in 1984) reflected the club-like character of most city institutions. Membership of Lloyd's Insurance Exchange was of a similar size, and other institutions, such as the London Metal Exchange and the London Commodities Exchange, were considerably smaller. Merchant banks were organized into an elite group of Accepting Houses, trusted by the Bank of England, and it used to be said that the Governor could assemble all the main bankers in London for a meeting in his office within half an hour.

These intimate and informal arrangements made the management of crises and the control of scandals and misconduct the easier – not that scandals did not occur but that informal collective decisions could be made as to how they should be dealt with.

The common culture generated by such a system was powerfully reinforced by a tradition of social exclusiveness. Membership of city institutions and especially senior positions in them was largely restricted to the upper and upper middle classes, educated in public schools and preferably the better of them, and followed by university education at Oxford or Cambridge and/or a brief career in one of the Guards regiments. The small-scale, officers' mess, club-like, male, upper-class and distinctively British culture of these institutions was hence carried forward throughout education and careers and finally reinforced by membership of the even more exclusive network of London's gentlemen's social clubs.

The specific control of the securities market was regulated by the Stock

Exchange rule book and by disciplinary proceedings before a panel of senior members. Perhaps more important, however, was the system of managing stock trading. Those actually dealing in shares who made their money from the difference in price between sales and purchases, the jobbers, were barred from selling shares direct to the public. This was undertaken by brokers, who were barred from dealing in shares, and acted only for clients. Their income came from commissions charged on the amount of share transactions they undertook, and they hence had an incentive to seek the best bargains for their clients and no incentive to unload shares they happened to have bought upon unsuspecting clients. Jobbers and brokers were organized in small firms, traditionally partnerships with unlimited liability, and with no ties to other investment institutions such as banks. These firms competed with each other for business and also specialized in shares of different kinds. Successful brokers especially might hope over the years to attract not only more but wealthier clients, and over the generations to move up the informal hierarchy towards its peak. At its peak lay the privilege of acting for the senior aristocracy and the Royal Family. The system was hence designed to be not only socially exclusive but uncompromised by other attachments. Minimum commissions were enforced to ensure that even those dealing in small amounts could offer a proper service. Foreigners were barred from membership of the exchange.

The Emergence of the New Regime

By the end of the 1970s these arrangements had come under great pressures, some of them the same as those leading to the American reforms of 1975. As in the United States, the rise of the big institutions dealing in large blocks of shares put pressure on minimum commissions. The Exchange remained adamant that the end of minimum commissions would precipitate a collapse of the other structural safeguards, because volume of trade and income-earning potential would have to be expanded to allow members to deal at lower margins. Change was therefore unthinkable. The institutions remained dissatisfied, and as time went on the threat began to emerge of them forming a parallel market to deal in shares with each other outside the Stock Exchange. In addition, with the abolition of currency exchange controls by the government in 1979, it became much easier to buy shares on foreign markets, particularly in New York. Given that blue-chip companies, in which the institutions invested heavily, were mostly quoted in New York as well as London, the danger was that business would be lost.

International competition was also growing in a wider sense. The banking sector had already become largely internationalized by the 1980s with London developing an increasingly significant Euro-dollar market, which diversified into other currencies traded beyond the restraints of their nations of origin. Banks had been attracted to London in increasing numbers in the 1960s and 1970s, and banking services and financial instruments had grown and diversified rapidly as they competed for business. Improvements in communication and information processing were clearly leading to the prospect of much greater international trading in stocks and bonds, which was of course facilitated by the ending of currency exchange controls. Europe was going to be a major market, with Tokyo and New York providing the other main bases backed by the world's largest economies. Although London had an established pre-eminence, it could not, however, expect to become the European centre for securities business unless it developed the capacity for the increased volume of trade.

This required a number of changes. First foreigners would have to be admitted to the Stock Exchange, just as foreign banks had been accepted by the London banking world. Secondly, the capitalization of Exchange firms would have to be greatly increased in order both to transact the much greater volumes of business, including large block trading for the institutions, and to compete with the major foreign (especially American and Japanese) securities and investments houses, which were tied to large investment banks. Thirdly, the regulatory regime had to be both credible and intelligible to newcomers. It would no longer be possible to assume that everybody shared the same values based on class and national culture; small-scale informality would disappear and clear rules and procedures would have to be substituted. Finally, care would have to be taken that a rapidly expanding market did not lead to the Exchange losing control of the market and various parallel markets and exchanges growing up.

The final nail in the coffin of the old regime was driven in by the Office of Fair Trading (OFT), which began a review of the Stock Exchange rule book in 1979 with a view to referring it to the Restrictive Practices Court as a restraint upon competition. The OFT compiled a list of 173 restrictive practices, but its objections centred upon minimum commissions, the jobber/broker distinction (single capacity), and the ban on access by outsiders. The Exchange looked set to fight the case line by line in court, when in 1983 the Chairman of the Stock Exchange reached an agreement with the Secretary of State for Trade and Industry and the case was called off. Under the deal all the main points were conceded: dual capacity, an end to minimum commissions, access for outsiders and the possibility of other financial institutions owning member firms. Initially it was hoped that the changes would be introduced by degrees, but it soon became apparent that events were moving too fast, and it was accepted that the system would change in one Big Bang on 27 October 1986. By that date almost every jobbing and broking firm had allied itself with a major banking or investment house, many of them foreign, and the new internationalized and larger-scale system was introduced.

To achieve success in this, however, it was necessary also to create a new regulatory system, and this proved just as fraught with difficulties as other reforms. The British securities industry had always done without a state regulatory agency, and the SEC was always looked upon with fear and loathing by British practitioners as representing the formalism, legality, bureaucracy and heavy-handedness that was the antithesis of the successful British regime. Quite apart from recent pressures for reform, the British system was not without its critics however, particularly as, in the course of the post-war years, public awareness of the financial sector began to grow. Direct participation in the securities market was, until the privatizations of the Thatcher government, quite small and traditionally the preserve of the wealthy, but the rise of the institutions – especially pension funds, unit trusts and life insurance – betokened the increasing participation of a large sector of the population, as investors at one remove from the securities markets themselves. Public and media interest in the stock market and in 'the City' more widely gradually began to grow, and with it a sensitivity to scandal. With the property boom and associated secondary banking crash of 1973/4 and the attendant stock market fall in the wake of the OPEC oil price increase, a considerable number of cases of serious misconduct were revealed to public comment, together with the dependence of fiancial institutions upon the competence and honesty of practitioners. The Bank of England was compelled to organize a multi-billion-pound rescue of the secondary banks to protect the banking system as a whole from a collapse of confidence.[7]

The Problem of Agreeing Standards

With the emphasis of the Thatcher government upon the extension of property-owning democracy through the encouragement of the maximum possible numbers of home owners and of increased share ownership through privatization of public utilities and other nationalized industries, sensitivity to scandal and concern for protection of investors against fraud and abuse naturally increased. This contributed to pressure for the introduction of a regulatory system that was more public and accessible and less the exclusive preserve of a social elite. One difficulty faced in doing so however was the establishing of agreed standards. As time went on and public debate continued, practices which in the past had been normal and acceptable came to be vilified as immoral and even crimi-nalized.

One example of this was insider dealing, that is taking advantage of privileged knowledge of information about a company that is likely to send the share price up or down, buying shares in advance of this information becoming public, and so making a quick and certain profit. Under the traditional system the social intimacy of members of city institutions naturally led to the passing on of tips about particular shares, which might well include 'hot' information. It would have perplexed leading members of these institutions up to the end of the 1950s to be told that they were doing anything reprehensible in acting on such information. It was precisely because of the access to such information that one was part of the

City, and one was part of the City in the clear expectation of making a considerable amount of money. Yet by the 1980s insider dealing had become a criminal offence in both Britain and the United States, and evidence of it was being constantly trumpeted in the press as a matter demanding prosecution in the interests of fair play for ordinary investors. Thus when an up-and-coming member of leading merchant bankers Morgan Grenfell was discovered using knowledge gained at work to make a killing, he was instantly dismissed and subsequently prosecuted and faced public vilification and personal ruin.

Similarly the practice of stagging was well established in the City as a means of making a quick profit. The object here was to pick a share or government bond issue that was likely to be attractive or oversubscribed. This meant that it would command an instant premium in the market, but the distribution of the bonds or shares would be in proportion to applications. Thus a stag might apply for 10,000 shares at the fixed offer price, in the expectation of actually receiving 2,000, which she/he would instantly sell at a profit. If she/he was wrong of course, and the issue was undersubscribed she/he would get the full 10,000 and have to pay for them. Nonetheless, at least in certain cases, this was not a very difficult judgement to make.

When the government began its programme of privatization, it faced the difficulties that the amount of money being raised by the shares issued was unprecedentedly large, and secondly, that it wished to encourage new small investors to subscribe. The logic of these pressures was to reduce the offer price to bargain levels. Given that the utilities constitute blue-chip investments, the institutions were bound to be strongly interested. In order to prevent them snapping up all the shares, the government offered small investors a privileged but limited allocation, the rule being that the fewer shares you applied for the greater the certainty of getting all you asked for. Because of the offer price and because of institutional demand, the privatization issues were, with one or two exceptions, a dead certainty for the stags, whose tactic was, as in earlier years, to make multiple applications, so that, even after restrictions in allocation, they ended up with a good parcel of shares for resale at a profit. The government rapidly designated this as unfair practice and began warning in increasingly stringent terms that multiple applications would be sanctioned, concluding within five years with a threat of criminal sanctions. In the end it was a conservative MP who was made an example of in 1987, when he was convicted of making multiple applications for British Telecom shares in 1984 and initially imprisoned, but released and fined on appeal. The appeal court explicitly referred to the wording of the BT prospectus in setting aside the prison sentence, and compared the more explicit warnings of criminal sanctions which were contained in later privatization issues.

It was against this background, as well as the rising case load of outright frauds being referred to police noted earlier and a number of other scandals and abuses in relation to securities which there is not space to review here, that the government requested Professor Gower to undertake a review of financial services and investor protection. Gower took extensive soundings in the City and issued an interim report, on which there was further consultation, before producing a final report which formed the basis of the Financial Services Bill introduced in 1985. Gower was in favour of a state regulatory agency with powers similar to those of the SEC, which would supersede the rather hesitantly used powers of the Department of Trade and Industry to institute inquiries when things went wrong. There was vehement opposition to such a move, and the system which was finally established left the DTI with some continuing powers and responsibilities and retained the emphasis upon self-regulation: a system, as it was called, of statute-backed self-regulation.

Regulation by the Securities and Investments Board

The central new institution is the Securities and Investments Board, whose members are appointed from City practitioners by the Secretary of State for Trade and the Governor of the Bank of England. The Board acts as a licensing and accreditation authority for a series of self-regulatory organizations covering the various sectors of the City. There was considerable bickering about the establishment of the SROs, and complaints about the inappropriateness or indignity of being associated with 'that kind of organization', but eventually there were five: The Securities Association (TSA), the result of the merger of the Stock Exchange and the International Securities Regulatory Association, the Financial Intermediaries Managers and Brokers Regulatory Association (FIMBRA), covering the very large numbers of financial and investment advisers, the Association of Futures Brokers and Dealers (AFBD), firms advising and dealing in futures and options, the Investment Management Regulatory Organisation (IMRO), representing mainly investment and unit trusts and pension funds, and the Life Assurance and Unit Trust Regulatory Organization (LAUTRO). Also recognized by the SIB were professional bodies, lawyers and accountants, and recognized investment exchanges including the Stock Exchange, the commodities and metal exchanges and the London Internatinal Financial Futures Exchange (LIFFE). Lloyd's insurance market was, despite acrimonious political debate, exempted from the system, because it had been subject to extensive reregulation on a somewhat similar basis under the Lloyd's Act, 1982.

Under the SIB regime it became illegal, and punishable by up to two years' imprisonment, to practise in the financial services sector without recognition either by the SIB or one of the SROs. The responsibility of the SROs is to devise rules of practice and membership and to ensure that practitioners hold themselves ready for both regular and random inspections. The licensing system was introduced in stages up to April 1988, by which time firms had to apply for accreditation. By this point the SIB had developed an extensive rule book and engaged in a number of extended negotiations with various SROs about particular features of rules and practice, not always to the satisfaction of practitioners. Under its first chairman, Sir Kenneth Berrill, the SIB made it clear that it would use its licensing powers to insist that rules were devised that gave adequate protection for investors, that ensured good practice in the conduct of business and that, as far as possible, eliminated conflicts of interest. All sectors were also required to establish a compensation fund to ensure that investors are protected in the event of fraud or failure in a member firm. By this point, as Berrill retired and was succeeded by a new chairman less given to tough talking, widespread hostility to the complexity of the rules under the new system had developed and its was castigated by some practitioners as unworkable.

Certainly, as in the United States, the price of heightened political awareness of the financial services sector, with its opportunities and risks, had increased media attention and public awareness of the regulatory issues, and increased demand for a regime that would give real investor protection both from business failures, that swallowed up investments, and from malpractices. At the level of the small investor, encouraged to have a go at riskier investments in the enterprise culture fostered by the Thatcher government, there was sustained cause for concern both at malpractices and at the ineffectiveness of the licensing arrangements administered by the Department of Trade before the new regime. It was failure in investment advisers Norton Warburg in 1981 that was one of the immediate causes of Gower's review of investor protection. Although only £12 million was involved, the liquidation revealed serious failings in the mixing of client and company accounts which essentially involved clients' investments being used to keep Norton Warburg afloat. Further, the Department of Trade had renewed its licence to act as an investment adviser only two months before the crash, having had a report on Norton Warburg for some time before that. In addition, the Bank of England had allowed NW access to its staff for investment advice when they were on the point of retirement or redundancy, thereby implying approval of NW's reliability.

Continuing Problems

In subsequent years similar tales of woe were repeated. Investment advisers Macdonald Wheeler went broke owing £9 million in 1986 and were able to pay out only a quarter of that two years later. In the OTC market two dealers went out of business amid numerous accusations of misrepresentation and share pushing, Prior Harwin and Ravendale Securities. The largest firm in the OTC market, Harvard Securities, came under sustained pressure from investors and was refused membership of the Securities Association. It continued to operate into 1988 under an interim licence from the SIB, but was the subject of a Department of Trade investigation and continued complaints from investors, who claimed to have been cajoled into buying stocks in which Harvard was a market-maker, only to find that future prospects touted at the sale were unrealized and that the shares were impossible to resell. Evidence was published that Harvard salesmen were told in writing: 'Your job is to sell the shares retailed by Harvard Securities. And only those shares.'[8] Although senior dealers were permitted to buy back 30 per cent of stocks sold, juniors were permitted to buy back only 10 per cent, after which commission was reduced pro rata.

In some of the stocks it sold, Harvard was also a major shareholder, so creating a conflict of interest. Clients hardly seemed likely to get fair treatment under these circumstances, yet at this very time major stock-broking firms were withdrawing from the small investors' market, claiming that the small bargains they were asked to process were not worth the trouble in commission. In September 1988 Harvard finally gave up the struggle, and closed down virtually all its share-dealing operations, leaving up to 150,000 clients to attempt to salvage what they could. In those cases where Harvard had been the sole market-maker in the shares that they had bought their prospects were bleak.

One of the more curious areas of difficulties was commodities and futures, a market that one judge in a case in 1983 likened to a jungle in urgent need of regulation. Futures are notoriously volatile, and as the saying goes, 'not for widows and orphans', who need a secure investment. Their attraction however is that volatility can mean large gains. This attraction was strongly emphasized in the sale pitch of LHW futures in the early and mid-1980s, whose clients were persistently phoned and persuaded to throw in more money to recover what had already been lost. Tales of woe proliferated in the press, and LHW came under pressure to stop its high-pressure selling, and also to moderate its very high commission rates, which some clients claimed absorbed all the gains which were made. Futures were certainly a lucrative business for some. Three former employees of LHW set up on their own as DPR Futures and began using the same techniques and generating the same complaints. DPR was eventually suspended by a winding-up petition from the SIB, having been the subject of an earlier DTI enquiry. LHW apparently reformed in the interests of achieving an SIB, or rather AFBD, licence, but by the time this happened in 1988, the two founders had withdrawn from active control. Accounts then released showed profits of £19.4 million in 1985/6 on a turnover of £36.5 million, and £10.6 million on £26.7 million in the following year. The two major shareholders, John Hughes and Jeremy Walsh, received dividends of £19.3 million between them for the two years. After staff cuts and reorganization, the revamped LHW was anticipating group profits of only £3 million in 1987/8. Following the revelation of these facts the two founders reduced their holdings to 14 per cent, and Clive Thornton, the former chairman of the Abbey National Building Society, was brought in to improve the chances of an AFBD licence that was essential for the business to continue. The SIB looked as though it was going to be more persistent and decisive than the DTI in policing the markets, but there was evidently still plenty of work to be done.

It has not only been marginal operators who have found the new regulatory regime demanding. In October 1988 Smith New Court, the City's largest independent market-maker was suspended for three months from being allowed to make markets in shares in companies involved in takeover bids where it was acting as stockbroker or financial adviser to one of the parties. This followed its purchase of a million shares in Ruberoid, which was being bid for, and their sale to a broker acting for Tarmac, which then made an agreed bid after agreeing not to sell to the hostile bidder, Raine. SNC was forced to unscramble the deal at a cost of at least £60,000 and was denounced for 'incompetence on the part of a number of people within SNC in an area which was of the utmost importance to the integrity of the market' by the Takeover Panel, which ordered the suspension under its new powers in the SIB regime. Conflicts of interest inevitable in financial conglomerates are supposed to be contained by professional standards and barriers to communication in such situations, and it was evident that additional training of staff was necessary to achieve the required standards.

Barlow Clowes

Just how weak the preceding regime has been was most dramatically demonstrated by the Barlow Clowes affair. This was a firm of investment managers which the SIB petitioned to wind up in June 1988 after it became subject to the new licensing system. The failings were serious in a number of respects. The amount of investments involved approached £200 million, put up by about 17,000 investors. More importantly, Barlow Clowes specialized in government stocks or gilt-edged securities that are a very secure form of investment. It offered however to invest both in Britain and offshore through its Gibraltar operation, and specialized in offering tax-efficient schemes, which enabled it to claim high returns for investors. Substantial offshore operations and the deliberate targeting of tax should have been enough to arouse suspicions among the authorities, and indeed it emerged that suspicions were rife but were not followed through with decisive action to protect investors. Although the principal, Peter Clowes, at first claimed that assets were realizable in full, given time, it soon became evident, first that very large sums had been spent on a lifestyle that involved the frequent hiring of executive jets, and second, that substantial amounts of offshore investments had not gone into gilts, but into less secure and realizable assets such as companies and real estate.

All the relevant authorities were aware that something was not well at Barlow Clowes, but none took decisive action. The police made inquiries as a result of information about the large expenditure on travel and expenses a year before the crash. The Inland Revenue was also alerted and made inquiries at the same time. More importantly however, the Minister for Consumer Affairs was alerted about concerns that BC was neither licensed by the DTI nor a member of the NASDIM (the precursor of FIMBRA). BC's auditors cited serious apparent irregularities in its offshore operation in September 1986. The Bank of England expressed doubts as to whether the rates of return on gilts offered by BC were legally attainable.

Above all the DTI, which had responsibility for licensing BC, made an error in 1974 which proved disastrous. BC started trading in 1973, at which time it enquired of the DTI whether it needed a licence. The DTI replied that it was unable to advise BC how to construe the Prevention of Frauds Investment Act, but added guidance which led BC to conclude that it did not need a licence. When, in 1984, the DTI was alerted to the dangers at BC, it recognized that its earlier letter could be construed as suggesting no licence was needed. It therefore granted a licence in 1985. It appears that it was only after that point that it began to accumulate evidence of irregularities, and as it did so it responded not by a swift and decisive inquiry and suspension, but by seeking assurances that all was well, which were freely given, but not honoured. It was also concerned that public intervention or refusal of a licence might precipitate BC's collapse. Since one of the civil servants involved in the licensing procedure reached the conclusion that, although BC was disorganized, Clowes was basically honest, it was hoped that firm guidance would better serve everyone's interests. A DTI inspection did not ensue until late 1987, and by the time that began to confirm fears, the new regime under the SIB was being implemented and the DTI seemed to be glad to pass on its responsibilities. The net effect of the saga was a special inquiry into the role of the DTI in the case and the threat by the associations formed to protect the interests of the investors in BC to sue the DTI for negligence.

Sir Godfrey le Quesne's enquiry was specifically limited, however, to ascertaining the facts, and he was precluded from making judgements, particularly as to whether the DTI's licensing procedures had been adequate.[9] His report confirmed information that had already been revealed and provided in its detail plenty of ammunition for those, notably the group of investors formed to seek compensation and the Labour opposition, who wished to accuse the DTI of negligence. It also showed that the licensing office was greatly overburdened, with only half a dozen civil servants coming by the 1980s to deal with hundreds of licences and so unable to give many of them the attention they deserved. This fact only reinforced one important point arising out of the case: what was the value to the investing public of a licence? Was it, as investors said, a mark of recognition by the state that the licensee had reached approved standards and reliability and was therefore to be trusted, or was it like the much-derided dog licence, something that was supposed to be applied for, but involved no vetting worthy of the name and was anyway ignored by many?

The new regime under the SIB was clearly intended to be the former, but the evidence of BC suggested that the DTI was closer to the latter, with BC being allowed to continue to operate without a licence, and above all with the Department demonstrating the inertia and unwillingness to respond effectively, for which City commentators had for so long critized it.

The government's response to le Quesne was to claim that the DTI's conduct had been reasonable – the word 'competent' was avoided – and that the government had no legal liability for compensation for negligence. This provoked outrage even among some Tory MPs, and the government offered two remedies. First it gave its support to efforts by private city institutions, who had been taken in by BC and directed clients to its schemes, to mount a rescue scheme to compensate the investors. Secondly, it suggested that if the matter were to be taken up by the Parliamentary Commissioner (ombudsman) and he found maladministration, the government might look differently upon compensation. There was a precedent for this. A small investment adviser in Torquay was the subject of an ombudsman's inquiry, and in 1986 he invited the DTI to reimburse investors because of the failings of the DTI's licensing department. The DTI paid up. Despite knowing in 1981 that the company admitted failing to keep proper records, and that substantial sums were owed to clients for which the principal was unable to account, the DTI took no action, because this evidence was given to it in confidence, and renewed the investment adviser's licence. The ombudsman concluded that the DTI had shown a 'lamentable lack of concern for the interests of those members of the public who had a right to assume that the department's licensing system offered them a reasonable measure of protection'.

BC's investors were certainly in need of something, most of them being small savers, some with most of their money at risk. BC's UK operation was set to pay out 75 pence in the pound, but the 11,000 investors in the offshore scheme stood to get only 30 pence. There were those, of course, who uncharitably said that investors, even small ones, who chose to go offshore in schemes offering returns above the going rate were being greedy as well as gullible, but there was little doubt that BC's demise resulted in genuine hardship for some, and it was upon this that media attention focused. It did not focus in any hostile fashion upon the responsibilities of investment advisers to evaluate the reliability of BC in directing naïve clients' money to it. Some of these advisers were shown to be unreliable and in too deep with BC, but others were substantial businesses with well-established reputations.

These troubles were all outside the ambit of the traditional and established city institutions and demonstrated the need for newer fringe operators to be brought under effective regulatory control. They do, however, indicate both the problematic nature of good or 'good enough' conduct in the financial services sector, and the vital importance of effective monitoring and compliance procedures to achieve it. Police prosecutions may satisfy some, but will not recover investors' money, nor are they feasible until clear evidence of wrongdoing is accumulated. Where the operation in question is an out-and-out fraud this may be rapid enough, but where, as in these cases, it was a combination of recklessness, incompetence and greed taking control in substantial legitimate businesses, the chances of indentifying anything of interest to the police at a stage early enough to prevent damage, or even usually to enable the recovery of losses, is slight.

Takeovers

As Marx noted long ago, it is a feature of competitive capitalism that the more successful enterprises which prosper drive the less successful out of business or swallow them up. The result is an increasing concentration of industry, sector by sector, in a few giant corporations, a trend to oligopoly and monopoly. One of Marx's interests in this process was what he took to be its political consequence, namely the increased solidarity of workers when all faced with the same employer and their more ready recognition of his exploitative powers, that is, increased class-consciousness. The problem which has given rise to more long-term concern, however, has in practice been the abuse of giant corporations' market power against the consumer. There have been those, such as J. K. Galbraith, who have argued that the interests of the giant corporation differ from those of smaller businesses. The modern corporation is too large to be highly flexible, and seeks stability and efficiency by sophisticated long-term planning, and attempts to predict and influence the market through the control of supplies of raw materials and advertising, for example. It hence acts to ensure as far as possible a peaceable and loyal work force by offering good wages and conditions and a variety of fringe benefits. The outcome of this may be products whose prices reflect a monopoly or cartel. If those products are more or less essential and demand is inelastic, this abuse of the market may have a marked impact, as the oil-exporting countries demonstrated when they successfully tripled the price of oil in 1973 after the foundation of the OPEC cartel.

Different sections of the industrial economy mature in this respect – that is, are susceptible to monopoly – at different points in industrialization, and generally the trend to monopoly and the formation of cartels did not pose a significant problem until the end of the nineteenth century. At that point the United States began to experience major problems of the abuse of market domination, notably in steel, railways and banking, and introduced anti-trust legislation, which required the breaking up of some of these monopolies and banned the circumvention of market pricing by cartel agreements. The legislation has been added to from time, but only intermittently enforced. The most well-known recent case of action to end a monopoly was the break-up of the American Telephone and Telegraph

(AT and T) telephone company into regional corporations. The most notorious case of anti-trust prosecution in recent years has been the heavy electrical equipment case of 1962, in which managers of leading American electrical equipment manufacturers were convicted of having held secret meetings to fix prices, despite overt company policy to the contrary.[10]

Other countries, however, have reacted to the problem in a quite different way, seeing oligopolies and cartels as a means for the state more easily to direct the development of the economy. This was the strategy of the Germans and the Japanese, producing a direct political and economic alliance between government and big business known as corporatism. Britain has taken a middle road. Industries which have been regarded as basic or as public utilities – gas, electricity, water, telephones, coal, railways, steel – have been nationalized as a means of safeguarding the public interest. Although there has been long dispute about some cases – notably steel – it has only been with the advent of the Thatcher government that utilities have begun to be sold off to come closer to the American model. Legislation has been limited. Cartels and price agreements are not necessarily illegal, but do have to registered with the Restrictive Practices Court. There is then a hearing on the desirability of the cartel arrangement in which manufacturers or suppliers of services – including potentially at one point the Stock Exchange, as was described above – can argue their case for price agreements as the means of securing quality and reliability rather than being an exploitation of the customer. Takeovers and mergers that seem likely to constitute oligopolies or monopolies are referred to the Monopolies and Mergers Commission, which inquires into the likely effect on the market and makes a recommendation. The final decision rests with the Secretary of State for Trade and Industry, which indicates the explicitly political character which the problem is held to have in Britain. References to the Commission on a proposed takeover can come either from the Secretary of State or from the Office of Fair Trading, the quasi-state agency established in 1973 to police competition and fair trading in the interests of the customer.

Certainly the basis for decisions on whether to permit takeovers and mergers may be very much wider than a formal calculation of the amount of the market for certain products that the new corporation would have. In the case of defence-related companies for example, the government may want to prevent a takeover by a foreign company. As the case of Westland Helicopters showed in 1986, the participation of friendly foreigners (in this case Fiat of Italy and Sikorsky of the United States) offering to rescue an ailing company and the prospect of future business may not necessarily be welcome, and in this case an almighty row ensued into the details of which there is not space to enter here. Political and economic considerations can also apply when mergers are proposed by companies in the defence-related sector, where both are nationals. In this and other cases where government is the main purchaser there is some interest in maintaining competition among suppliers since, as recent events in the defence industries in both Britain and the United States have shown, corporations producing weapons systems and aircraft to government specification and with heavy research expenditure not infrequently exploit the deep pockets of the state and its lack of direct involvement in manufacturing and pricing.

Political and economic considerations enter in all sorts of other complex ways also. The proposed merger between British Aerospace, a recently privatized and successful corporation, and Austin Rover, the also recently privatized but legendarily weak car manufacturer, was presented with enthusiastic remarks about the complementarity of technologies by the chairmen of both boards, but the political benefits to the government in disposing of a lame duck and at the same time giving it a degree of economic protection were evident in the substantial package of cash and debt write-offs that the corporation chairmen expected of the government. In another direction, the takeover by Nestlé of chocolate manufacturers Rowntree Mackintosh was the cause of a furore over hostile bids by foreign companies, especially those carefully structured themselves to be immune from takeover. On the other side it was argued that Nestlé's cash and market power would improve the marketing of Rowntree's products, and that in any case the confectionery market was near maturity, with international sales increasingly dominated by a few giant corporations. Those who did not become part of one of these faced extinction.

Much the same arguments have been applied to the media industry, but with different political implications. The success of Rupert Murdoch in putting together a £3 billion newspaper and television empire, starting in Australia and now encompassing Britain and the United States, has evoked anxiety not only about his economic exploitation of the market position, but about the political desirability of having one man in control of such a large sector of the media worldwide, and so capable of influencing what is reported as news and how it is reported, particularly given Murdoch's known firm, right-wing views. Doubts have also been expressed about the quality of the output of his papers and broadcast stations, and his emphasis upon profitability regardless of the quality of the journalism involved. This anxiety has been further fuelled by the vaunting ambitions of Robert Maxwell, who has declared his objective of developing an empire parallel to that of Murdoch, but based in the printing and publishing (books and magazines) sector of the media. This has coincided with an emphasis upon high-pressure marketing of 'blockbuster novels' and a shift to retailing books like any other commodity, and no longer in a specialized way and with limited general profitability as a part of Culture.

This group of political and economic problems related to takeovers is quite well recognized and has given rise to control institutions in most industrialized countries, even though enforcement is by no means rigorous. The issues are inevitably complex and even nebulous and can be dealt with only by government intervention by law or policy. There are two other well-established problem areas in which takeovers also produce problems, and a fourth which has recently been the centre of great difficulties, but which is much less clearly identified and almost entirely uncontrolled.

Regulating the Bid Process

The first of these concerns the way in which a takeover bid is conducted. Takeovers tend to take place in waves. Macro-economic factors such as the maturation of the market sector may be important background influences determining where bids will come, but bidding depends upon the bidder being able to raise the money necessary for success. This in turn depends in part upon the state of the economy: if it is booming, profits will be high and these can be retained to finance a bid. In part also it will depend upon the stock market: if there is a bull market with prices rising, the bidding company will be the more able to offer its shares in exchange for those of the target company at a high price – much less painful normally than offering cash. Finally, the cost and availability of credit from bankers to finance a takeover bid will also influence when takeovers happen. The late 1980s, with stock markets which had experienced the longest bull market in most practitioners' memory, starting in 1973–4 and lasting until the crash of October 1987, have been a period of takeover booms.[11]

Table 8   Recent takeovers and mergers

	1988 (10 months)		1987	
	Mergers	Value (£)	Mergers	Value (£)
Europe into UK	68	4,782	45	1,654
US into UK	33	1,148	32	749
Rest of World into UK	125	6,474	96	3,976
Total	226	12,404	173	6,379
UK into Europe	188	1,877	142	1,209
UK into US	317	12,891	263	18,106
UK into rest of world	605	17,653	471	21,578
Total	1110	32,421	876	40,893

Souce: Acquisitions Monthly, November 1988

In markets in which bid succeeded bid with ever-increasing speed and size and with constantly new tactics being employed to achieve success, the difficulties of control became even greater. The means by which fairness is achieved vary on different sides of the Atlantic, but, as one

Table 9   Changes in takeover and merger activity within the UK

	Total of all takeovers and mergers				% Expenditure	
	No. acquiring	No. acquired	Value (£m)	Cash	Issue of ordinary shares	Issues of fixed interest securities
1973	929	1,205	1,304	53.0	35.7	11.3
1975	276	315	291	59.4	32.0	8.6
1980	404	469	1,475	51.5	45.4	3.1
1982	399	463	2,206	58.1	31.8	10.1
1984	508	568	5,474	53.8	33.6	12.6
1987	850	1,125	15,363	32.2	62.3	5.5

Source: British Business, 5 August 1988

commentator has remarked, the principles which the control systems seek to protect are the same in Britain and the United States. Hurst identifies four:[12]

1   To protect the right of the target company shareholder to be the ultimate party determining the success or failure of the offer by making the decision to tender or not to tender his shares while possessed of all the material facts and in an atmosphere free of undue coercion or time pressure.
2   The regulatory authority . . . should primarily be concerned with ensuring that the parties to the offer provide information to the shareholders to enable them to judge the merits of the offer for themselves. To this end both British and American schemes require detailed disclosures of things such as the identify of the offerers and his associates, sources of financing for the offer, the ultimate objective in acquiring the offeree's shares and any relationship or understanding with the offeree's management.
3   Both countries are concerned with protecting the position of the minority shareholder following completion of a takeover in which the offerer has acquired a controlling interest.
4   Both countries are concerned with defensive measures which may be undertaken by the management of the offeree to impede the success of the offer. The courts in both countries have held that any action taken by management of the target which is motivated primarily by the desire to retain control of the company to preserve their jobs and not because they believe it is in the best interests of the corporation to do so is a violation of the Director's fiduciary duty to the corporation.

The overriding principle which sums up all four of these objectives is shareholders' sovereignty. It is for the shareholders to decide by a majority vote whether or not to accept the bid. The difficulties which have arisen have largely revolved around the ways in which this majority is achieved and the possible oppression of the interests both of the company itself and of minority shareholders in the process. In practice the protective arrangements of the schemes in both Britain and the United States are directed mainly at the interests of minority shareholders. As will be shown later, although the corporation has a legal identity, its interests are rarely given much protection in takeovers.

The protective measures in the United Sttes are largely legal, under the 1934 Securities Exchange Act and SEC regulation under it, as well as legislation by individual states. Remedy has hence been strongly perceived to lie in recourse to the courts by way of an injunction or by civil suit for damages. This tactic is widely used, both by shareholders who feel their interests have been abused, and by corporate management resisting a bid which they will claim is unfair or illegal in some respect. The effect of legal action is to lengthen the bid process and to apply leverage: legal actions are used to obtain changes in the terms of a bid and sometimes to get it called off. In a case where the bid is a hostile one, i.e. has not been agreed privately with the target company before being made publicly, the target may adopt a number of defensive tactics. It may seek a friendly takeover by another company, known as a white knight, on terms which it regards as more favourable to it. It may seek to borrow enough money to purchase a controlling interest in its own shares, a tactic known as the leveraged buy-out, which frequently involves the company going heavily into debt to raise the necessary cash. Finally, it may adopt one of the variety of spoiling tactics designed to make it unattractive to the bidder, such as the poison pill device of declaring an extraordinary and massive dividend to existing shareholders.

The market is allowed considerable freedom of operation as regards takeovers in the United States, and there is a substantial tolerance of foreign bids, a fact of which a number of British corporations have recently taken advantage. The market is left to decide who should own and control a corporation within fairly broad limits and this has led to considerable problems, currently being debated in the United States, but far from resolution. The British system, by contrast, involves detailed informal regulation.[13] In the course of a previous takeover boom in the 1960s, the Department of Trade and the Bank of England became concerned at the tactics being used by some bidders and encouraged the formation of a panel of senior City figures to draw up a code of conduct in takeover bids. The City Panel on Takeovers and Mergers has developed and survived and has now been given legal recognition under the Financial Services Act. Its regulations have gradually become more extensive and formal, and it has responded to a series of undesirable innovations in takeover practice and to constant criticism that it is ineffective at controlling abuses. Although it has limited direct legal powers, it does have what might be called decisive influence. Members of self-regulatory organizations and particularly of the Securities Association are bound by their rules to respect and abide by the rulings of the Panel on pain of suspension or expulsion. The chances of any corporation being able to escape compliance without leaving its advisers in serious trouble and its shares suspended from quotation are hence slight.

The regulation administered by the Panel is now extensive and seems responsible for the less wild takeover market in Britain. In particular, a specific rule has for some time banned the target company from any defence activity during an offer which may preclude shareholders from deciding on the merits of the offer unless the defensive measure is approved by a shareholders' vote. Regulation requiring disclosure of the facts of the bid and the protection of the rights of minority shareholders have been stimulated by a number of recent practices that the Panel has attempted to outlaw. Takeover by stealth has been a particular problem, with bidders quietly building a substantial holding in a target prior to making a bid, at which point the share price of the target will normally rise sharply. This practice was banned by requiring holders of 5 per cent of the company to declare their holding and holders of 30 per cent to make a bid for the entire company, so that control should not be acquired on the cheap. This resulted in concert parties, groups of associates buying up just short of 5 per cent and holding them in readiness for the bidder, and dawn raids, in which vast sums were unleashed on an unsuspecting market to snap up as many shares as possible before it reacted and the price rose. Both these practices are now banned, but not always easy to detect and sanction.

The Guinness Affair

The importance of the panel's regulatory system and its rulings was illustrated on a large scale in Guinness's contested bid for Distillers in 1986.[14] Contested bids are the most prone of all to abuse, since not only is the target company resisting the bid, but there are two (rarely more) bidders chasing the shares. Distillers was the result of a series of past amalgamations and takeovers of the Scotch whisky industry, with the notable exception of Bell's, which remained independent and the leading brand. The world market for alcoholic drinks was showing distinct signs of maturation in the 1980s, with bids in the beer-brewing end of the market as well as the spirits end proliferating, and encompassing Australia, Britain, Europe, the United States and Canada. Distillers, although in a very strong market position, given the export success of Scotch, was widely held to be weakly managed. Guinness was in a similar but even more vulnerable position, dependent mainly upon the one distinctive brand-name beer, and still controlled by the Guinness family. It had responded by expanding its international sales and by acquiring a very large number of mainly small-scale companies, most of which had little or nothing to do with brewing or the drinks trade.

Fearing for the worst, in the 1980s Guinness brought in new management headed by Ernest Saunders as chief executive. He decided upon a strategy to secure Guinness by widening and building up its drinks side and dispensing with other activities. This he did with despatch and success, selling off most of the non-drinks-related companies rapidly, and then setting his sights on taking over the bulk of the Scotch whisky industry. This was an extremely ambitious move for a company of Guinness's size, since it would involve bidding for a company larger than itself. The danger, however, was that unless it achieved a major success of some sort, it would itself become a bid target. Bell's was the first and obvious objective and the bid succeeded, not without considerable efforts, but without a major furore; the question about tactics then used were raised later in the light of the Distillers bid.

Distillers was a much larger company than Bell's, and there was the added difficulty of a rival bid from the food retailing group Argyll, headed by the able and determined James Gulliver. Argyll had the added advantage of being Scots, and undertook to preserve the Scottish headquarters of Distillers. Many details of the takeover are still contested, but two points which illustrate the problems that can arise in such situations are fairly well established. In the first place both Guinness and Argyll were offering shares as a large part of the takeover bid. Both conducted vigorous publicity campaigns designed to show that theirs was the superior company in terms of management ability, and that it had the capacity of improving Distillers' performance. The shares of the companies continued to be traded on the stock market. It hence became a vital matter that the bidders' shares should not fall in value, since if they did the value of the offer would fall and the other bidder gain advantage. The share price should have reflected only the sentiment of the market as to the merits of the bidders. In practice it is alleged that Guinness organized a share support scheme, spending £25 million in arranging for friends and associates to buy Guinness shares and guaranteeing them against loss in doing so, so as to ensure that Guinness share prices rose, or at least did not fall. Since this was of course done covertly, it took a considerable amount of investigation by the City authorities to uncover what looked like evidence of a share support operation. If true, this could mean that a false market existed, and that holders of Distillers shares were persuaded to favour Guinness when the true situation would have led them to accept Argyll's bid.

Secondly a decisive parcel of 10.6 million Distillers shares was purchased in the closing stages of the contest and was bought at 75 pence above the cash alternative price of Guinness's bid. The value to a bidder of the last few shares necessary to obtain control is obviously much greater than the remainder of the shares, and Panel regulations are designed to ensure that all shareholders get fair treatment. A Panel inquiry ruled that the ultimate purchaser of these shares was acting in concert with Guinness – it did not need the shares itself, only the vote of the shareholder to approve its bid. If the Panel enforced its regulations to the full this could involve requiring Guinness to pay other shareholders the same price, amounting in all to between £100 and £220 million. Guinness appealed against the Panel's ruling to the High Court, in itself a relative innovation. The Court found that the Panel had not acted improperly.

Just what constitutes fair treatment of all shareholders, what is a fairly conducted bid, and how to prevent abuse are hence increasingly complicated and contested matters, which have vital implications, not only for shareholders' personal financial advantage, but also for the survival of companies and the restructuring of entire sectors of the economy. For the most part regulation of takeovers is a matter of public policy making and administrative regulation with some legal backing. Sanctions, where they are applied, are predominantly civil and administrative, and the basic issues are fairly well understood and widely debated even though, particularly on the question of monopoly, unresolved. In one area of difficulty arising out of takeovers criminal sanctions are applied, however, and a great deal of publicity has recently arisen about them.

Insider Dealing

A bid almost invariably results in a rise in the share price of the target company. Anyone buying shares ahead of a bid can hence usually make a substantial short-term profit by reselling the shares at the height of the bid. At times speculators anticipating a bid on the basis of analyses of likely targets and market rumours may push share prices up, only to be left holding on to them as the bid fails to materialize. It is hence easy to lose money by hanging on to the coat tails of takeovers as well as to gain it. Certainty comes from privileged information about an imminent bid and those with such inside knowledge, notably such advisers as merchant banks, stock brokers and accountants, are under strict obligations not to take advantage of it. It is, however, very difficult to detect insider dealing with certainty if the share purchase is made through a third party unconnected with the bid, though the circumstantial evidence may be strong. The certainty of the quick profits to be made, the unfair advantage of the insider and the abuse of trust involved combined to lead governments in a number of countries to make insider dealing an offence over the past 15 years. Governments and prosecuting authorities in both Britain and the United States have become increasingly vociferous about the wickedness of the abuse, and frequently reiterate their determination to prosecute. Financial institutions have made it plain that employees thus betraying their trust risk instant dismissal and, because subject to less rigorous standards of proof than a court of law, have in a number of cases implemented the threat. Because of the difficulty of proof, legal cases have largely depended upon admissions by offenders and have not been very frequent.

That these abuses can be both systematic and lucrative was illustrated by the cases of Dennis Levine and Ivan Boesky. After an earlier position at Citicorp, Levine moved to the brokerage and investment house of Smith, Barney, Upham and Co. in New York, where he began to have regular knowledge of impending takeovers. He later moved on to Drexel, Burnham, Lambert the organization of the so-called junk-bond king, Michael Milken.[15] Levine came from a modest background, but Boesky had an inheritance of $700,000. Between 1980 and 1985 Levine traded in 114 stocks making over $11.5 million. Boesky turned his inheritance into a fortune of $200 million, giving Levine 5 per cent of his profits for inside information provided.

The Levine–Boesky example, far larger than anything so far brought to light in Britain, but by no means isolated in the United States, demonstrates that insider dealing can involve serious money and clearly requires control. That control is now exercised not by threats from governments and prosecutors, but by stricter compliance and monitoring procedures by banks, brokers and investment houses and regulatory agencies, and most vitally of all by the computerized records of share transactions held by the exchanges. These provide an audit trail vital to the success of later inquiries and, when backed by legal disclosure requirements upon the buyers and sellers, constitute a reasonable basis for a successful inquiry once suspicions have been aroused. These suspicions are constantly tested by the monitoring of share price movements to pick up anything unusual, especially just before the bid, the main difficulty being that speculators may legitimately anticipate a bid and also that information about it may leak inadvertently.

Corporate Raids

Unfairness and betrayal of trust are the obvious reasons for vilifying insider dealers. The absence of an obvious victim of their activities, however, and the novel status of the abuse as illegal gives the condemnation a somewhat rhetorical air. Much more genuinely problematic are a set of takeover-related activities that are for the most part legal and vigorously defended. This vast and largely unregulated area of abuse might be said to focus on the question: When is a bid not a genuine takeover bid?

There are many reasons for bids. Some, as has been seen, are the outcome of the maturation of a sector of the economy. Some are the consequence of the egotism of a tycoon. Some are the result of a desire to snuff out a potentially dangerous competitor who has developed a radically new product or production process which is patented. Some are by contrast the outcome of weakness and the desire for absorption into a larger, better financed corporation. All these kinds of bids, however, share the common characteristic that the bidder intends the bid to succeed and to acquire control of the company, and subsequently intends to integrate its activities into existing ones, thereby making more rapid growth possible. All are based on the value to the bidder of the target as a going concern.

Others, however, make bids principally with the object of a substantial short-term profit. Normally this will be preceded by a careful analysis of a target to determine the risks of a bid. Favourite targets are those which are for one reason or another underrated by the stock market in relation to their asset value. Provided the bidder's analysis is correct, and he has the finance necessary to mount the bid, he is almost guaranteed a substantial profit. If the bid succeeds, he will dismember the company into its component parts and sell them for more than he paid.[16] This was Asher Edelman's avowed objective in making a bid for Lonrho in 1988. Lonrho's shares were subject to depression because of the company's controversial history. In the 1970s it became involved in an imbroglio involving sanctions-breaking in Rhodesia and was castigated by the then Prime Minister, Edward Heath, for paying part of its directors' fees into the tax haven of the Cayman Islands: he called this the 'unpleasant and unacceptable face of capitalism'. In the 1980s it was involved in a long-running and acrimonious battle for control of the Harrods store-group, House of Fraser. It has been dominated by its creator, Tiny Rowland, a tycoon who developed Lonrho from beginnings in Southern Africa, expanded by developing good economic and political contacts throughout Black Africa, and consolidated Lonrho's position in the later 1970s and 1980s by expanding in Britain and America. Lonrho remained a conglomerate encompassing very diverse activities held together by the energy and ability of its founder, and included leisure, wines and spirits, mining, manufacturing, agriculture, financial services and motor distribution. There was certainly a question whether these disparate concerns could be made to function harmoniously and prosperously in Rowland's absence.

Lonrho's defence inevitably consisted of persuading shareholders that Edelman's bid greatly undervalued them, in order to force him to increase his bid to the point at which his analysis of the dismemberment value of Lonrho began to be reached. If Edelman were to succeed at less than this price he could sell off Lonrho and make a profit, or keep it or parts of it – no doubt the most profitable parts – and earn the annual dividends. If he failed, he could sell out his stake at a much higher price than he paid. Edelman had done just this with the truck makers Fruehauf in 1986, when they were forced to take on a debt of $1.5 billion in an attempt at a leveraged buy out. In the end it failed and Fruehauf had to sell 31 per cent of its equity to investment bankers Merrill Lynch.

In the event Edelman backed off rapidly, selling a 5.8 per cent stake in the face of competition from Australian Alan Bond, who increased his stake in Lonrho to 20 per cent, so becoming the largest shareholder and overtaking Rowland himself, who had long held 15 per cent. Bond showed every sign of being determined to mount a hostile bid, having earlier been encouraged to go into the market for Lonrho's shares by Rowland as a counterweight to Edelman. Bond was hard hit by the October 1987 stock market crash and was widely regarded as being heavily in debt, but a careful marshalling of his resources was enough to convince his bankers to back him, and so turn him in Lonrho's eyes from a friend to an enemy.

Examples could be repeated many times over in the takeover boom of the 1980s: Sir James Goldsmith's $4.7 billion bid for Goodyear Tire and Rubber in 1986 for example, which he claimed was made in anticipation of success, but from which he eventually withdrew $600 million richer. Where a bid fails in this manner it is referred to rather as a corporate raid. Whatever the name, such activities divert the energies of corporate management to dealing with a bid while it lasts, which may be for an extended period, and often lead to the company becoming heavily burdened with debt. Investment in long-term research and planning is frustrated the wider the process spreads, as companies are constantly warned not to present themselves as bid targets and to ensure that annual profits and dividends are maximized to keep their share price protectively high.

Corporate raiders' reaction to criticism is on the whole truculent. What they are doing is nothing more or less than what stock markets permit: buying and selling shares and companies at market prices. Most soundly castigate the greedy and inefficient management of the companies they raid, and chide them for not being more aware of their obligations to shareholders to make money, obligations which the raiders see themselves fulfilling. Thus T. Boone Pickens, whose company's investments had produced $13 billion for three-quarters of a million shareholders by 1986 without ever winning a takeover bid, including a gain of $760 million in a bid for Gulf Oil in 1983: 'Managements cry-baby around complaining that they have been burdened with excessive debt and that they are going to have to look at their projects more closely in future. Hell, they should have been looking at them anyhow.' Similarly Carl Icahn, who came from nowhere to a successful takeover of Texaco for $1,223 million in 1987/8, picking up TWA on the way, after starting in 1979, remarked: 'Texaco is a great collection of assets – without the management. They're a bit like the boy who kills his mother and father and then says: have pity on me I'm an orphan'.

Britain has been less troubled by the greater excesses of corporate raiding. Probably the leading experiment in a genteel fashion is Hanson Trust, which rejects the term 'asset stripping' in favour of 'asset management'. Hanson certainly has built up his empire by genuine takeovers rather than raids, and by retaining a substantial portion of his purchases – the most profitable parts are retained and the rest resold at a profit. It is this eye for a corporate bargain that is the key to Hanson's success. United Drapery Stores, for example, was bought in 1983 for £260 million. Hanson quickly sold several of the chains of clothing stores, leaving a chain of department stores and duty-free shops which then made more profit than the whole of UDS before acquisition. The same was achieved with battery makers Berec (Ever Ready) bought in 1987 for £95 million. Now that overseas companies have been sold, the parent in Britain makes three times the profit of the whole group in 1981. In the United States Hanson brought SCM for $930 million in 1985. He then disposed of companies generating 40 per cent of SCM's profits for $926 million, leaving him with the remainder, which generate annual profits of $100 million. He achieved the same with Imperial, rapidly selling brewers Courage for £1.4 billion to the Australian Elders IXL and, with other disposals, cutting the net costs of retaining the bulk of Imperial to £850 million. Whether this is corporate restructuring and revitalizing the industrial economy or an old-fashioned eye for the main chance depends upon your vantage point, but Hanson is clearly a step above the raiders.

A step below them are the arbitrageurs. It was here that Boesky made most of his money, albeit with inside knowledge as well. The arbitrageur buys a block of shares in a company she/he knows or conjectures is a bid target. If she/he has enough cash she/he may be able to stimulate bid rumours by the very size of his/her stake. Formally she/he is speculating that a bid will emerge so that she/he will then be in a strong position to negotiate a large gain on his/her holding, and the importance is not the size of the stake but its strategic position. A successful arbitrageur can stimulate sufficient interest in the target by others to push the share price up at least temporarily and so be certain of a profit. And of course the shares themselves do not have to be bought, only an option to buy at a fixed price for a limited period. But by these means a company may find itself manoeuvred into the takeover market where expectations are so aroused as not be capable of being dampened by any statement from management, support from major shareholders, or plans for development.

It was in this position that the Midland Bank found itself in 1987. Not only is it the smallest of the big four British clearing banks, it made a disastrous purchase of the Crocker National Bank of California, which was heavily exposed to third world debt. Even when the bank was sold off again, much of the debt burden remained on Midland's books. Its investment banking arm, Greenwell Montagu, was one of the damp squibs of the Big Bang. It took remedial action by selling off three subsidiaries in Scotland and Ireland for £400 million and raised £700 million in a rights issue, but with its share value falling 45 per cent after the stock market crash, more was needed, and the vultures were circling. Hanson acquired 6 per cent of its shares and Robert Maxwell 2.5 per cent. Saatchi Brothers, the advertisers, even proposed a merger. 'You have no idea how demoralizing it is to the staff, the managers, the customers and shareholders to face this endless drip of threats, half-truths and inspired gossip', said the chairman, Sir Kit McMahon. In market parlance, Midland was 'in play' as a takeover target. The remedy adopted was a link-up with the Hong Kong and Shanghai Bank, which has quite different markets and welcomed the access Midland offered to Europe. For Midland it involved a capital injection of £383 million, a greatly increased collective asset base, and an agreement not to increase or dispose of the holding of 14.9 per cent of Midland for three years, so making it difficult for a bidder to build up a stake.

No doubt Midland would have in time traded out of its difficulties, but in the predatory atmosphere of the time it needed a powerful ally. McMahon's former colleague at the Bank of England, the Governor, Robin Leigh Pemberton, was clearly perturbed at this kind of problem earlier in 1987. He remarked,

> Some takeover bids appear to have been launched not so much in response to evidence that a company's management is not up to the task, or in the belief that its business would do better in different hands, but in order to reap a once and for all capital advantage. There have been situations recently where opportunistic creditors have sought to use the considerable platform and influence of a minority shareholding to unsettle the management of a well run company. The expression 'putting a company into play' is as unpleasant as the idea behind it.[17]

The Governor offered no remedies other than a vague warning of sanctions if matters did not improve. That surely is scarcely enough. The calculated effect of corporate raids and arbitraging is essentially to create a false hyped up market in the shares for the purpose of enriching the operators and regardless of the interests or welfare of the company, its staff or its clients. In comparison with these forms of licensed greed and exploitation of the securities markets, insider dealing seems paltry indeed.

Considerable attention has been given to takeovers as a specific example of a problem area in the securities markets, and the financial sector more widely, because the problems of regulation are extensive and important. They concern not merely the control of greedy and ruthless individuals, but the well-being of the industrial and the financial sectors and the balance between them.[18] Assets diverted to dealing with raids and takeovers cannot be productively invested in industry. The issues raised are complex in principle, and even when issues of principle such as what constitutes a bona fide takeover bid are resolved, the measures required to manage them are not easy to envisage. The financial sector is peculiarly one in which matters of control become quickly politicized and lead into wider questions of economic and political policy. The passions aroused are great and the rheotoric deployed, using terms such as 'criminal' and 'dishonest' may be vehement, but there are few easy distinctions to be drawn and even fewer straightforward criminal cases to be mounted. Of course this does not mean that straight frauds do not exist and cannot be prosecuted as such, only that, substantial and numerous though they are, the problems of control of abuse are not remotely to be identified with them.

NOTES

1 S. Sharpiro, *Wayward Capitalists*, Yale University Press, 1984, ch. 1.
2 The account of the development of securities regulation in America draws upon the researches of Michael Moran. See his 'Investor Protection and the Culture of Capitalism', in Leigh Hancher and M. Moran (eds), *Capitalism Culture and Economic Regulation*, Oxford University Press, 1989; 'An Outpost of Corporatism: The Franchise State on Wall Street', *Government and Opposition*, 1987, no. 1; 'Regulating Britain, Regulating America', in C. Crouch and R. Dore (eds), *Corporations and Accountability*, Oxford University Press, 1989.
3 The most accessible account of the great crash is that of J. K. Galbraith, *The Great Crash 1929*, Penguin, 1961.
4 Shapiro, *Wayward Capitalists*.
5 There are a number of accounts of the Equity Funding affair. See, for example, R. L. Dirks and L. Gross, *The Great Wall Street Scandal*, McGraw-Hill, 1974. A briefer account is W. E. Blundell, 'Equity Funding: "I did it for the Jollies"', in J. M. Johnson and J. D. Douglas, *Crime at the Top*, Lippincott, 1978.
6 This account of the British regulatory system draws on the more detailed information in M. J. Clarke, *Regulating the City*, Open University Press, 1986.
7 For an account of this period see M. J. Clarke, *Fallen Idols: Elites and the Search for the Acceptable Face of Capitalism*, Junction Books, 1981.
8 *The Sunday Times*, 25 September 1988.
9 Sir Godfray le Quesne's Report on Barlow Clowes was published by the Department of Trade and Industry (HMSO), 1988.
10 See 'The Heavy Electrical Equipment Anti-trust Cases of 1961' by Gilbert Geis in M. B. Clinard and R. Quinney (eds), *Criminal Behaviour Systems*, Holt, Rinehart and Winston, 1967; and in G. Geis (ed.), *White Collar Crime*, Atherton Press, 1968.
11 The question arises, of course, why the takeover boom of the 1980s should have continued beyond October 1987. The crash, which took perhaps a third of the value off shares in most stock markets, was experienced as a set-back, but by mid-1988 takeovers were again in full swing and scaling new heights in terms of the size of individual bids. Stock markets had recovered, but not to pre-crash levels, and the trend of interest rates, especially in Britain, was upwards. This problem is beyond the scope of full comment in this book, but two suggestions seem worth making. In the first place, it may have come to be seen to be possible to offset weakening performance by companies by an aggressive policy of acquisitions, which can keep total profits rising even if percentage rates do not. In the second place, and more persuasively, the boom had arguably become self-sustaining by 1987, and companies, as is described below, came to see the options not any longer in terms of the cost of making a bid and the rewards of success, but in terms of the necessity of demonstrating strength by bidding, lest others bid for them. In a market driven no longer by the pursuit of profit, but by the maxim 'eat or be eaten', the costs of borrowing to finance a bid and the track record of the bidders' profits became of lesser importance. Useful information on takeovers and mergers by British companies is to be found in *British Business*, 5 August 1988, pp. 28–9, and 28 October 1988, pp. 26–8, London, HMSO.

12 T. R. Hurst 'Self-Regulation versus Legal Regulation', *Company Lawyer*, 1985, pp. 161–2.
13 The progress and development of the City Panel on Takeovers and Mergers has been widely and regularly commented on in the financial press. A good review of its development can be found in B. A. K. Rider, 'Self-Regulation: The British Approach to Regulating Conduct in the Securities Business with particular reference to the Role of the City Panel on Takeovers and Mergers in the Regulation of Insider Trading', *Journal of Comparative Law and Securities Regulation*, 1978, pp. 319–48. Comments on this and more recent events are also to be found in M. J. Clarke, *Regulating the City*, pp. 105–14.
14 A journalistic, blow-by-blow account of the Guinness affair is available in N. Kochan and H. Pym, *The Guinness Affair*, Christopher Helm, 1987. See also P. Pugh, *Is Guinness Good for you?*, Blackstone Press, 1987.
15 Two useful sources on these and related events are C. Bruck, *The Predator's Ball: The Junk Bond Raiders and the Man who Staked them*, American Lawyer/ Simon and Schuster, 1987; J. Brooks, *The Takeover Game*, E. P. Dutton, 1987.
16 No doubt takeover bidders have, on occasion, been women, but rarely.
17 *The Times*, 12 March 1987.
18 A work which deserves mention as dealing with aspects of the status of the financial sector in Britain on which there is not space to comment in this chapter is G. Ingham, *Capitalism Divided? The City and Industry in British Social Development*, Macmillan, 1984.

9 The Regulation of Industry: Safety versus Profits

As the title indicates, this chapter presents the regulation of health and safety issues in industry as a struggle between the profit-seeking objectives of business and the interests of employees and the public in physical and psychological protection. To demonstrate the entrenched nature of this tension, the chapter begins with an account of early British factory legislation and then goes on to point to the similar problems posed by the development of the oil and gas industry in Britain in the 1970s and 1980s. In both periods the extended political struggle over the nature, extent and control of regulation on safety matters is evident.

Much of the research on this topic has been concentrated on the work of inspectorates, but it is important to recognize that health and safety issues are by no means always managed in this way. Political campaigns over how to deal with particular problems may produce a decisive result in the short or medium term, as the campaigns over the elimination of lead in petrol and aspects of car safety illustrate.

Many health and safety issues do require inspectorates to manage them, however, and the rest of the chapter is concerned with the ways in which and the conditions under which they cope with their responsibilities. Achieving compliance with the regulations laid down is an especial difficulty for inspectors, and there is wide agreement in the literature that this is usually achieved by persuasion, sometimes backed by threats, rather than by coercion and prosecution, even though many inspectorates have legal powers. The most important reasons for this are the limited manpower and resources of inspectorates and their aim of achieving compliance over the long term on the basis of a practical agreement, which the punishment of specific offences does not necessarily achieve.

None the less businesses do at times act in a purely calculative way with the objective of maximizing profits, regardless of health and safety matters. The response of legislators has been to attach strict liability to offences, so that pleas of ignorance or honest intent cannot be used to counter allegations of failure to achieve standards. Although appealing in terms of obtaining convictions, and hence, in theory, commanding the respect of business for inspectorates, this turned out to be an unsatisfactory tactic, because it tended to reduce the room for negotiation between the two parties.

In recent years, as industrial processes have become more diverse and complex, the need for negotiation to identify and achieve standards adequate to protect employees and the public has become more and more evident. The freedom of inspectors to engage in such negotiations has hence become more widely recognized, though still subject to restraint by political campaigns, in which business is depicted as ruthless and amoral and responsive only to continual prosecution.

As the final examples of British Environmental Health Officers and the American Food and Drugs Administration show, such an emphasis upon litigation is misplaced. What is important is the political ascendancy of the inspectorate and evident public demand for effective regulation, which leads to regulations and standards that are not unduly favourable to the industry in question, and an adequately funded and staffed inspectorate with sufficient administrative powers to intervene and make life uncomfortable for the recalcitrant company.

At the end of the chapter attention turns to more detailed suggestions on how the relationship between business and inspectorates is best managed. It is suggested that encouraging companies to write their own detailed health and safety codes, subject to the inspectorate's approval, may well offer advantages in terms both of acceptability and enforcability.

In the Beginning . . .

As far back as the first half of the nineteenth century, industry demonstrated an incapacity for self-regulation in respect of health and safety. New entrepreneurs hiring labour by the day or the week to work in their factories were sufficiently single-minded in their pursuit of minimal costs not to hire men where women or children could do the job more cheaply, nor to protect the limbs of their workers from moving machinery nor their lungs from cotton, coal and other dusts, and to require them to work hours so long that they became at risk of injury from exhaustion. It was government inquiries into conditions in factories and mines that led to the first of what was to become a continuing stream of legislation regulating conditions in workplaces to protect the health and safety of employees, of customers from unsafe products, and of the public from pollution, explosion and other hazards.

Marx and Engels, who were formulating their analysis of capitalist society as these first reports were published, interpreted them in the light of the relationship of employer and employee, in contrast to the traditional one of master and servant. The master had a diffuse relationship with his servant, whose skills, abilities and efforts he called on, and to whom in return he owed a duty of care and maintenance. Thus it was not easy to say in many situations where the master's rights to require the servant's co-operation ended, but on the other hand it was understood that a servant, much like a horse, would not perform well unless properly fed, housed and trained. Capitalist factory production changed all this. The worker was hired for a precisely specified job for which she or he had the necessary abilities and skills, and was paid not according to any reference to a 'living wage' but to what a competitive labour market would bear. In times of slump, wages were cut and in times of boom, as labour became more scarce, wages rose.

Marx and Engels perceived that it was only by combining together that workers could hope to defeat the immiserating operations of the market, which they saw as the real tyrant. It was not, they argued, that factory owners were especially greedy or cruel, but the competition compelled them to cut costs wherever possible in order to produce at a price in line with others. As the more ingenious introduced innovations in productive technology, in factory organization and in marketing techniques, they gained a competitive advantage for which the rest could compensate only by further cutting wage rates and refusing expenditure on improved factory conditions. In the longer term these less able industrialists would be driven to bankruptcy as their capacity to compete on price grew more marked and their poor machinery and worn out labour force turned out products of lesser quality. In the process, and exacerbated by business cycles which forced cost-cutting on all manufacturers, many of their workers would be stricken with industrial diseases, be maimed, and die.

Reports of the conditions in mines and factories stimulated a considerable parliamentary reaction, which in the long term was to have political consequences more potent than was envisaged by Marx and Engels. The Tory party in particular saw an opportunity to use the reports as a stick to beat their Whig opponents, many of whom were associated with the factory movement and *laissez-faire* capitalism. The Tories represented the traditional rural economy, and were simultaneously involved in a long and ferocious debate over what was in effect a price support system for grain, which was directed at maintaining an adequate supply to feed a nation recently at war, in the face of the vagaries of the British climate. Tories were well aware from long historical experience that bread, or the lack of it, was the basis of riot and rebellion by the poor in Britain. In the factory owners they saw a new urban class of masters who had abandoned their wider obligations to their servants and treated them worse than animals, since they failed to accept that workers cannot work unless they also eat, sleep and maintain their health. The humanistic and moral outrage expressed at the conduct of the manufacturers was hence in part disingenuous, as is described in detail and with subtlety by Carson.[1] None the less the campaign was effective. The Tories lost their battle over grain prices with the repeal of the Corn Laws, but they won that over factory conditions with the Factory Acts, which laid down basic conditions regarding hours and safety, and in particular restricted the employment of women and children.

It was not a campaign won in one battle, however, nor without the realization by the opposition that there were advantages to making certain concessions. The larger factory owners were better connected with Parliament, some of them even sitting as MPs. They realised that their public moral position was untenable if they opposed regulation root and branch. They also realized that they would suffer politically for sins they did not personally commit since they would be condemned for defending practices and conditions in the worst factories, which were mostly small. In their larger factories, built to accommodate larger and more modern machines, conditions were better, and there was more concern to hire a competent labour force at wage rates that would maintain health in order to ensure that the machines were operated with adequate skill and care. Further, in boom times, their capacity to dominate the market and to maintain profitable prices was compromised by the competition of the smaller producers. Regulation would have the effect, they calculated, of imposing the costs of improving conditions disproportionately upon the smaller manufacturers, who fell further below the new standards than the larger ones, and who were also less able to bear their costs. The result would be that many would go out of business, leaving the market to the larger manufacturers.

It was not, however, quite as simple as this. After initial legislation was passed it was assumed that the problem was dealt with, at least in the sense that industry would gradually improve its standards. The Whig factory owners avoided opprobrium and might anticipate a more secure economic future. Not surprisingly the manufacturers under most pressure from the new regulations and most at risk of bankruptcy were extremely reluctant to conform, and further inquiries following the initial Act showed that standards were not improving as required and that the law was being flouted. Manufacturers evidently could not be relied upon to obey a new law where it conflicted severely with their interests, and it became plain that a means of enforcement would be necessary. It was only after further legislation to establish an inspectorate to enforce the Factory Acts that real progress began to be made.

Carson distinguishes the two phases of regulation as symbolic and instrumental. In the first phase the political pressure was to denounce the unacceptable and set civilized standards; in the second the means were devised to set about realizing the objectives that had been set. In the case of the early industrial regulation, the distinction between the two elements was clear; in later years, with the general acceptance that regulation usually requires an inspectorate to administer it, the distinction has become less obvious, but it remains important. The public and political campaigns to achieve legislative action to control hazards may well result in symbolic victories expressed in ringing phrases by politicians. Thus when the Piper Alpha oil rig blew up in the North Sea in 1988 with the loss of 168 lives, the worst disaster in the oil industry to date, the Secretary of State for Energy was predictably quick to announce an inquiry in order to learn the necessary lessons to prevent such an event ever happening again. Yet the history of safety regulation in the British offshore oil industry was not such as to inspire great confidence that this desirable end would be achieved. Here again, the research work of Carson is illuminating.[2]

Oil and Gas

Gas was discovered in the southern North Sea in substantial quantities in the early 1960s, and it was recognized by the oil and gas industry (oil industry for short) that there was a good chance of finding oil also. Two other vital facts were also well indentified. First, offshore drilling is extremely hazardous in all respects. The rigs required needed to be much larger than those in the relatively shallow and usually calmer waters of the Gulf of Mexico and the Arabian Gulf, where the industry already had some experience, partly because of the greater depth of the sea (600 feet) but mainly because of the frequency of storms in the North Sea, which can produce winds of up to 160 miles an hour and waves up to 100 feet high. Production, supply, maintenance and safety would need to be able to be maintained in these conditions and in consequence there was much talk of rigs 'operating at the frontiers of technology'. Calculations were made, but no one knew for certain what would the capacity of the vast new rigs to withstand winds, tides and currents, whether their tubular steel construction would prove to be strong enough, or what safety measures against blow-outs could be effectively installed. Two major incidents demonstrated the reality of these hazards. The jack-up rig, Sea Gem, collapsed and sank in 1965 with the loss of 13 lives, and in 1980 the Alexander Kielland accommodation platform in the Norwegian sector of the North Sea capsized with the loss of 123 lives. Engineers were reported at the time as saying that no realistic tests into metal fatigue and potential buckling of hollow steel components such as the rig legs were conducted until 1977. The Norwegian inquiry found that one of the rig's legs had been weakened by being cut to introduce a hydrophone and subsequently rewelded to a poor standard. The rig developed stress fractures at the weld, and was not designed to remain upright when one of its five legs failed.

As Carson remarks, this bears out his analysis of safety regulation in the North Sea oil industry. Despite the talk of rigs operating at the limit and indeed beyond what was known of engineering technology, the immediate cause of the collapse of the Kielland was well within the knowledge of the industry, and proper attention to the maintenance of standards in cutting and rewelding the major structural rig member should have prevented disaster.

For the second major feature of the North Sea oil exploration was time pressure. This pressure was evident and strongly expressed by the Treasury from the first round of licensing in 1964, because of the enormous benefits oil revenues were expected to bring to the British economy, then, as ever, suffering from balance of payments problems. These pressures were greatly enhanced by the oil crisis of the early 1970s, when the formation of OPEC led to an enormous increase in oil prices and was instrumental in the stock market crash of 1973/4 and the subsequent sterling crises, culminating in the ignominious application for support from the International Monetary Fund in 1976. Oil was accurately perceived by Governments and the Treasury as the means to keep the British economy afloat, and hence progress from exploration to production was encouraged to take place as fast as possible.

This suited the oil companies in two respects. In the first place, oil exploration is highly risky financially. Vast investments have to be made in drilling what may be dry holes, and these were disproportionately greater in the North Sea because of the conditions. Further, the investment is nearly all 'up front' in advance of any return. The costs of financing it hence have to be borne from an early stage, but revenue starts coming in only when oil begins to be pumped. Until it does, interest charges accumulate. Secondly, the oil industry has traditionally guarded its independence from outside regulation, cultivating a macho image of high risks and rewards, and emphasizing its monopoly of knowledge of the peculiar difficulties and hazards of oil drilling and of the means to manage them. Offshore operation provided significant advantages in maintaining this independence, since the rigs are private structures beyond the easy reach of government inspectors.

This combination of factors proved decisive in preventing the development of a rigorous, government-controlled regulatory system, and indeed delayed the implementation of any regulatory system considerably. The initial problem was that offshore structures did not immediately fall under existing health and safety legislation. Although the extension of civil and criminal law was later construed as giving Scottish legal authorities powers to investigate fatalities, offshore installations did not fall within the definition of a factory, and the Factory Acts were hence inapplicable. When the Sea Gem collapsed in 1965, the inquiry pointed out that health and safety protection was provided only by the model clauses incorporated into licences for oil exploration granted by the Government, and that the only sanction for ensuring the proper operation of safety procedures was the revocation of the licence. The inquiry recommended a statutory code, backed by usable sanctions, and a bill was prepared which was finally enacted in 1971 as the Mineral Holdings (Offshore Installations) Act.

It was, however, the detailed regulations under the Act which implemented health and safety controls and these were developed, in close consultation with the industry, only gradually. Thus those concerning inspection and the reporting of casualties did not become operative until 1973, those concerned with operational safety, health and welfare, not until late 1976, and those concerning fire-fighting equipment, not until 1978. It looked at one point as though this process was to be superseded as a result of the decision by the Government to apply new general legislation on work safety, the Health and Safety at Work Act 1974, to the North Sea oil industry, and an announcement to this effect was made in 1976. The Act was extended to the continental shelf in 1977.

The question was, however, who was to administer the regulations, whether those particular to North Sea oil rigs, or those they shared with other factories and workplaces. The oil crisis of 1973/4 led to the reorganization of ministries and the establishment of the Department of Energy, within which the petroleum exploration division (PED) was charged with responsibility for administering North Sea oil development. It was this Department which was active in the negotiation and enforcement of health and safety regulations. Although a decision in principle was taken in 1976 to transfer responsibility for inspection and enforcement to the Health and Safety Executive (HSE), the umbrella health and safety body formed in the wake of the 1974 Act to co-ordinate the factory and other inspectorates and achieve improved regulation, this was met by sustained opposition from the oil industry, supported by the PED, which emphasized the unique problems of oil exploration and the absolute necessity of specialist expertise.

What ensued was a dispute between the HSE and the PED which was finally resolved only with the reaction of the new Conservative government in 1980 to the Report of the Burgoyne Committee, established two years earlier 'to consider so far as they are concerned with safety, the nature and effectiveness of the Department of Energy's regulations' in the light of the 'tangle of divided responsibilities'. Burgoyne concluded that there was an overwhelming case for regulation to be concentrated in the hands of a single agency, and that the choice lay effectively between the HSE and the Department of Energy. It recommended that the job go to the Department of Energy, and the government agreed. The regulatory system, when it was finally established after 1980, hence represented total victory for the oil industry. The same Department responsible for promoting rapid exploration was also responsible for health and safety regulation.

The grounds cited for this arrangement have consistently been that offshore exploration poses unique problems, and that in particular the difficulties of controlling blow-outs and fires in installations processing vast quantities of oil and gas in production conditions that are constantly changing require very specialized expertise, which does not exist outside the oil industry. In some respects this is indeed the case, but it is equally the case that a major fire or blow-out is a catastrophe not only for the rig workers but for the oil company, which faces the loss of a huge investment, the costs of controlling the fire, and heavy claims from the dependants of the dead and from the injured, besides the adverse publicity. It would be surprising if the industry did not take, in the language of health and safety regulation, 'all practicable measures' to prevent disasters. Major disasters have been relatively rare, and that of Piper Alpha unprecendented in its extent.

What Carson is able to show, however, is that none the less the oil industry has been extremely hazardous for workers, not as a result of the exceptional conditions and major hazards of offshore exploration, but as a result of weak regulation and enforcement of safety, and constant pressure on workers to get on with the job of production. Far more workers have been killed and injured in routine accidents resulting from lack of adequate safety provisions and procedures wholly comparable to those in onshore manufacturing and construction than have been affected by major disasters unique to offshore oil rigs. Between 1974 and 1976, for example, the risk of death was six times that in quarrying, nine times that in mining and eleven times that in construction; when diving is excluded, the risk reduces to four, six and eight times respectively. Carson gives a specific and vivid example of how these risks were taken:

> In late 1974, this particular installation was inspected while it was still, in effect, little more than a maritime construction site; and it was noted that the intention was to house 122 persons in temporary 'portacabins', six to ten to a cabin, during the construction phase. However, no Certificate of Fitness under the Construction and Survey Regulations (1974) was required at this point, because the absence of any 'oil related function' on an installation in this stage of development had been interpreted by the department as exempting it from this requirement, and because, in any case, the deadline fixed for certification by the regulations was August 1975. Such a certificate, with its prescription of appropriate accommodation standards, escape routes, and protection from hazards such as fire, would therefore become necessary only when drilling commenced, a stage that was reached in June 1975, some eight or nine weeks before the deadline was due to expire. During an inspection carried out at this point, it was noted that 120 men were still housed in a three-tier stack of portacabins; and the inspector suggested that 'it would be very difficult to evacuate this installation quickly and safely should an emergency arise'. As one of his superiors baldly noted on the file's minute sheet, 'they are *drilling* with 330 people on board.'
>
> Some three weeks before the certification requirement was due to take effect, the platform was visited again; it was noted that the first well was about to be perforated, with 214 persons still on board, and that, indeed, *production* was now expected to begin before the end of the month. The inspector recorded his personal view that to embark on this phase of the operation while construction (not to mention drilling) was still in progress would be 'hazardous' and of debatable good sense 'from other than an economic point of view'. But the platform received its Certificate of Fitness some ten days after the prescribed date, as a result of the department having instructed the certifying authorities 'to virtually ignore' temporary accommodation carried over from the construction phase into the drilling and subsequently into the production phase on this and other northern North Sea platforms. Approximately one month later, a further visit confirmed that production had commenced, although completion was 'still

months ahead' and although at least 55 construction workers were still on board.[3]

The Politics of Regulation

Carson's work illustrates important points about the regulation of industry in respect of health and safety which are not always evident in what is now a substantial Anglo-American literature covering a considerable number of industries and inspectorates, which can inevitably be drawn on only selectively here. The political element in the regulation of industry is always well identified in his writing where, in the studies of many inspectorates, as in the day-to-day working of the inspectorates themselves, this tends to recede into the background. Many studies are concerned with a regulatory regime that is already established, without considering how and why the regime came to be instituted in the first place, and how extensive and important the lobbying of the industry concerned was in the establishing of the regime. This can vary in at least two dimensions. In the first place the industry can lobby more or less successfully for control of the content of regulations and the stringency of the standards involved and can further negotiate more or less successfully a weak regime of enforcement. As will be illustrated below, regulatory systems may also change in their style and effectiveness over time as a result of changes in political climate and governmental policy shifts, sometimes in response to major disasters where regulatory effectiveness is shown to have been poor. Although major political mobilization is hence normally necessary to introduce regulation of an otherwise unregulated aspect of safety in an industry, the regime, even after it becomes experienced and settled in, remains subject to change under political pressure.

Secondly, industry can lobby on the principle of regulation, and that involves a contest which may vary at one extreme from concern with the nature and extent of the continuing regulatory regime to, at the other, a once-for-all regulatory decision. Not surprisingly, academic researchers have concentrated on how regulatory regimes work, but other kinds of regulatory decisions are also important. A political campaign, for example, not to develop nuclear power in a country will, if successful, preclude the development of a nuclear regulatory agency. The recognition of the hazards of lead poisoning resulted initially in the phasing out of lead water-pipes and later in the elimination of lead in most paints. More recently it has resulted in the phasing out of lead in petrol as a result of vigorous campaigns in Britain and especially in the United States. The American campaign is particularly noteworthy and interesting because of the constraints involved.

Political debate in the 1970s on the pollution of the environment developed very rapidly and produced an entirely new rhetoric including words such as ecology, environment (and environmental impact), finite resources, pollution and recycling, and stimulated an awareness of man's relationship to the planet. This has come to be seen as one of successful manipulation, as a result of such technical achievements as the conquest of space, mass air and road travel and increasingly sophisticated means of the technological domination of nature, from air-conditioning to freeze-dried foods, from the high-yield crops of the green revolution to heart transplants. The tendency of Governments, notably American ones, and industry to declare man's increasingly comprehensive domination of nature was suddenly challenged by the findings of scientists. On the one hand global problems of water and air pollution, consumption of finite hydrocarbon energy sources, devastation of large areas of wilderness by devegetation and so on were drawn to the public's attention. On the other hand there was a recognition of the more proximate dangers posed by nuclear power generation, toxic waste disposal, use of pesticides and fertilizers, and hazardous chemicals produced by industry. The outcome was environmental and ecological awareness, followed later by the formation of 'green' parties in Europe, and a wave of political enthusiasm to regulate the hazards involved. In America this involved the foundation of the Environmental Protection Agency with a federal remit to vet all new industrial developments for their environmental impact and a focus of environmentalist pressures.

Car Safety and Leaded Petrol

One of the specific problems requiring immediate confrontation was air pollution from car exhausts. Car ownership had grown steadily throughout the post-war years and by the 1970s was the primary means of transport for most Americans. Petrol, most of it home-produced, was cheap and the road system had been continually expanded and upgraded. Nemesis came in Los Angeles, the city of the car, with its freeways crisscrossing the city with no single centre, thanks to the peculiarity of the local climate: exhaust-based smogs began to become intolerable in their frequency and density. A partial remedy to this was the catalytic convertor, a device inserted into the exhaust system to absorb some of the more noxious gases. After some debate and hesitation convertors became compulsory on all cars sold in the United States. Once convertors were established, however, pressure increased to ban leaded petrol, for the convertors rapidly absorbed the lead from the exhaust emissions which coated the catalytic plates and prevented them from working properly. The car industry non the less complained that cars would not run properly on unleaded petrol, because the lead was added to enhance the octane level of the petrol. Refining petrol to the necessary octane level would be difficult and costly, and damage to car engines would likely result. People would just have to replace their convertors more often.

This was not a plausible argument in engineering terms. American cars with their large, slow-running, low compression engines use a lot of petrol, but they are easier to adjust to running on lead-free petrol than European and Japanese cars with smaller, faster-running, high-compression engines. Further, the campaign against lead began to generate research indicating that atmospheric environmental lead levels were high, particularly near major roads, and that car exhausts constituted the major source of ingested lead. Secondly, research increasingly showed that, contrary to what had been accepted as the basis of evaluations of lead in the past, there are no safe, i.e. non-toxic, levels of lead ingestion. In particular, for children the dangers of brain damage exist, even at levels well below those where clinical symptoms of lead poisoning are evident.

That children were particularly at risk was a potent argument, and in combination with other factors was sufficient to get a decision in the 1970s to eliminate leaded petrol by requiring new cars to run on unleaded.

When Reagan succeeded Carter as President in 1981 and immediately turned his attention to reducing the regulatory burden upon industry as a means of freeing it to generate more wealth, leaded petrol was an early target. A Reagan-nominated appointee took over as Director of the EPA and it seemed that a policy reversal would follow a wide-ranging review of the issue. By this time, however, things seem to have moved too far, and the EPA's review of over 1,100 written comments and testimonies by over 110 witnesses concluded that the evidence was overwhelmingly in favour of eliminating lead in petrol. Whatever the views of the Director, the staff of the EPA proved committed to the ideals of its foundation and refused to compromise, and the agency finally adopted a position of intransigence. It correctly calculated upon the political weight of public support on the issue, and on the political leverage of the scientific evidence on the damage caused by lead which it had accumulated. The White House chose not to join battle on the issue, and the EPA emerged victorious.

When the issue was taken up in Britain in the early 1980s, the basis of the successful campaign was hence well established, even against determined opposition from the Thatcher government and the oil and motor industries.[4] The latter argued, as in the United States, that it would be extremely costly to retune engines to run on lead-free petrol and to produce lead-free petrol of adequate quality. Both these contentions were subsequently shown to be false, provided the industries were given a reasonable time to change to the new regime. By this point the battle in the United States had been won and accepted by Reagan, and other European countries were falling into line. British scientists began monitoring lead levels and came up with horrifically high readings in urban areas, including school playgrounds near main roads. Atmospheric lead from vehicle exhausts was initially claimed by industry to be only a minor source of blood lead levels, but this was shown not to be the case. This accumulating evidence was co-ordinated into a campaign for lead-free air (CLEAR), led by Des Wilson, the highly experienced campaigner on issue-based politics, who first made his mark in the 1960s with the foundation of Shelter, the campaign for the homeless. Mrs Thatcher had no more stomach for an increasingly plainly unpopular and unnecessary struggle, and the government conceded the necessity of phasing out leaded petrol.

Such regulatory battles are by no means always won by regulatory campaigners, nor are they usually as simple as that over lead in petrol, where the choice was effectively to keep it or to phase it out. The campaign over car safety started by Ralph Nader in the United States in the 1960s is an example of one in which there were both gains and losses by the campaigners. The American car industry's attitude to safety up until the late 1960s was that it was not an issue for them, but that it was up to governments to build safe, well engineered roads, and to drivers to drive competently and carefully. Nader's scathing analysis of the Corvair, published at book-length in *Unsafe at Any Speed* demonstrated the industry's refusal to consider car safety. Nader maintained that the makers knew that the Corvair had a tendency to roll over when cornering, as a specific result of its suspension system, which was designed to produce a car appealing to the eye and giving a soft ride.[5]

As the campaign for safer cars gained momentum, attention focused on restraining systems for drivers and passengers to minimize injury in the event of an accident. The outcome was the fitting of the seat-belts familiar today; but few modern drivers will probably be aware of the safety devices which could have been accepted then, but which were rejected after industry lobbying, partly on the stated grounds of additional cost, but in reality more because they drew attention to the fact that driving a car is an enterprise that risks death or serious injury. The first was an interlock of the safety belt with the ignition to prevent the car being started until the seatbelt has been buckled on. The second was an alternative safety system which research showed offered considerably better protection in an accident than seat-belts. This provided for an air bag to be installed under the dashboard that was inflated on impact and filled up to form a large cushion halting the dangerous forward motion of the driver into the steering wheel and dashboard. All these examples indicate the way in which health and safety issues can be resolved, positively in the case of leaded petrol and exhaust emission, and negatively in the case of seat-belt interlocks and air bags, as a result of political campaigning on specific issues, and without the need for inspectorates to enforce the decisions reached.

Inspectorates

Many aspects of health and safety relating to industry require continuous management and are not to be resolved at the political campaigning stage. As was seen from the example of the British factory inspectorate, acceptance of the necessity for regulation in a given area in principle is followed by a debate about just what is to be regulated and to what standards. Whether these standards are enshrined in the legislation or whether, as is more frequently the case, a regulatory code is subsequently negotiated, industry input is usually substantial. The industry's legitimate interests are accepted, and it should not be required to meet standards either so tight that the benefits, in comparison with laxer standards, are disproportionately low and the costs of meeting them high, or to meet standards which exceed what is technologically feasible. The interests of industry in minimizing the costs of meeting the standards are recognized as legitimate, subject to the objectives of health and safety being met.

Just how tight is the regime which is ultimately imposed depends very substantially, however, upon public political pressures, which in turn usually reflect the extent of public risk in the industrial process in question. Where the public becomes acutely aware of the risks, and where anxiety is enhanced by safety failures, political pressure can increase to the point where it may threaten the future of the industry. This has happened with asbestos, for example, where, although the industry was aware of the dangers of disabling and life-threatening diseases consequent upon inhaling asbestos fibres, workers were told not to worry, and asbestos continued to be used in highly dangerous locations such as the insulation of heating pipes in schools and hospitals. Only when organized labour gained access to the research on the hazards and began to bring suits against employers did the wider public begin to become aware of the dangers. In response to public outcry, the uses of asbestos have become much more selective and the asbestos-processing manufacturers, like the tobacco giants, have diversified away from a pariah product.

A somewhat similar situation, though much more highly contested, prevails in respect of nuclear power. Here the dangers of radiation were always well known, and elaborate safety regimes established from the start, which in any case had the secondary function of improving the security of nuclear plants against unauthorised intruders, who might have more interest in the weapons-making aspects of the plants than in their power generation. The position adopted by the industry has hence been not that of denying that hazards exist, but of accepting that they are great, but claiming that they are carefully controlled. So great are these dangers, however, that some countries have been reluctant to develop nuclear power stations at all. In recent years the industry has come under pressure in two technical directions. In the first place, major failures in safety, such as that at Three Mile Island in the United States, or worse still Chernobyl in the USSR, which made sheepmeat unfit for human consumption as far away as Britain, have cast serious doubts upon nuclear safety, particularly since human error seemed to play a substantial part in both disasters. Safety systems may be technically effective, but if their procedures are not complied with because of laxness and incompetence they will provide no protection. Safety cannot be reduced to technique.

This has led to a more critical awareness of what is meant in engineering terms by 'safe'. If an industrial process is to pose no risk at all, it must be abandoned; any process which entails hazards can be contained only within more or less calculable limits by the application of engineering knowledge. Thus safe nuclear power generation does not involve no escapes of radiation into the surrounding areas; it involves escapes within agreed and established limits. Debate has hence moved to focus upon whether nuclear plants are actually keeping to agreed limits, and the minor failures and problems that any hazardous major industrial process routinely faces have become the object of greatly enhanced public attention.

For most hazards the regulatory regime established under legislation is successfully administered by an inspectorate so as to keep the dangers to an acceptable level and incidentally prevent them from becoming a political issue again. As was seen in the case of oil, there is a danger that the specialization and closeness of the inspectorate could result in it becoming over-friendly with industry and more sympathetic to its problems than it should be. Where this is compounded by the prospects of a job with the industry at much higher rates of pay in the latter part of an inspector's career, the dangers of 'capture' are great.

Anyone who has visited or worked in an industrial plant posing obvious physical hazards – a foundry, a construction site, a trawler, a mine – becomes immediately aware of the competing demands of safety and production. The hazards of the working environment are painfully obvious and provoke a natural anxiety and caution, both of which impede the workers' application to production. Workers none the less seem blasé about the dangers, and most men indeed go for years without an accident; major disasters are even rarer. Safety procedures are routinized by a combination of compulsory measures – searching miners for smoking materials before descent into the pit, for example – recognition by workers of safety practices, and workers' skill and experience in managing real risk *in situ*: this machine kicks back when performing a certain process whereas that one does not, this area of floor becomes slippery at certain times, and so on. Safety is hence routinized and work could not continue unless it was. In the case of some industries, such as food and chemicals processing, the dangers are not immediate but deferred, and routinization is even easier to achieve. It is the function of the inspectorate to ensure that this routinization does not exceed regulatory limits, and that workers incorporate protective safety routines into their working habits. In doing so they may come to constitute a nuisance for workers and management: protective clothing is uncomfortable, stringent testing of batches of products tedious when results always show adequate quality. Speed and efficiency, and hence earnings, exert constant pressure against safety.

Not that safety, particularly as it affects customers and the public rather than workers, may not have its economic benefits. Factory owners in the nineteenth century realized the benefits of safety and health legislation in imposing financial pressures upon their smaller competitors to their own advantage. In addition, regulatory regimes agreed with the state and administered by an inspectorate may be used as a seal of approval to enhance public confidence in the industry and its products. Kolko's analysis of the meat-processing industry in the United States, and in Chicago in particular, in the early years of the twentieth century illustrates this principle.[6] The industry was initially reluctant to accept regulation, but mounting public concern, fuelled by Upton Sinclair's factual novel *The Jungle*, detailing the grotesque abuses of hygiene and quality standards prevalent in the industry, led the larger companies to realize that the benefits of an inspectorate outweighed the costs. Smaller plants would not be able to raise the investment necessary to meet new standards of hygiene, and in addition the inspector's stamp of approval upon each can of meat provided a formidable marketing weapon for export purposes, particularly given the competition from the rapidly expanding Argentinian meat industry. Of what value after all was an Argentinian government inspector's stamp? Much the same is true today of the American pharmaceutical industry. Because the Food and Drugs Administration (FDA) licensing procedures are recognized as among the toughest in the world, many countries which do not have licensing authorities which are backed with a full testing and evaluative capacity rely upon FDA approval to license the distribution of a drug in their own country.

Compliance and Deterrence

How then do inspectorates exercise control over the industries they police? This has been the question at the centre of a great deal of recent research, all of which has produced variants of the same answer. Inspectorates are reluctant to use their legal powers to impose sanctions, especially sanctions involving legal proceedings, and above all criminal proceedings, upon manufacturers and businessmen. Rather they seek to gain the confidence and co-operation of industry to manage an agreed regime. They would sooner act as advisers, keeping managers alert to the dangers and preventing them being unduly diverted by production objectives, than as policemen intervening to stop production and initiating proceedings every time. Despite this finding in the detailed studies of a variety of industries and inspectorates by able scholars, surprise seems to persist as to why this should be so, even in the face of the equally regularly repeated reasons which are elicited. There are hence two questions to be asked about inspectorates' management of hazards: why they should opt for a compliance strategy, and, given that they have good reasons for doing so, why anyone should expect a more punitive and legalistic approach.[7]

The reasons a compliance strategy is adopted are partly the objectives of regulation and partly a reflection of comparative resources. Safety is achieved by a combination of routine procedures designed to minimize known hazards and alertness to recognize and respond to new ones where they arise. Although an inspector may be able to refer to a procedure required by the regulations or to suggest a routine that would secure safe operation in some respect, he is well aware that this may impose costs upon the plant, especially in terms of the extra time involved, and also that it is important that the routines are followed even when he is not present to verify them. He is also aware that serious accidents tend not to happen as a result of one lapse in safety procedures, but as the outcome of an accumulation of lapses: the platform should not have been allowed to become slippery, but the death of the worker was caused by his slipping and falling against a guard rail, which had failed because it had not been maintained. The inspector's objective is hence to persuade, advise and negotiate: to advise and educate as to where dangers lie and how to avoid them; to negotiate an acceptable set of practices and standards in the plant which minimize risks but allow production to take place efficiently; and to persuade workers and management that safety is a real issue they need to take into active consideration, because failure to do so may lead to catastrophe, personal in terms of accidents, and plant-wide in terms of damages claims, halting of production and adverse publicity, besides any sanction the inspector may impose.

If the preferred role of inspectors is that of adviser, maintaining awareness of dangers, they are none the less aware that co-operation will not be achieved in all cases. Some plants will feign co-operation and engage in the most outrageous abuses as soon as the inspector leaves, to counter which she/he may adopt a pattern of unannounced visits at unexpected times such as nights and weekends. Others still may simply be obstructive about compliance, belligerently questioning the necessity for new equipment or altered practices, vaguely promising to make amends but never doing so. Surely in these circumstances the inspectors must use their legal sanctions? Indeed they do, but usually only with the greatest reluctance, and a number of studies report that resort to legal sanctioning procedures is regarded as failure. There are good reasons for this. In the first place, sanctions are imposed for specific events: a plant was found at a specific date to be in violation of specific regulations, which may lead to a fine and a court order to make the necessary modifications by a given date. A co-operative business may be shamed by the publicity surrounding a court appearance and conviction, but an intransigent one is likely to be indifferent and to carry on more or less regardless, making only the modifications absolutely necessary. The inspectorate's only recourse is greatly to increase its rate of inspection of the recalcitrant business and to threaten continual legal proceedings; if it has the powers it may also threaten to close the business until it has made the necessary amendments and come up to standard.

This combative relationship with the business is extremely time-consuming for the inspectorate, and if, as is usually the case, it involves legal proceedings, it is even more time-consuming. Cases prepared for trial have to be approved by senior inspectors and referred to lawyers, and evidence must be meticulously accumulated in order to convince a court and gain a conviction. The net effect is to divert the energies of a number of inspectors from other inspections and to stretch their resources even more thinly. The conviction of one cowboy may be achieved at the expense of allowing a dozen others to flourish unchecked. And at the end of the day the courts impose sanctions frequently amounting to a very little more than a small fine. It follows that unless inspectors have substantial administrative powers, for example, to close a plant with dangerous levels of toxic chemical pollution or refuse to approve a batch of products for public consumption, their leverage against deviant businesses may rest on the refined threat of the use of their legal powers rather than their actual use. Presenting legal action as something so profoundly horrible that no sane businessman would willingly put himself at risk of having it visited upon him is much the same psychological tactic as the threat of the use of the cane in schools and the threat of imprisonment for conventional petty criminals. The punishment when it comes is not pleasant, but it can be endured, and most importantly it passes fairly quickly; those who have endured it are not deterred but inured.

The most difficult decision faced by inspectors is whether to insist on improvements which they know the business in question cannot afford, and which will hence close the business, perhaps adding to local unemployment. They may take action to enforce standards in the public's and employees' interests, but they may court unpopularity in doing so. If other businesses also begin to fear the imposition of expensive requirements to improve standards, they may become more devious in allowing inspectors access to information about hazardous aspects of their operations on which they might have otherwise sought their advice. Inspectors are hence constantly aware that whatever their rights of entry and inspection, the plants are the source of the information they require and often in a good position to conceal it if it is compromising. In the case of some advanced manufacturing processes the inspectors may simply not have the knowledge of new materials and processes, which remain trade secrets. Whether they are divulged in consultations with inspectors is a matter of the confidence in which the inspectorate is held.

In a variety of respects then, persuasion, albeit backed by the threat of sanctions, is a strategy normally preferred by inspectorates. The alternative punitive and deterrent strategy is widely perceived to be ineffective in so far as it can be adopted, and limited in capacity because of the time taken to process legal cases and the limited size of inspectorates. As will be seen in examples below, inspectorates do vary considerably in the extent to which they are reluctant to impose sanctions and in the range and power of the sanctions at their disposal, and they also vary over time in their relative willingness to impose sanctions. There are also differences in style and propensity to sanction between the United States, where business has traditionally been antagonistic to state regulation, and Britain where attitudes have been more co-operative. As Reiss points out, this difference is manifested in the way in which regulations are framed.[8] In the United States statutory standards for pollution control, for example, have sanctions attached to them, whereas in Britain pollution statutes set only general standards, deliberately leaving detailed standards and regulations to be developed by the inspectorate in negotiation with the industry. Pressure exists in the United States, therefore, for inspectors to issue citations for violations of statutory standards, where British inspectors are at more formal liberty to negotiate both what are reasonable standards for this plant at present and how those standards are to be improved in the future. In practice, however, American inspectors informally use statutory rules as bargaining chips to achieve compliance, and agree not to issue citations providing plants make real efforts to improve. In neither case do the inspectors emulate the police, whose instinct is to charge an offence if there is clear evidence that it has been committed.

Corporations as Amoral Calculators

Why then the expectation that legal sanctions will be used? The reasons are both commonsensical and historical. Whilst many industrialists and businessmen are honest, responsible and law-abiding, not all of them are. Hence, although it may be congenial and effective for inspectors to spend most of their time advising, cajoling and perhaps threatening, this may greatly underestimate the tendency of some businesses, including major corporations, to act, in Kagan and Scholz's phrase, as amoral calculators.[9]

This is certainly what Ford did over the Pinto car.[10] The Pinto was introduced under considerable time pressure at the lower end of the market, with senior management insisting that it must meet the requirements of weighing no more than 2000 lb and costing no more than $2000.

It was launched successfully, but after a while began to be associated with horrific burn-outs after rear-impact accidents. Analysis often showed that even at relatively low speeds the petrol tank, which was located across the back of the car, crumpled and was pierced in rear-impact collisions, and if conditions were favourable, as they usually were in the hotter and drier of the American states, the petrol ignited and incinerated the occupants of the car. It was shown that the original design of the car included a strengthening bracket which better secured the petrol tank and prevented it being dislodged and punctured on impact. This bracket had been withdrawn in the final model to conform with the price and weight guidelines. Further, when Ford became aware of the dangers of explosion with the Pinto it decided not to recall all the cars to modify them, and to risk a number of suits for damages from individual victims. It took this decision because of a financial calculation that the costs of recall and modification would exceed the costs of litigation and damages in the number of cases likely to arise.

Instances such as these arouse considerable public passions. Ford was indicted on criminal charges of reckless homicide but eventually acquitted. Similarly in Britain the sinking of the cross-Channel ferry, *Herald of Free*

Enterprise, in 1987 with the loss of nearly 200 lives generated a considerable furore. The ship sailed with open bow loading doors leading on to a car deck, which on a roll-on-roll-off ferry runs uninterrupted from one end of the ship to the other. As the ship picked up speed the bow began to dip and water flooded in, causing it to founder extremely quickly. The crew members immediately responsible, including the captain, were rapidly sanctioned through their professional licensing bodies, but the inquest upon the victims was persuaded to go further than that and return verdicts of unlawful killing upon many of them, implying a potential charge of manslaughter. What seems to have angered the jury and certainly angered relatives of victims was that there was no means by which the bridge could be certain that the bow doors were shut. Evidence was produced that masters had requested the installation of a simple set of warning lights for this purpose and received rejections from the company in terms that were authoritarian and contemptuous. More widely, the design of roll-on-roll-off ferries was called into question as inherently unstable and liable to quick capsize in the event of water getting into a car deck unrestricted by the watertight bulkheads which are a safety feature of most large ships. Why was design not questioned, particularly given an accident only eighteen months previously in which a similar ferry had been holed and had capsized rapidly, though on that occasion fortunately without loss of life? What were the responsibilities of the company and the relevant inspectorate in reassessing the risks of the roll-on-roll-off design and ensuring that remedial action in the form of the installation of removable bulkheads was undertaken? Was not the design aimed precisely at maximizing speed of loading and unloading and providing maximum accommodation space at the price of safety? The natural reaction of those directly affected, and perhaps of a wider public, to such a disaster is to seek to attribute blame and to claim culpable negligence, but as even the above details suggest, it is likely to be exceedingly difficult in practice to attribute it upon clear legal grounds to the satisfaction of a criminal court 'beyond reasonable doubt'.

There are none the less cases, usually involving smaller businesses, where flagrant disregard for safety is manifest. Dumping of toxic waste is a perennial example, with fast money to be made by the unscrupulous who will take dangerous industrial waste from a small plant for a fee less than the substantial amount it would cost to dispose of it safely, and then dump it in a landfill site as non-hazardous waste and hence for minimal costs. Such deliberate profiteering at calculated risk to public health surely demands criminal sanctions. No doubt, though, the public would probably be more reassured if an effective licensing regime had prevented such an operator from ever returning to the waste disposal business.

Strict Liability: A Blind Alley

Although licensing has played an increasingly important part in the regulation of business, reliance on the extensive administrative discretion of licensing authorities has been a relatively recent trend. As Frank points out, confirming the similarities between Britain and America, initial legislative reaction to health and safety issues was symbolic: 'The laws that were passed frequently contained ambiguous sanctions or no sanctions at all.'[11] When in due course it became evident that the laws were not being respected, inspectorates were founded to enforce them. This did not happen on a significant scale until the twentieth century in the United States. When inspectors began their work they rapidly found that the enforcement of criminal sanctions was impossible on a conventional basis because it was only too easy for businessmen to argue lack of intent. The reaction of legislators was to strengthen an already existent tendency to impose strict liability to maintain standards and a duty of care to ensure them at all times, so that ignorance and inadvertence could not be pleaded. This was a simple and attractive solution. After all, it was the continuous maintenance of standards that was important, and legislators and the public certainly did wish to impress upon industry their constant obligation to remain alert to maintain the required standards. It was hence only just that they should be punished not only for deliberately flouting the standards – there were enhanced penalties for this – but also for simply failing to attain them.

Strict liability coupled with criminal prosecution became the favourite tactic for keeping deviant industrialists in line and redressing the imbalance in resources between them and what was usually a limited inspectorate. It was also a means of avoiding granting extensive discretionary powers to the inspectorate which could be argued to be the basis for the bureaucratic suffocation of industry and a violation of the rule of law. In fact strict liability turned out to be a blind alley. In Britain, a report by the lawyers' pressure group Justice said that by 1975 there were over 7,000 separate criminal offences, almost half of which did not require proof of intent.[12] Of these, 4,386 had been created between 1961 and 1975, a period of rapidly increasing regulatory intervention by the state. By 1980, the objections to strict liability had become well articulated. To accuse someone of a crime, when only guilty of the violation of a technical regulation, made a mockery of the notion of criminal guilt. The distinction between offences long agreed to be criminal and immoral, *mala in se*, and those merely banned by technical legislation, *mala prohibita*, might not be defensible as an absolute one, but it retained conceptual importance. There was something decidely contradictory about arraigning businessmen and industrialists in court on criminal charges, upon which no defence of lack of intent (*mens rea*) was permitted. In Britain, even a defence of due diligence, that the defendant had taken due care to conform to regulations, was not available for many offences, since safety was held to require absolute adherence to standards. And as Levi shows, the criminal law certainly has not been enforced.[13] In 1982 there were 1,640,066 conventional criminal cases and 17,602 regulatory ones, almost all of them in magistrates' courts. Sentences were almost invariably fines, and fines were usually low, and at times derisory, in relation to the resources of the business involved. Between 1976 and 1979, fines on companies for breaches of the Health and Safety at Work Act, 1974, never exceeded 16 per cent of the maximum, which rose from £400 in 1976 to £1,000 in 1977.

Inspectors, as has been described, are reluctant to take cases to court, and courts are evidently reluctant to impose severe sanctions. As Frank (p. 232) puts it in respect of the United States, with improvements in the technical training and knowledge of inspectors in the mid-twentieth century and incipient professionalization, coupled with a degree of delegation to them of rule-making authority,

> Inspectors began to define their rule as one of technical consultation rather than law enforcement . . . Professionalisation had the effect of making inspectors identify more with science and engineering, more prestigious fields than policing . . . Most businessmen, they said, were willing to comply with the law. They only needed to be shown how . . . This approach was reinforced by the technical complexity of health and safety rules. Inspectors had to make more exacting measurements which increased their workload. Second, increasing complexity substantiated industrialists' complaints that they did not know they were violating the law.

Political Campaigns and Regulatory Methods

The shift to administrative regulation and away from criminal sanction has not, however, been quite the continous process, expedited by the realization that the benefits of strict liability were illusory, that Frank implies, particularly in the United States. Politics has remained important and has played a significant part in retaining an emphasis upon criminal sanctions. The consumerist and environmental movements of the 1960s and 1970s have frequently adopted a criminalizing rhetoric in relation to all kinds of business misconduct. Ralph Nader in particular has frequently made no bones about his desire to see corporate offenders convicted in criminal courts and visited with severe and credibly painful sanctions. In cases where the harm done is substantial, the motive greed, and the state of mind of the offender reckless or malevolent, such rhetoric is of course persuasive. Crusading lawyers make a good press. As Katz has pointed out in the course of an account of the social movement against white-collar crime in the United States in the 1970s that is too particularistic in its references to be commented on at length here, federal institutions such as the Internal Revenue Service, the Securities and Exchange Commission and especially US attorneys, took the lead in attacking cases of corporate misconduct. In some cases this was the result of the liberation of earlier enthusiasts, who had been restrained in their attacks on elites during the Nixon years, with their political emphasis upon street crime. To some extent also, though, it was the outcome of entry into public service in the 1960s of able and well-qualified lawyers with liberal sentiments. Finally, it reflected the fact that the anti-white-collar crime movement was manifestly case-oriented and lacking in the institutional reforming zeal of its early predecessors in the New Deal years of the 1930s.

> It was natural that a group of prosecutors who regarded themselves as the best would seek opportunities to dramatise their excellence. White collar crime cases were likely to be seen as especially difficult, in part because they had to be uncovered and 'made', and in part because they brought an unusual quality of defence counsel to the other side. Political corruption prosecutions would especially dramatise the office's professional integrity and independence from politics . . .
>
> The case for emphasising white collar crime was put as a matter of enforcement philosophy rather than mere self-celebration: federal prosecutors should reach where state prosecutors jurisdictionally cannot, and the best federal prosecutors should reach crimes inaccessible to lesser staff. In a sense the most serious crimes are those which attempt to make use of politically powerful and economically elite positions to frustrate detection and prosecution.[14]

Katz ranges widely over offences in his review, but the reaction he refers to had its impact on health and safety-related offences and the regulation of industry.

One regulatory agency founded in the period he describes, during which the environmental lobby grew to a formidable strength, was the Office of Surface Mining, whose subsequent career was researched by Shover et al.[15] The initial recruitment of staff attracted those committed to environmentalism, who were encouraged by the political climate to adopt a stringent enforcement-oriented approach to the OSM's work. A centralized and hierarchical organization developed, which gave a dominant role to the legal department, because of the agency's limited resources and the continental territory it was required to administer. The net result was a loss of discretion for inspectors at individual mines as cases were referred upwards for legalistic decision-making on the reported facts in the manner of the police. In time, as the influence of the environmental movement waned, that of the surface mining industry grew, and the OSM found itself increasingly isolated in the face of political attacks. It gradually softened its regulatory stance, but had by now acquired a reputation as an example of over-regulation, so that when Reagan became President in 1980 it was a prime target for 'deregulation'. The staffing of the OSM was cut back sharply, limiting its inspection and enforcement capacity, and the two top jobs were political appointments filled by individuals committed to a persuasive approach to regulation. The agency found its strength much reduced and underwent a major change of enforcement strategy as a result of failing to recognize the importance of the prevailing political climate. Unlike the EPA referred to earlier, it had not established itself sufficiently with the public to be able to mobilize support against an antagonistic presidency and succumbed to the influence of industrial concern for 'reasonableness' in regulation.

Just how dramatic and extensive was the move to stringent penal enforcement in the early 1970s, and hence how likely the swing back in favour of industry is indicated by Kagan and Scholz:[16]

> Suspicious of regulated firms ability to 'capture' enforcement officials, reformers prevailed upon the federal government in the early 1970s to take over or strictly supervise state enforcement of legal standards governing workers' safety and health, air pollution, nursing homes, blood collection, and numerous other regulatory programmes. Statutes and regulations were enacted prescribing nationwide rules, sometimes denying enforcement officials any discretion to grant exceptions or to take compliance cost into account. Inspectors in some programmes were legally prohibited from making appointments for inspections in advance, and instructed to issue citations for or write up *every* regulatory violation they saw (as opposed to merely issuing warnings for 'first instance' less serious violations). In some programmes monetary fines for violations have been mandatory, thus limiting the discretion of agency officials and judges to suspend fines in cases where businesses undertook (or could be induced to make) a good faith effort to comply. Many statutes have increased the authorised level of fines to up to 25,000 dollars *per day* for continuing violations. To reduce legal delays agencies have been granted more powers to impose fines and issue summary orders without first having to seek a court order. Citizen complainants have been authorised to bring law suits to compel enforcement officials to issue citations and prosecute violations more vigorously.
>
> Interviews with inspectors and regulated firms confirm that such laws have produced marked changes in enforcement procedures. Bargaining between inspectors and business managers has been widely reduced in many programmes.

So far attention has been concentrated on the circumstances giving rise to industrial regulation and the strategies adopted to maintain it. Implicit in this discussion has been an argument that regulation is the art of the possible, and that regulatory success in achieving and maintaining or improving adequate standards must be seen against the relevant political background, both the macro-politics of the issues regulated and the micro-politics of the interaction between the regulatory agency and its industrial clients. Both of these may change over time but they may also have stable features of some significance. The final part of this chapter will address the question of effectiveness or 'what works' more directly in the light of this analysis, providing two contrasting examples of regulatory agencies with major public remits: British Environmental Health Offices and the American Food and Drugs Administration's control of the pharmaceutical industry.

Environmental Health Offices (EHOs)

Hutter's study of four Environmental Health Offices describes in some detail the work of the officers and abstracts two dominant strategies which reflect their circumstances. As in other studies, effectiveness is understood not in the abstract but in the real situation in which EHOs work, and which sets limits upon what can be expected. What is particularly striking, however, are the limits to effectiveness which are built into the EHO's remit. Although there is a national body representing all EHOs, the Institute, it is not a regulatory agency and wields little influence. It does not even train officers, most of whom are non-graduates, and who get their technical training in short courses and part-time study during their work as EHOs. They see their work as a practical job, not as a vocation. EHOs are employed not by central government, but by local authorities, and hence their status, funding and independence may vary over time and from authority to authority, and reflect changes in political control of authorities. Further, EHOs have extremely diversified responsibilities. Although much of their work is in practice concentrated upon food hygiene and housing matters, they are also responsible for aspects of industrial pollution and noise problems, as well as public environmental health matters, such as refuse collection, street lighting, crematoria and cemeteries. Regulations is some areas are straightforward to enforce but in others, especially industrial pollution, they are not, and assistance is often required from independent analysts and other agencies, such as the Health and Safety Commission, with whom they share responsibility. Finally, penalties in the cases which they take to court are statutorily limited to relatively small fines, dealt with normally in magistrates' courts, which rarely impose the maximum.

EHOs have a vital public job to do in ensuring that the public as customers and employees are not poisoned by substandard food from shops, restaurants and canteens, and ensuring that tenants, especially those in difficult circumstances, such as the elderly or single parents, do not suffer from damp, structural defects, and the failure of landlords to maintain properties. Yet the chances of their achieving anything like rigorous enforcement are remote indeed. The number of premises constituting potential sites for inspection is vastly greater than can be coped with on a regular basis, and the most that inspectors can hope for is reasonably regular inspection of food outlets, and response to other issues, particularly housing, via complaints. Legal action is deterred by the limited nature of the penalties involved and by the diversion of time from inspection which preparing a case for court entails. In addition, inspectors complained that magistrates treated them without the deference they accorded to the police, and regularly questioned the adequacy of their evidence and asked whether warnings had been given. As Hutter notes, the police do not warn. In one incident she described, an EHO was called by the police to deal with an unlicensed stall-holder selling fish in the street. The inspector pointed out various defects in his stall and equipment, and the stall-holder responded compliantly, but requested permission to sell off the remainder of his fish as he had not much left. The inspector was happy for him to do this, but the police reacted by saying that unless he moved immediately he would arrest him for obstruction.

In addition to these difficulties, the local authorities exercised at times very intrusive control, not only of the policy on prosecution and inspection, but in individual cases. Three authorites vetted every case going to court, and by no means always approved the Chief Inspector's proposals, producing evident conflicts of interest in some instances, given that the businessmen and traders were not infrequently known to the councillors on the Environmental Health committees.

Not surprisingly the EHOs were cautious about bringing cases to court, but there were some where prosecution was essential as a counter to persistent and flagrant violation of regulations with serious risk to public health. EHOs hence particularly resented vetting by councillors, whom they castigated as ignorant. As Hutter points out, their work would be made much easier if they were given licensing powers, particularly over food outlets, since they could then enforce minimum standards before allowing outlets to open, and threaten revocation of the licence, which the licensee would have to appeal against, rather than going to court and obtaining a derisory fine. The inspectors' strategy was hence necessarily based on persuasion and bluff, with threats to have recourse to prosecution being used as a lever to obtain compliance and a careful avoidance of specification of the penalties if convicted.

The nature of this persuasion varied interestingly, however, as between the two rural authorities and the two urban ones that Hutter studied. In rural areas the persuasive strategy was full-blooded, as Hutter puts it:

> Officers educate, persuade, coax and control offenders into complying with the law. They explain what the law demands and the reasons for these legislative requirements and discuss how improvements can best be attained. The whole strategy is premised on patience and understanding, and gaining compliance is regarded as an open-ended and long term process.
>
> Those adhering to this strategy emphasised that legal action, especially prosecution, is literally a last resort which should only be used when other methods have been exhausted.[17]

To this end an extensive hierarchy of formal letters having the appearance of official enforcement notices was developed to pressure the recalcitrant, the actual legal enforcement notice coming only at the end, after an extended series of reinspections. Legal enforcement was something of an embarrassment in rural areas, which were relatively close-knit. Offenders were sometimes well known to inspectors, who might come into contact with them socially. In addition, compliance and information on regulatory offences were held to be likely to weaken if a strigent enforcement policy were to be adopted. Inspectors genuinely expected the persuasive strategy to work precisely because of the socially integrated nature of rural areas.

In the urban areas, by contrast, not only was such social integration lacking, but the basic level of properties and food outlets was lower, poverty a much more substantial problem, and environmental health issues much more likely to feature on the political and media agenda. Not only was a full persuasive strategy hence less likely to achieve results, but there was a lack of basic security in respect of standards, that the minimum had already been achieved, and in respect of political support, that persuasion would be approved of. Inspectors felt bound to be more aggressive, because they came across more bad cases, and because they feared that over-tolerance would be interpreted as softness. Indeed, different types of inspectors were attracted to the different types of local authorities, with the urban ones dismissing the rural as 'soft', and the rural deriding the urban as 'little Hitlers'.

But what could the urban inspectors do, since they were equally lacking in resources and arguably even more overwhelmed with offences than their rural colleagues? Their response was what Hutter calls the insistent strategy, which does not involve a great increase in prosecution, but is much more active in its threats of it. Rather than controlling and educating, inspectors laid down what they required to be done and the date by which it was to be done, and followed this up with a much shorter series of enforcement letters before arriving at a legal notice of enforcement. This did not, however, involve the elimination of negotiation and bargaining, both on the basis of bad cases as opposed to minor ones and on the basis of what the resources of the offender could reasonably by expected to produce over what period of time by way of improvement. Although tougher than the full persuasive strategy, urban inspectors were hence still markedly compliance-rather than deterrence-oriented. Table 10 illustrates the consequences in terms of prosecution outcomes, Departments A and B being rural and C and D urban.

Hutter's work points out the difficulty of evaluating what constitutes effective regulation. The departments in her study evolved strategies that were directed at maximum effectiveness, given their circumstances. There is no provision for regulatory effectiveness to be independently monitored,

Table 10   Probability of prosecution of food premises

Department	1977	1978	1979
A	1:1327	0	1:322
B	1:171	1:257	1:147
C	1:66	1:47	1:88
D	1:35	1:42	1:68

Source: Hutter, *The Reasonable Arm of the Law?*, table 22

and objective surveys of any comprehensive nature are lacking. Clearly, effectiveness could be increased if EHOs were given greater powers and independence. Given their very wide-ranging responsibilities, many offences are inevitably undetected – landlords notoriously fail to comply with the law, for example, and inspectors are largely dependent on tenants' complaints to identify the deviant.

The Food and Drug Administration

A marked contrast is provided by the case of the pharmaceutical industry, studied by Braithwaite, whose work covers Britain and Australia also, but concentrates upon the American base of a substantial number of multi-nationals, and the FDA as the regulatory agency.[18] Unlike the EHO's, the FDA's clients are a known limited number of companies with whom regular contact is maintained. Further, the FDA has very substantial administrative powers, both over licensing individual drugs and over licensing production facilities. In modern times the company has been required to show, on the basis of research evidence, that a new drug is safe, effective and better than existing drugs before it is given a licence. Manufacturing facilities are regularly inspected and required to keep detailed records, and to maintain a quality control and compliance unit.

The reason for this is the pre-eminence of pharmaceuticals in modern health care. Since the development of penicillin saved the lives of thousands of combatants in World War II, the pharmaceutical industry has made enormous strides in developing drugs to treat a vast range of ailments, including not only infections treated by vaccines and antibiotics, but such disorders and conditions as epilepsy, depression, anxiety, schizophrenia, ulcers, heart disease and cancer. Not all are equally effective, but collectively they have been effective enough, in conjunction with advances in surgical techniques, to support a public expectation of the rescue of the individual from morbidity and mortality in almost every case of ill health until extreme old age. In consequence the pharmaceutical industry has a very high public profile and is exceedingly profitable.

It is also extremely expensive to run. Not only are the costs of production of some drugs relatively high and the investment costs of building modern production facilities to adequate standards great, but the costs of research are enormous. Most importantly, research is not usually productive of a new effective drug. Research operates from two strategic points: into the disease or disorder in order to pinpoint the precise mechanisms involved, the manipulation of which can lead to a cure; and into the structure of complex chemical compounds, based on a knowledge of the biologically active qualities of related compounds. It is on the latter that the pharmaceutical industry concentrates.

One general rule about the nature of pharmaceuticals is that if a substance is active it is also toxic. Many, if not most, of the compounds produced in research will prove to be inactive. When an active one is synthesized, efforts are hence concentrated on attempting to identify precisely what its effects are. If it can be shown that these are in some respects beneficial, an elaborate balancing exercise then ensues to evaluate these against the unwanted toxic effects. This is most widely acknowledged in treatments for such conditions as cancer and AIDS, which modern medicine cannot fully control, but all drugs are dangerous as well as beneficial. It is important therefore that as much as possible is known about side-effects, as they are politely called, overdose effects, contra-indications, such as patients suffering from other weakness or diseases than that treated by the drug in question, 'cocktail' effects of the drug's interaction with other medications, and the differing reactions of the old, the young and the unborn. It is recognized that much of this information cannot be obtained from the animal studies which are the basis of drug research, and that it cannot be complete until evaluations of the drug in use in the general population have been undertaken. The longer a drug has been in use, the better its risks and benefits are understood.

This implies a very long step-by-step approach to pharmaceutical development. The more extended this process, the higher the costs of development. In practice, the formal constraints are limited to two major licensing stages: clinical trial and general release. By the time a company has reached the clinical trial stage it has reached certainty that it has an active substance to market and has spent a great deal of time and money selecting that substance and rejecting many others. From that point on it will be willing to countenance specific and limited contra-indications, and recognize limited side-effects, but is increasingly reluctant to recognize serious dangers which might compromise the drug's future.

This is the more so where the drug is that rarity, a leader in the field. Most new drugs are in fact variants upon existing ones, which are claimed to be safer or more effective than their predecessors; these products compete in an already congested market. Where a breakthrough is achieved with a genuinely original compound, the profit potential is hence enormous if the disease or disorder treated is widespread in the western world, where there are incomes to pay for it. Zantac, the leading treatment for ulcers developed by Glaxo, and how the main foundation of its profits, is an example of this. Zantac is now the world's best-selling drug, sales of which exceeded £1 billion by mid-1988. Librium and Valium, the benzodiazepine minor tranquillizers developed by Hoffman La Roche, and prescribed on an awesome scale for anxiety and depression until recently, is another example, and one which indicates how far things can go wrong. Librium and Valium were widely prescribed on a repeat basis to patients for years, because research showed them to be safe and effective; in particular there was no lethal dosage level, and side-effects and complications were said to be few. What was not recognized until recently was that long-term use of them can create serious dependence with horrific withdrawal symptoms if supplies are suddenly withdrawn. As a result, Librium and Valium are now prescribed much more cautiously, but Roche's patent has run its twenty years, and its profits have been made.

The regulatory agency hence stands between the drug company keen to exploit its new product and the public eager to benefit but at risk from the dangers. As Braithwaite's research shows, the fatal weakness of the FDA in the past was its relatively passive dependence upon the research of the drug companies to provide information by which to evaluate drugs to be licensed. Adequate information is so costly to generate that even the American agency cannot hope to be voted the funds necessary to undertake its own evaluation studies and must rely on requiring information to adequate levels from the industry. The key to effectiveness has hence lain in ensuring that this research is of an extent and quality necessary to be reasonably sure that a new drug is safe and effective. Braithwaite uncovered a range of misconduct in the pharmaceutical industry that leaves no doubt as to the strength of its profit motivation and of its assertive and at times combative attitude to regulation. The size and corporate arrogance of some of the multinationals and the fierce competitiveness of most drug companies produced practices that are by no means conducive to health: doctored research results; suppression of reports of dangerous side-effects; manipulation and deceit of inspectors; well-staffed legal departments; dumping substandard products on third world countries, with few regulatory controls, whose populations are also used as the testing ground for new products; even the creation of a 'Vice-President responsible for going to jail', who is designated as the executive who will admit to guilty knowledge, so saving the skins of the rest.

Why is it then that the FDA is now recognized as the most effective regulator of the drugs industry in the world, whose approval is often taken by poorer countries as the sole basis for approving the release of a new drug? The answer lies in a series of disasters and near-disasters in the 1960s and 1970s. MER/29 (triparanol) was a drug developed by Richardson Merrell to reduce blood cholesterol levels, which went on sale in 1960 and within a year was used by 300,000 Americans. It generated a flood of adverse reports, including baldness, skin damage, changes in the reproductive organs and the blood, and the production of eye cataracts. Only after it was withdrawn did it become evident on inquiry that information about these effects was known even at the animal research stage, and was surpressed.

Richardson Merrell was also the licensee in America that sought to release thalidomide in the early 1960s, a drug that produced nearly 8,000 deformed children worldwide. Thalidomide was produced by a small German pharmaceutical company which claimed it to be an extremely safe hypnotic. The company resisted acting upon reports of peripheral nerve damage and birth deformities, and hoped to make a huge profit if the drug was sold on licence worldwide through major pharmaceutical houses. Richardson Merrell was delayed in gaining a US licence by a meticulous official at the FDA who insisted that inadequate information on the drug's capacity to pass through the placenta to a foetus was available, and the delay was enough for the information about birth deformities to break through, initially in Australia and then in Germany, which led to the drug's withdrawal.

Finally, in the mid-1970s G. D. Searle was shown to have falsified research results on at least two of its products, Aldactone and Flagyl, both of which were carcinogenic. Searle executives were subject to withering interrogation by the Senate's subcommittee on health, under the chairmanship of Senator Edward Kennedy. Criminal charges against Searle were not approved by a grand jury, but the pressure and publicity of the hearings resulted in a major shake-up of the corporation, including the replacement of its president and the establishment of a sophisticated corporate compliance unit.

There is not space to detail fully these and other cases described by Braithwaite of the dangerous, unscrupulous and incompetent abuses in the American pharmaceutical industry. Their exposure and the publicity surrounding them, and the horrifying effects that some of them had on patients, provided a political mandate for a much greater stringency by the FDA. It is important to note that this did not involve resort to criminal prosecution. In almost the only case in which the FDA did prosecute a major company, it lost. Abbott, the major supplier of sterile intravenous solutions, was prosecuted along with five of its executives in 1971, after eight deaths in three months at one hospital and 45 other cases of blood poisoning as a result of contaminated Abbott fluids. It was only the latest in a series of failures, including mislabelling, inadequate sealing of bottles and contamination, which went back as far as 1964. As Braithwaite puts it, 'there was not the evidence to link the specific good manufacturing practice violations reported by the FDA's district inspectors as the cause of the sterility problem' (p. 117). None the less, Abbott later estimated the cost of FDA regulatory action at $480 million, a no doubt exaggerated figure, but almost certainly very much higher than any fine a court would have imposed.

The FDA obtained improvements by exercising the enormous leverage it has over licensing new products and by being able to recall batches of products if manufacturing defects are detected. Although it benefited from additional legislation in the wake of the MER/29 and thalidomide cases, it successfully exploited its public ascendancy by negotiating improved structures and practices in companies which would lead to tighter controls: quality assurance units within drug testing laboratories, for example, established on an independent basis from management with direct referral to the top of the organization. It has managed to achieve compliance in most quarters by demonstrating that if its exacting standards are adopted as recommended, the company acquires an enhanced international reputation for quality which helps to sell its products, including standard preparations in competition with those of other companies. Negatively compliance is obtained by reacting to deviousness and truculence with a blitz of inspections, complaints, citations and requirements to improve, which can cost the company dearly in executive time, in production lines at a standstill, and in additional expense to implement remedies.

This tactic, however, is possible only given adequate staffing of the FDA, strong licensing powers to exercise regulatory control over manufacture, and the compliance of the majority of companies. Overall, the FDA is in an unusual position in relation to the drugs companies in having established a reputation as a guardian of a vital public interest to whom significant administrative discretion is to be allowed. That discretion is today being questioned in some quarters, especially with the advent of AIDS, on the ground that FDA caution leads to delays in the licensing of valuable new drugs, but the FDA has remained strong enough to be largely protected from the Reaganite wave of deregulation. Of course, it could also be pointed out that only a country as rich and large as the United States, which devotes such a large proportion of GNP – much greater than Britain – to health care, could afford the costs the FDA imposes on the pharmaceutical industry, which are recouped in the price of its products. Whatever the immediately obvious costs, effective regulation does not come cheaply.

Regulatory Effectiveness

Braithwaite concluded his study of the pharmaceutical industry with the assertion that 'clout is what counts' in effective regulation, and that the most effective regulatory system is one that gives the agency extensive discretion, but permits redress, regulated by various review channels (p. 380):

> The best guarantees against abuse of administrative descretion are provided by diligent investigative journalists, active oversight committees of elected representatives, vocal consumer and trade union movements, aggressive industry associations, which are willing to use the political process to defend their members against such abuses, freedom of information statutes with teeth, free access of the scientific community to the raw data on which regulatory decisions are based, and requirements that regulatory agencies publicly justify the decisions and publicly hear appeals against them.

This sounds like protesting too much. Braithwaite is aware that legal appeals against administrative discretion would paralyse a regulatory agency, hence his recommendation of the political process. But pharmaceuticals are a privileged case, not only in the heightened public attention that they have had in recent years, but in their inevitable public involvement. Where it is only the safety of workers that is at issue and the product poses no immediate public hazard, as in the oil and mining industries, for example, industry pressure for restraint in the use of discretion is likely to prove effective sooner or later, as the OSM example indicated.

Braithwaite subsequently went on to study coal mining, as a result of which he was led to modify his views and to develop the only fully articulated regulatory control package that argues for maximum effectiveness.[19] Many *ad hoc* ideas for corporate regulation have been proposed in the past decade and a half, and some of them incorporated into legislation. Stone, for example, devotes a substantial proportion of his analysis of corporate excesses to suggesting remedies, some of them more plausibly effective and politically feasible than others, but with no overall strategy other than improving corporate public accountability.[20] Braithwaite's solution is the more interesting in that it is the outcome of long-term reflection on the problems discussed in this chapter. Compliance achieved by persuasion is the method universally favoured, and will be effective in so far as it encourages the development of institutions and practices which build health and safety routines into business. Compliance will not be achieved in all cases, however, unless the regulatory agency has the necessary leverage – clout, as Braithwaite calls it. That can be constituted by powers of legal sanction or by administrative discretion. Legal sanction, as has been seen, is ineffective – agencies are outgunned in the courts, their time and personnel tied up in legal arguments, and at the end of the day what has been achieved is the imposition of sanctions on an act, not always resulting in the achievement of a reformed practice, and by no means certainly the achieving of a change of attitude by the business. If, on the other hand, extensive discretionary powers are given to the regulatory agency, they have either to be appealable, in which case the courts triumph again, or they are negotiable only through the political process, which may lead to wild oscillations in the levels of support for either side over time.

What emerges from this is the question of what is the most effective means of achieving business compliance. Braithwaite's answer is to get companies to write their own rules. The case of coal mining makes this particularly apposite. It is an especially hazardous industry, and he is able to produce vivid statistics to show that increased regulation in both Britain and the United States produced declining death and injury rates in so far as compliance with improved standards was achieved (not all legislation to this end has been effective). However, conditions in different mines vary very widely – some are deeper than others, some are more at risk from gas or water, some work in stable geological strata, some in unstable. This means that whilst reasonable standards on certain risks – precautions to ensure gas detection early and to eliminate naked lights below ground, for example – are necessarily universal, others, such as the frequency and strength of roof props, should vary with local conditions. Such variations are, in practice, usually negotiated with the relevant inspectorates, but Braithwaite's proposal is to formalize this by allowing individual companies to write their own detailed safety regulations in the light of nationally agreed general standards, which would then be approved for implementation.

Once approved these regulations would have legal force, and violations of them would be sanctionable by administrative action – suspending working – or legal action. Braithwaite points out that by getting the company to write its own rules, it would find it difficult to object to them as unnecessary or irrelevant, and would have no excuse for not keeping to them: voluntary compliance should be more easily achieved. To ensure compliance Braithwaite proposes (p. 126) an internal compliance unit

> to monitor observance of the rules and recommend disciplinary action against violators. Should management fail to rectify violations or to act on recommendations for disciplinary action, the director of compliance would be statutorily required to report this fact to the regulatory agency. This provision would make compliance the line of least resistance for corporate offenders in most circumstances, that is the cost of yielding to the compliance director would generally be less than the costs of fighting the investigation, prosecution and adverse publicity that would almost certainly follow rejection of the compliance group's recommendation.

Another benefit of this system is that, because it allows for health and safety regulations to be written for local application, it can permit the specification of detailed requirements which achieve the general principles laid down in legislation. This then makes legal action for non-compliance much more a matter of straightforward fact, for example, that roof supports are at a specified distance and no greater, rather than that roof supports are adequate to ensure the safety of miners. This in turn will focus the collective mind of the company on devising an adequate and comprehensive safety system when drawing up and negotiating their regulations.

Braithwaite's scheme is appealing, even if not without objection. It will be returned to for consideration in its implications of wider issues in the control of business crime at a later stage, but at this point a brief comparative reference to the financial sector is pertinent. The new regulatory regime in Britain under the SIB bears marked similarities to Braithwaite's enforced self-regulation which, as he says, is in essence operative to a substantial extent in coal mining in the United States and Australia. The difficulties which have arisen over the SIB arrangements now subject to objection by the regulated, that the rules are too many and too complex, seem to have to do partly with the new and untested interrelationships between financial institutions which new arrangements are required to regulate, and in part to do with the balance of power as between the regulators (the SIB) and the regulated. If the regulator is lax, it will allow approval of detailed regulations which do not give adequate protection; if it is too tough, it will refuse to approve schemes until they are so stringent as to be denounced as overburdensome and hence invite cheating. Clearly there are some nice judgements to be made.

Power at the Top

This Chapter should not close without mention of some research which raises a matter often taken to be beside the point by commentators. It is axiomatic to most social scientists that institutions are more important and powerful than the men who lead them, and it is frequently asserted by corporate chiefs that they did not know of the misdeeds that their underlings were perpetrating. As Braithwaite showed of the drugs industry, this can be an artificial appearance at times, and guilty knowledge is often deliberately withheld from senior personnel: 'Give me deniability', as President Nixon is supposed to have said. Clinard interviewed 64 retired middle managers of Fortune 500 companies with an average period of service with a single corporation of 32 years. They had hence seen several chief executives come and go. He puts one of his conclusions as follows:

> The general theme expressed by most middle management executives was that top management, and in particular the Chief Executive Office (CEO), sets the corporate ethical tone. These views were not found to be due to antagonisms or jealousy of top management as such: the respondents simply felt that top management completely dominated the overall ethical tone of their corporation. Over half the interviewees went even further, believing top management to be directly responsible for the violation of government regulations. In fact top management's influence takes precedence in their view over the possibility of a pre-existing ethical (or non-ethical) general corporate cultural pattern. One executive described the prime role of management succinctly when he said: 'Ethics comes and goes in a corporation according to who is in top management. I worked under four corporation presidents and each differed – the first was honest, the next was a wheeler dealer, the third was somewhat better and the last one was bad. According to their ethical views pressure was put on middle management all the way down.'[21]

Clinard's managers were commenting much more generally than on health and safety issues, but these were included within the ambit of their remarks. Whatever institutional or legal changes are proposed for securing improved compliance it would seem that attention to persuading the CEO would be a useful beginning. Whether such logic can be applied in reverse, when sanctions are involved for misconduct, is regrettably less likely. Recent history indicates that, because the corporation is so closely identified with its chief executive, he will be heavily protected against forced admissions of guilt. Motivation to cut costs in business in the pursuit of profit, including the costs of maintaining standards of health and safety, can never be eliminated, but can at best be contained by effective regulatory agencies which are supported by health and safety compliance units within the organization, which are not subject to line management and have access to the top of the organization. Such arrangements will not resolve the problems associated with small businesses, where the adequate funding and staffing of inspectorates and their arming with credible powers of sanction is the only way to ensure clout. What is certain is that criminal prosecution, though no doubt still useful as a symbolic bludgeon, is more of a diversion of resources and attention than an effective weapon in the struggle.

NOTES

1 W. G. Carson's work on the Factory Acts is to be found in 'Symbolic and Instrumental Dimensions of Early Factory Legislation' in R. Hood (ed.), *Crime, Criminology and Public Policy*, Heinemann, 1974, pp. 107-38; also in 'White Collar Crime and the Enforcement of Factory Legislation', *British Journal of Criminology*, 1970, pp. 383-98; 'The Sociology of Crime and the Enforcement of Criminal Law' in P. D. Rock and M. Mackintosh (eds), *Deviance and Control*, Tavistock, 1974; and W. G. Carson and B. Martin, *The Development of Factory Legislation*, Martin Robertson, 1975.

2 Carson's work on the oil industry is to be found in 'Legal Control of Safety on British Offshore Installations', *Contemporary Crises*, 1980, reprinted in part in P. Wickman and T. Dailey (eds), *White Collar and Economic Crime*, Lexington Books, 1982, pp. 173-96; and in *The Other Price of Britain's Oil*, Martin Robertson, 1982.

3 'British Offshore Installations', in Wickman and Dailey (eds), *White Collar and Economic Crime*, p. 188.

4 The British campaign against leaded petrol is forcefully presented with an opening chapter on the American experience in D. Wilson, *The Lead Scandal*, Heinemann, 1983.

5 Ralph Nader, *Unsafe at any Speed*, Grossman, 1965.

6 G. Kolko's comments on Chicago meat processing are in *The Triumph of Conservatism*, Free Press, 1963. See also his *Railroads and Regulation*, Princeton University Press, 1965.

7 One of the most interesting collections of essays on inspectorates is K. Hawkins and J. M. Thomas (eds), *Enforcing Regulation*, Kluwer Nijhoff, 1984, especially the editors' introductory essay; A. J. Reiss, 'Selecting Strategies of Social Control over Organisational Life'; R. A. Kagan, 'Regulatory Inspectorates and the Police'; and R. A. Kagan and J. T. Scholz, 'The Criminology of the Corporation and Regulatory Enforcement Strategies'. Reiss's review of Hawkins's monograph on pollution, *Environment and Enforcement: Regulation and the Social Definition of Pollution*, Clarendon Press, 1984, is worth reading in its own right, and appears under the title, 'Compliance without Coercion', *Michigan Law Review*, 1985, pp. 813-19. Other works in this well-researched area are: N. Gunningham, *Pollution, Social Interest and the Law*, Martin Robertson, 1974; G. M. Richardson et al., *Policing Pollution*, Clarendon Press, 1983; E. Ashby and M. Anderson, *The Politics of Clean Air*, Oxford University Press, 1981.

8 Reiss, 'Compliance without Coercion'.

9 Kagan and Scholz in Hawkins and Thomas (eds), *Enforcing Regulation*.

10 M. Dowie's, 'Pinto Madness', the first full report of Ford's excesses, appeared in *Mother Jones*, September/October 1977, and has been widely reprinted and adapted, for example in J. H. Skolnick and E. Currie, *Crisis in American Institutions*, Little, Brown, fourth edn, 1979; see also F. T. Cullen et al., 'The Ford Pinto Case and Beyond', in E. Hochstedler (ed.), *Corporations as Criminals*, Sage, 1974.

11 N. Frank, *From Criminal Law to Regulation: An Analysis of Health and Safety Law*, Garland Publications, 1986, p. 230.

12 *Breaking the Rules*, Justice, 1980.

13 M. Levi, 'Business Regulatory Offences and the Criminal Law', *Company Lawyer*, 1985, pp. 251–8.

14 J. Katz, The Social Movement Against White Collar Crime, in *Criminology Review Yearbook* 1980, pp. 174–5. See also N. Abrams, 'Assessing the Federal Government's "War" on White-collar Crime', *Temple Law Quarterly*, 1980, pp. 984–1008.

15 N. Shover et al., *Constructing a Regulatory Bureaucracy: The Office of Surface Mining Reclamation and Enforcement*, National Institute of Justice, 1982.

16 Kagan and Scholz, 'The Criminology of the Corporation and Regulatory Enforcement Strategies', p. 70.

17 B. Hutter, *The Reasonable Arm of the Law?* Clarendon Press, 1988, p. 132.

18 J. Braithwaite is an energetic writer and researcher with a greater penchant for analysing the problems of effective control than most academic commentators, no doubt because of his role as Director of the Australian Federation of Consumer Organisations. See, in the immediate instance, *Corporate Crime in the Pharmaceutical Industry*, Routledge and Kegan Paul, 1984.

19 Braithwaite's idea of enforced self-regulation was initially presented at length in 'Enforced Self-Regulation: A New Strategy for Corporate Crime Control', *Michigan Law Review*, 1982, pp. 1466–1507. This was applied to an empirical study of coal mining in *To Punish or Persuade: The Enforcement of Coal Mine Safety*, State University of New York Press, 1985.

20 C. Stone's *Where the Law Ends: The Social Control of Corporate Behavior*, Harper and Row, 1975, provides a useful analysis of why regulation is necessary and why the law is ineffective.

21 M. Clinard, *Corporate Ethics and Crime*, 1986, Sage Publications, pp. 132–3.

PART III

Control

10 Control

No attempt has been made in the preceding chapters to instantiate in detail the points made about the nature of business crime in Part I for each area of business crime discussed. Not only would this have been tedious and lengthy; more importantly it would have tended to impose a rigid similarity upon kinds of business crime which each have their distinctive characteristics and control problems, and it has been upon these that attention has been primarily concentrated. This is not to suggest that the categories in Part I do not apply; direct and oblique references to their application have been made throughout; but they do not apply in the same way nor with the same force in each area. The analysis in Part I was rather used as guidance in the exploration of successive empirical areas in Part II. In this final Part conclusions will be drawn in the light of Parts I and II which can be divided into three areas. First, what general or strategic conclusions as to the ingredients of how business crime is controlled may be reached on the evidence? Secondly, what, given the evidence of the nature of business crime and the problems of its control, should be the objectives of control and how are they to be achieved? Thirdly, what are the prospects of moving in such a direction and what indications are there that aspects of the analysis developed here are already beginning to be recognized and influential?

Strategic Conclusions

Comments have been made throughout the investigation of different areas of business crime about the particular problems of control posed in each case and some of the methods adopted. Two more general conclusions are possible, however, one negative and one positive. The negative one concerns the law, and particularly the criminal law, whose role has been seen to be limited, even when sustained and deliberate efforts have been made to make it a prime means of control, as for example in the case of industry in the United States on health and safety issues. In each case it has been clear that legal control is impossible and in some respects undesirable. The private context of business offences, their complexity and frequently their ambiguity make the formality and precision characteristic of law difficult and require the extensive commitment of resources, which, as in all legal enforcement systems, are limited. Further, legal proceedings tend to polarize the parties involved so as to entrench antagonisms, which may be acceptable for some business offences sufficiently serious to warrant the ejection of the offender from the privileged business environment and his public stigmatization, but in most cases polarization conflicts with the negotiated character of business crime. In all the areas considered, though not, certainly, in all instances of offences, strong grounds have been shown to exist for dealing with misconduct by negotiation rather than simple condemnation and sanction. There is in almost all cases more to play for than obtaining a judgment or conviction. Part of this is captured in Reiss's dichotomy of compliance and deterrence.[1] Business crimes more widely than those which he discusses (that is those subject to regulatory agencies) tend to be matters where compliance with an accepted way of doing things over the longer term is regarded as a matter of greater importance than the detection and sanctioning of an individual offence. It is hence not just that the law is hard to apply as a prime means of control for business offences, but that even its successful application does not resolve the principal issues raised. Compliance as an objective derives from the contested and ambiguous nature of many business offences. What is at issue is not the condemnation of an act, but the negotiation of an agreed practice. It matters greatly not just that the offender committed the act and knew what he was doing, but also how he construed his action.[2] In law categories of right and wrong are (or are supposed to be) laid down and certain, whereas in business offences they are frequently contestable.

A further aspect of the inapplicability of law and particularly of criminal proceedings is that even where the public interest is involved, as for example in the case of industrial regulation, relations between the parties, the enforcer and the offender, revolve very largely around resources. To put it in a criminal law metaphor, the concern is reparation and recovery of property, not fines and imprisonment. This in turn gives a private character to business offences which marginalizes the public interest. Thus employers seek primarily to minimize damage done by predatory employees and to recover losses, and see prosecution in the light of its effect on their reputation, not (or not only) as a matter of the public interest in the repression of crime. Insurers are glad to settle many frauds without reference to the police for similar reasons. Even inspectors in health and safety matters negotiate with a business as to what can be achieved in the way of improvement, given the resources and capacities of the business, rather than enforcing strict standards in the interests of employees and the public.

The Role of the Law

If business crime has a largely private and negotiated character, what role, if any, is left for the law? The law remains important in two ways. In the first place it remains an important sanction of last resort. In those areas where the negotiation of the offence and the reform of practice break down, recourse to law may become vital as a means of enforcement, both to resolve the private struggle over resources and to require compliance by a legal injunction. Criminal prosecution also remains an essential means of enforcement for extreme cases. Simple villainy is possible in a business environment like any other, and deserves criminal sanction. Achieving this may be difficult, but it is not inappropriate: where the offence involves calculated exploitation and causes significant damage to the legitimate interests of others, prosecution is not a route that should be eschewed simply because of the business context.

The important matters are, first, not to suppose that it is only such extreme and clear-cut criminal cases which are significant in business crime, or even of prime significance. On the contrary they are tangential to the public good, both because they are exceptional and because, by their brazen and calculated exploitation, they declare themselves to be not genuinely part of business. The scam operator who collects public subscriptions for a venture – jobs, shares, business franchises, even a purported charity – with no intention or capacity to provide the goods or services specified, and then disappears with the subscriptions is much less of a danger than a legitimate operator who does provide the service specified, but falls foul of strong competition, or introduces his/her own innovations and so exposes the subscribers to risks way beyond those which they could reasonably have ancitipated. What is important in such circumstances is to have means of establishing and constantly developing standards of good practice and the means of evaluating innovations as acceptable or dangerous.

The reader may object at this point that the straight subscription fraudster is a menace who may pose no less a threat to the public good, given that there is evidence that some such criminals are repeat offenders who make fraud a way of life. This is true, though the scam is likely to be more short-lived and hence involve fewer subscribers than that of the basically honest but reckless or over-confident operator. More importantly, it reinforces the need for something more than the criminal law to deal with such offenders to ensure that they do not return to offend again. Discussion of this aspect of the matter must be deferred to the next section.

Besides remaining as an appropriate sanction for clear cases, the law can also act as a background to business crime, both in the sense of providing a framework for understanding, debating and identifying misconduct, and as a resource in negotiation. Threat of recourse to the law is certainly a useful weapon in achieving compliance, though on the evidence reviewed in earlier chapters, it is frequently not in practice much to be relied upon. Insurers might threaten litigation, but are in practice reluctant to go to court; tax authorities have extensive legal powers, but use them sparingly; environmental health officers threaten prosection, but the costs are so great and the penalties so limited that it amounts largely to bluff. None the less the threat of legal action is an important weapon in the armoury, part of Braithwaite's 'clout'. It imposes costs and delays on the opposition, involves potential public stigmatization, and can have quite severe long-term consequences for the offender's employment, trade or profession as a result. In this sense the law is a weapon to be used in a larger number of cases, but not to be relied upon by itsdelf to achieve the desired result.

A final respect in which the law may play a part in business crime is in providing a framework for identifying offences. There is a sense, of which lawyers are fond, in which nothing is finally settled until an authoritative legal judgement has been delivered upon its principles, and in societies subject formally to the rule of law this is inevitably so. It may also be that particular developments in the law have a marked effect on what is or is not an offence. This has been true extensively in respect of tax law in Britain; a more limited example is provided by legal decisions that in insurance claims exaggeration is not fraud.[3] The law does not necessarily aid and inform a conclusion as to what is and is not an offence or misconduct, however, and there are increasing respects in modern industrial societies, of which business crime is but one, in which the rule of law is a fiction given no more than a deferential nod and in practice by-passed. At times this by-passing may be deliberate, as under the extensive devolution of rule-making to regulate financial institutions in Britain through the agency of the Securities and Investments Board and the self-regulatory organizations. Where the criminal law is used as an instrument of enforcement, particularly where there is an overriding political motive in seeing that enforcement is made to bite, where an abuse has been a source of political embarrassment in cases where what is acceptable or unacceptable practice is still open to debate, and still more so when the issues are complex, the law is in danger of confusing rather than clarifying. The issues of multiple share applications and insider trading have something of this character. Cases where what is at issue are complex matters of legitimate conduct involving such matters as corporate finance and takeovers will almost inevitably confuse rather than clarify.

Awareness

If the negative conclusion is the limited role of the law, what is the positive conclusion? It can be summed up in the word 'awareness', which has ramifications in several directions. Most obviously, the non-self-disclosing nature of most business offences means that unless steps are taken to uncover them they will continue unidentified. It has been pointed out on several occasions that this is not a matter of simple alertness, as it is for example of a policeman noticing evidence of a break-in, but rather of a suspicious cast of mind capable of detecting the slight signs that what appears generally legitimate is not quite right. Doing this involves awareness of business offences in the sense of actively accepting that such behaviour may take place in the midst of a basically legitimate enterprise. This is difficult and requires a conscious effort and a careful allocation of time and specialized personnel. As was pointed out in respect of employee crime and insurance fraud, it is impossible to be constantly suspicious: to doubt everyone and verify everything would quickly bring business to a halt and alienate the honest. What is necessary therefore is, first, an institutional arrangement devoted to identifying misconduct: a compliance officer or unit and a manager with responsibility for fraud control. Secondly, routine verification procedures have to be established to cover the main opportunities for offences. This may be achieved by the visits and reporting requirements of an outside inspectorate, or it may be the outcome of internally maintained checks, but unless points of vulnerability are identified and collectively policed, trouble, if it arises, will probably take time before it is recognized, if it ever is. If, however, compliance routines and checks are established, the sting is taken out of doubting the honesty of others: it is not that you are not trusted with the petty cash, it is just that it is routine to have two signatures to gain access to it.

Once awareness in this fundamental sense is achieved, the very possibility that abuse of trust and deceit could take place in an organization is recognized and the groundwork is laid for the development of awareness as a more extensive means of control. If the organization contains an established capacity and obligation to identify and monitor opportunities for offences, its next step, after identifying the obvious targets, is to consider the more nebulous issues. Awareness hence involves stimulating debate on features of the business that could give rise to dishonesty, conflicts of interest and exploitation. Such debate will not necessarily reach definitive conclusions even over a relatively long term, but it will have the decided merit of alerting everyone to the dangers of a particular area of business and play its part in helping to ensure that all are kept abreast of changing standards. In some cases it will be effective in achieving clarification and establishing new rules and conventions as to acceptable practice, if only by managerial or other authoritative fiat.

Stimulating debate on matters that might be regarded as wrong may well be regarded as a limited benefit, and by some even as a waste of time and a diversion from the goals of production and profitability. Besides attempting to persuade as many as possible that such goals should not be pursued regardless of the interests of others – customers, clients, creditors, employees, the public – informed debate on matters of crime and misconduct has the considerable merit of limiting the capacity of those subsequently accused of offences to plead ignorance or to offer hoary defences long ago discredited as unacceptable. If all are obliged to recognize the importance of clarifying new standards of conduct and of being aware of contested issues, and of the consequent obligation to exercise due restraint and caution, not only will the area of clarity as to what is and what is not legitimate be extended, but the freedom of manoeuvre of the deviant, exploitative, arrogant and reckless will be constrained. Offences will be easier to pin down and offenders easier to identify as such, not only for being shown not to have been in compliance with a required set of procedures – such formal arrangements are not always possible – but by having their arsenal of argument depleted.

Finally, this somewhat negative presentation of awareness as recognition of misconduct has its positive side in the identification and specification of good practice. This has a double aspect. In the first place, it may be possible in many cases to develop codes of good practice which should normally be adhered to and deviation from which will require explanation. Secondly, even where this is not possible, an environment in which acceptable conduct is the norm makes unacceptable conduct the more noticeable by contrast. This feature of awareness hence feeds back into the first of those mentioned. The successful establishment of good conduct makes the basic awareness of bad conduct the easier. If the issue is never raised, and the organization is just committed to 'getting on with the job', this is much harder.

How is awareness of business misconduct achieved, and hence the means developed to control it? When this question is posed, the necessarily somewhat abstract discussion of awareness so far can be translated into more practical terms. Whilst some, especially larger, businesses may be able to do a considerable amount by their own efforts, and whilst the detailed control of some types of offences and misconduct will of course only be possible as a result of the detailed appraisal of specific features of the individual organization, most businesses and most defences will benefit greatly from, if not require, an external input and stimulus. The extent and stringency of this external influence will vary according to, first, how great a problem the business thinks it has, both in terms of its damage potential and in terms of its lack of internal expertise. Thus, it is not uncommon today for businesses to call in computer security consultants to advise on the control of abuses of computerized records and accounting systems, not only because the losses are potentially great, but because the business has no in-house expertise in the matter.

Secondly, the extent of external intervention and control will vary according to the degree of public interest in the offences in question. Where the public interest is minimal, as in employee theft for example, the business will be free to act as it wishes, either on its own, or by calling in outside help from management consultants and the like. Where, on the other hand, the risk to the public interest is great, as in industrial health and safety, state agencies are established with legal rights of access and powers to intervene to require detailed standards and procedures to be complied with, on pain, at times, of suspension of business operations.

At one extreme there are hence strict licensing arrangements which are

Table 11   External intervention in the formulation of business standards

High		Degree of Stringency		Low	
formal licensing	state inspectorates	enforced/statute-backed self-regulation	state as stimulus to self-regulation (OFT)	trade associations' code of conduct	informal industry debate

imposed externally, over the formal requirements of which the business can exercise only limited influence (though the details of compliance may be more open to negotiation); at the other pole lie businesses relying on their own efforts at control. In between are matters regulated by inspectorates which have powers of intervention but not full licensing powers – environmental health officers are an example. Then there are statute-backed, formal self-regulatory systems, such as the SIB or Braithwaite's enforced self-regulation. Here intervention in the affairs of the individual organization is by a self-regulatory body, but this body in turn is actively regulated by a specialized statute and by a state or quasi-state agency. Less stringent still is the intervention of the trade association, which carries membership requirements that are not very demanding, but may be instrumental in developing codes of conduct for business in its sector, which come in time to be more or less binding on individual organizations, and which stimulate improved standards and recognition of problem areas. In Britain the Office of Fair Trading has been active in promoting the acceptance of codes of conduct as a more effective and acceptable alternative to detailed legislation, especially in areas subject to sustained consumer complaint, for example car and electrical appliance repairs, footwear retailing, home improvements, mail-order trading. At the least stringent level all industries generate their own gossip and debate, including discussions of scandals and court cases, and word circulates and has its influence by such informal means. The message may be distributed by this means that it is no longer acceptable practice to, for example, fail to give estimates for work to be undertaken. Such messages convey a meaning which is as much economic – that customers will look askance at a business that fails to come up to the new standard – as ethical.

An obvious corollary of this, and something that has been evident throughout the review of the evidence, is the central place occupied in the control of business crime by business itself. Whatever the efforts of outsiders – legislators, police, inspectorates, the media, pressure groups – it is only when business itself takes the control of offences seriously and engages its energies and resources that real progress can be made. It is not just that as a matter of fact business takes the leading part in controlling business crime, but that it necessarily does so, because of the closed and private nature of business and the complexity of internal operations. True, external pressure may be brought to bear to bring about reforms in conduct and standards, but only by increasing the costs of not taking pressure for reform seriously can outsiders coerce reform.

So much seems evident from the empirical material reviewed. Before passing on to a consideration of the objectives of control, it may perhaps be worth presenting the issues involved in a different light, since this will lead on to a wider conclusion that is not without interest in respect of the final section, which considers the prospects for the future.

Professional Ideals and Business Conduct

One form in which the debate about business crime has been manifested in the United States has been as a discussion of the place of ethics in business. This is seen as particularly appropriate because of a kind of business crime not reviewed here which has an obvious ethical aspect, namely corruption and abuses by professionals, particularly doctors and lawyers. The United States has always had a serious corruption problem in many of its governmental institutions. Machine politics, until the reforms that did not finally succeed until the demise of Mayor Daley of Chicago in the 1970s, routinely involved corruption of all kinds. It is not to be forgotten that Gerald Ford became President only because Spiro Agnew was disqualified from succeeding Richard Nixon because he was involved in corruption as Governor of Maryland. From the Lockheed and other foreign bribery scandals of the 1970s, to the widespread abuses of Medicaid and Medicare in the 1980s, to the wild overcharging of the federal government by defence contractors, a stream of misconduct has captured public attention in the United States which has involved gross violation of public trust by individuals and organizations which clearly knew better. From the Foreign Corrupt Practices Act onwards one response has been to attempt to spell out clearly what expected standards of conduct are – in this case that bribery of foreign governments to obtain sales is illegitimate, even if others do it. Although, as has been argued above, stimulating debate on standards and attempting to formulate them and to ensure that all participants are aware of them is an important aspect of achieving control, most social scientists would regard a simple emphasis upon moral debate and reform as inadequate. It is one thing to arrive at clearer standards, but another to enforce them, a matter which requires a diversion of resources on a permanent basis to establish institutional arrangements to ensure verification and compliance. It is one thing to give public voice to acceptable sentiments, and quite another to put them into practice under the everyday pressures of work. Only if checks are installed to ensure detection if practice does not follow rhetoric is real compliance likely.

Debate about business ethics does, however, raise an interesting issue in itself. Why should anyone suppose that business has any need of ethics? Is its job not to get on with producing, selling and making a profit by whatever ingenious means it can devise, save that it must stay within the limits of the law? And the latter has conventionally been taken to mean, not to use outright force or brazen trickery. If this image was ever accurate, the review of different kinds of business offences in the preceding chapters has made it plain that it is certainly no longer so. The objectives of profit, security and growth are required to be tempered by due concern for the legitimate interests of employees, customers, creditors and the public at large. Business is, in other words, increasingly under pressure to exercise self-restraint and to ensure that it does not exploit and oppress others with whom and through whom it works.

Such restraints are reminiscent of those characteristic of the professions, and it is ironic that the debate on ethical restraint should have been stimulated in part by professional abuses. For the *quid pro quo* of a profession's control over the market-place for its services is restraint. Professions provide services in areas of life regarded as of vital importance: the maintenance of health, the representation of a client in a court of law, the evaluation of safe engineering designs, the appraisal of accounts as 'true and fair'. The knowledge disposed of is relatively complex and extensive, and standards of competence to act professionally are ensured by the professional body. This gives professionals a powerful market advantage, which they are traditionally restrained from exploiting to the full by agreed scales of fees. Further, they are subject to elaborate codes of conduct as to the confidentiality of information supplied by clients, requirements to make themselves available to all who seek their assistance, and to exercise due diligence on clients' behalf. It is implicit in the institution of the profession that, whilst a minority of clients may have the money and skill to shop around to ensure that they receive adequate advice, many will not, and will have no means of knowing this until it is too late, by which time catastrophic damage may be done to clients' interests. The essence of the profession is hence control of the market accompanied by self-imposed restraint in the conduct of professional business.

This is not to say of course that the professional ideal is necessarily lived up to. Professional monopoly leads to complacency and arrogance, and to restrictive practices that have recently come under sustained pressure in Britain from the government through the Office of Fair Trading. None the less there are features of the professional ideal that sit well with the emerging obligations of business to have regard to the interests of others. Business can never be professionalized, because business remains a central part of a market economy. The professional ideal is, however, one that is likely to prove increasingly attractive to businesses, and especially to managers keen to present themselves as ethically sophisticated and reliable, and as capable and willing to take more into account as the wider obligations of business than the simple pursuit of profit. It is hence not without significance that the Confederation of British Industry should at present be pursuing the notion of the chartered manager, based upon the establishment of a charter group of companies, which would establish a code of professional practice and seek to apply it to both large and small organizations.

Put more widely, these ideas are part of the process of bringing business into public accountability, an issue that will be taken up more fully in the concluding section, but which involves the recognition by business that it does not operate in an environment peopled only by other businesses, but in a society containing other institutions and social groupings which have quite other and equally legitimate activities and purposes, which business must recognize practically, and to which it is increasingly required to account for itself. These however are large issues. Before commenting further, something more specific needs to be said about the objectives of the control of business crime.

A Prescriptive Strategy of Control

It has been a prime objective of this analysis to show that whilst controls currently exist for different kinds of business crime that are not often given public recognition, they coexist with other legally based controls that are regularly given public emphasis. The outcome is confusion as to what is an appropriate means of control and about what it is supposed to achieve. Criminal sanctions against offenders reflect the public interest through public punishment and hopefully the deterrence of others. Civil penalties may be used to more or less the same end, for example in the practice of the Securities and Exchange Commission, though with somewhat less dramatic force. Legal sanctions have, however, been shown to be usually only resorted to with reluctance, or where the public interest is strong. Thus, employers would usually rather settle a case by using their own resources than go through the courts, but industrial corporations have at times and in some countries come under great pressure to conform to acceptable standards in protecting the interests of the public as regards pollution and product safety and to be subjected to criminal proceedings if they do not. Even here however there has been a powerful tendency to revert to semi-private negotiation with regulators in order to settle offences. Such a practice is the norm in tax matters. It has been argued that there are good reasons for this tendency, which amount to the fact that legal sanctions are ineffective as a primary method of control.

If less formal, more private, negotiated and administrative means are to be used, however, questions arise as to whether the public interest is protected. If an employer negotiates with a deviant employee and concludes with terms that remain secret, how are the interests of the next employer who takes him/her on, and those of clients/customers, secured? If an inspector reaches agreement as to what a reasonable safety or emission standard is for a particular plant in the light of its resources, does this not reflect more the practicalities of the working life of inspectors rather than the protection of the public by the achievement of publicly notified standards? Should a citizen who has cheated the revenue over an extensive period be permitted to settle the case privately? Is the revelation of his/her identity not in the public interest?

On the other hand it has been shown that much of the impetus for solutions to business crime has derived from the fact that the interests of those directly involved can thereby be protected. Losses can at times be recovered, techniques of offending identified and prevention achieved for the future. Negotiated solutions seem to be more affective in compensating for losses and in the prevention of a future recurrence of the offence, matters which are not a major concern of criminal legal proceedings and are frequently not achieved in civil ones. Could such preventive and protective methods be reconciled with a fuller recognition of the protection of the public interest and be developed into a single consistent and effective strategy?

The remarks in the preceding section suggest that this might be possible. There it was claimed that misconduct can be to some degree prevented by an awareness of what it consists in, that is, by debate which clarifies and publicizes the issues and leads to the establishment of agreed standards, backed by well understood rationales. Secondly, such an awareness can be extended to pin-point the main opportunities for misconduct and to ensure that they are well recognized as such and subject to additional checks. This, however, essentially deals with the problem from the point of view of the system rather than the individual (whether that individual is a person or a corporation). Individuals commit offences, and it has been argued others are at risk as much from their incompetence, negligence and recklessness as from their calculated exploitation. An effective control system must take account of this. Protection and prevention will not be achieved without a capacity to identify offenders and ensure that they are not permitted to return to the field and offend again. This can be achieved by the implementation of three primary principles, identification, accreditation and exclusion, and two subsidiary ones, compensation and rehabilitation.

Identification

Business crime lends itself particularly to the exploitation of changed identity. The employee who wreaks havoc at one workplace and is thrown out will be able to gain re-employment much more easily if she/he adopts a new identity, which may not be comprehensive. If she/he has not been prosecuted, she/he may find simply moving to a new region or sector of industry or commerce is enough to provide protection against any revelation of his/her past depredations. The entrepreneur is in an even more privileged position. By adopting new trading names and operating behind the protective façade of the company form she/he can go from disaster to disaster without customers, employees or others having any knowledge of his/her past. This is a sufficiently well recognized problem in respect of tax that individuals (though, thanks to limited liability and insolvency law, not companies) will find it quite difficult to escape their liabilities by changing their identity. The problematic paradox is that so long as an individual offender remains within the business context in which she/he has committed the offence – as an employee, trading as the same company or as a corporation under the same ownership – she/he is relatively accessible to pressure and control. It is when she/he moves on to start anew that the dangers arise, but it is also at this point that civil liberties considerations arise of pursuing an offender with a record, which may reflect in part at least the politics of the offence and its history as private negotiations, rather than a public and formally established record as is the case with legal proceedings. The principle that participants in business must be formally identified and publicly registered in a reliable way over the long term is a necessary feature of effective control, but one that carries with it dangers.

Accreditation

For this reason the second principle, accreditation, is the more important, for accreditation is not for all purposes, but for a particular purpose. Accreditation may be nominal or substantial, and it may be technical or moral. Thus, for example, anyone may set up in business as a window cleaner or a toy retailer, even though one might wonder whether convicted burglars and paedophiliacs should be allowed to. One may not however practise as a doctor or as an investment manager without both demonstrating a recognized training, and perhaps other requirements such as capital adequacy, and being recognized as a fit and proper person, that is, lacking in any moral failings relevant to the occupation. Where technical accreditation is positive, moral accreditation is negative, all being acceptable until shown to be otherwise. The importance of accreditation is that its extent and detailed requirements are a reflection of the requirements and moral risks of the job. The requirements for being a doctor are different from those for being an investment manager, though clearly there are overlaps: a solicitor disbarred for abusing clients' funds would find it hard to gain accreditation as an investment manager.

Another advantage of accreditation is that it relies on disclosure. For positive accreditation of technical competence this disclosure amounts to showing that the necessary training has been undergone, finances have been raised, premises are adequate and so on. On the moral side it involves a response to questions put about the candidate's record. Records which are held on the delinquency of practitioners will be held by sector and have consequences on further participation in that sector. Thus insurers can circulate records of those who have attempted to defraud them, tax offices circulate details about bad payers, and self-regulatory bodies in the financial sector keep records about offenders against their rules. Civil liberties problems of identification and the potentiality for tendentious black lists arising are hence mitigated by the sectoral character of accreditation. In certain cases of course traditional checks, for example of criminal records or county court judgements may be made, where the extent of the trust involved in the business or position is great and the consequences of abuse substantial. In general however, the disclosure system operates in such a way as to permit a degree of deliberate deceit, at the risk of sanctions should this be exposed, but with the objective of eliminating not the primary but the repeated offence. For commission of an offence leads to the withdrawal of accreditation and hence to the prevention of further offences by the prevention of further practice in the sector.

Exclusion

The sanction essential to the success of this control strategy is hence exclusion. It is a quite different sanction from that visited by legal proceedings, which impose penalties for specific offences (punitive or compensatory), but make no attempt to prevent the individual continuing in business. It is vital for the protective and preventive success of the proposed control strategy that exclusion be capable of being effectively imposed. This implies an effective system of monitoring offenders after the offence to ensure that they do not alter their identities and return to cause further trouble. Effectiveness is also vital to the deterrent aspect of exclusion. Exclusion must be recognized by practitioners to mean that all the benefits deriving from training, experience and investment of time and money in a business will be put at risk if an offence is committed. That threat must include permanent exclusion from the sector in which the offence was committed and the possibility that the damage will spill over into the refusal of accreditation in a number of other sectors. Only if exclusion is effective will the sector be secure from the arrogant offender who concludes from the experience of being detected only that she/he will not make that mistake again and next time will know how better to avoid detection.

Rehabilitation

Exclusion, however, cannot of course work only on a permanent basis. If it is necessarily permanent it is so severe a sanction that there will be reluctance to use it. Temporary exclusion is also necessary, coupled with rehabilitation. There is little point in merely imposing a period of suspension. This will be experienced as punitive and the income lost will be avidly sought after as soon as accreditation is restored. In the mean time nothing will have been learned. If suspension or restriction on accreditation – permission to continue business subject to restraint – is accompanied by rehabilitative efforts, some benefit may ensue. Offenders may hence be required to learn in some detail of the errors of their ways and to participate in taking the steps necessary to minimize the chances of repeat offences. This is particularly important in developing competence and rational self-evaluation, as well as impressing upon the offender that further deliberate deviance could lead to permanent exclusion. Nor is there any reason why the offender should not contribute to the costs of such rehabilitation as the price of being permitted to continue business in the sector in question.

Compensation

The question of financial contribution leads to the final principle, that of compensation. It will be subject to the constraint of the resources of the individual or organization involved, but the element of compensation present in many informally negotiated kinds of business offence should not be ignored in a system which is intended to be protective as well as preventive. Whether compensation by the offender is supported by a sectoral compensation scheme for the victims of offences is a matter that will vary according to the circumstances of different business sectors.

Achieving Acceptable Regulatory Systems

Statement of principles inevitably involves putting issues in a more stark and extreme form than may be appropriate to their implementation in particular cases. The points made about a preventive and protective system so far sound rather like a simple licensing system. Whilst this is indeed operative in certain sectors of business, surely it is far too onerous and restrictive to be generally applied? Even if one points to the fact that licensing regimes proper seem to have made substantial advances in recent years, notably in the case of the financial sector in Britain, there is no supposition that they are to become the norm for all sectors and levels of business. On the other hand, if the principles outlined above are not to be put into operation with the stringency of a full licensing regime, can they be made to work at all? It is because of these responses that attention has been directed to the objectives of the proposed system. How easy it is to achieve the objectives of prevention and protection to within acceptable levels will vary from sector to sector according to the risks, opportunities and problems involved.

For the system is implicit in the continuum of external intervention in business regulation outlined in the preceding section. How extensive accreditation and identification procedures are will depend upon the nature of the trust involved and the risk of its abuse. State-managed licensing systems constitute only one extreme of a method of control, which in more limited versions can act to give protection also through codes of conduct sponsored by trade associations. Whether a more stringent regime is developed because of the ineffectiveness of the first will depend upon the perceived acceptability of the regime. It will, in other words, be a political matter. If, for example, traders in a particular sector fail to abide by a code of conduct, and customers and the public continue to suffer, pressure may grow for the substitution of a code that will be respected. At the extreme it may be based on a specialized statute enabling a minister to create a legally binding code. Less stringently, it may improve its effectiveness by intra-sectoral agreements, such as the Association of British Travel Agents' code of practice covering retail travel agents and tour operators. This prevents members selling package holidays promoted by non-members and is registered with the Restrictive Practices Court as being in the public interest. The toughening of the regime to improve the reliability of the code in protecting the public was undertaken after a series of failures of tour operators, leaving holiday-makers stranded.

Although state-administered licensing is the fullest version of the control system, it is hence not necessary or appropriate to all sectors. Most, including the financial sector, can be managed with the business sector undertaking the bulk of the administration of the system. Some sectors, despite known and persistent problems of abuses, seem not to generate the political pressure for effective controls. Second-hand motor car sales for example, despite the size of the outlays by consumers, seem to rely largely upon free market principles and a healthy caution by customers, and codes of conduct remain weak. So culturally entrenched has the expectation of abuse become here that it was even possible for a compaign advertisement against Richard Nixon to portray him as shifty and unreliable by asking 'Would you buy a used car from this man?'

Making Business Accountable

There should be no evading the point implicit in this remark. Achieving control of business crime is part of the wider process of making business more accountable, both to the public at large and to an increasing number of constituencies within it. Business is no longer constrained only by accountability to shareholders. It is required to take account of the legitimate interests of employees, customers, clients and creditors, and in some cases the public at large, and such requirements have become increasingly formal. Legislation on pollution, dismissal, equal pay for women, worker safety, product safety, and insolvency, to cite just a few examples, has proliferated in the post-war years as business has been increasingly made to recognize that business activity, if not now a privilege, has at least become a right with considerable attendant obligations.

It is significant that the swing to the right of the industrialized west in the 1980s, accompanied though it has been by rhetoric about deregulation and the virtues of the free market, does not in practice involve anything so straightforward as the return to nineteenth-century simplicities. True, there has been a degree of deregulation and, accompanied by the recession of the early 1980s, organized labour has been hit hard by it. Even right-wing governments in the industrialized world depend upon elections, however, and the basis of the Thatcher–Reagan electoral success has been the mobilization of an affluent majority of voters. This constituency has been rewarded by tax cuts, not assaulted by the consequences of deregulation. Where deregulation has gone further, as in some aspects of the financial sector in the United States, it has provoked such a series of disasters, in savings and loans institutions in the south, and in banking more widely, as well as in investment banking and securities, as to generate a considerable momentum for revived regulation by Congress, if not by the President, at the end of the 1980s. And in Britain the Prime Ministerial emphasis upon Victorian values is taken to include a respect for honesty, probity and hard work. Increased efforts at regulation and accountability have accompanied tax reductions, privatization and reductions in trade-union rights.

One way of expressing these changes is to identify them with consumer-ism and the consumer society. It is, after all, the more affluent half of society that accounts for the greater part of the purchase of consumer goods and to whom the lavish expenditure on advertising is directed to sustain demand and manipulate taste. Consumerism should not be interpreted too narrowly, however. It is true there has been a development of pressure for consumer protection in the post-war industrialized west, with most countries enacting laws which contrive, directly or indirectly, to put the onus on the manufacturer to produce safe and reliable goods which perform as specified. More widely used items are expected to perform to standards of accredited reliability and safety, as in the British Standards system, whose kite mark and serial number appears on many goods today. The rule of the market place, *caveat emptor*, is increasingly regarded as unacceptable, and customers expect to be able to purchase items without a detailed and informed appraisal of their quality and to be entitled to replacement, repair or refund from retailers if they fail to work properly. The extent to which this process has developed is illustrated by the activities of the Office of Fair Trading which, having negotiated codes of conduct in more than a score of business sectors since 1974, beginning with the servicing of electrical appliances and package holidays through shoe repairs and laundering and dry cleaning to party plan selling and double glazing in the 1980s, moved a step further in 1986 to propose a general duty to trade fairly. This would require legislation, but would be implemented through the introduction of enforceable codes of conduct sector by sector:[4]

It is appropriate that the consideration of codes of practice under a general duty would include, but not be limited to relevant trade associations. It is proposed that legislation would require the Office to involve other suitable parties, including organisations representing consumers. In this way the setting of standards sector by sector would build on the existing self-regulatory approach and would represent an attempt to achieve a consensus, with no association or organisation having a decisive influence, or a power of veto. The sectors for which codes would be first introduced would be those where consumer problems were most intractable and the prospective benefits would thus most clearly be likely to outweigh the compliance and enforcement costs.

The Office envisages approved codes containing a statement of general principles of fair trading pertinent to the sector but not being excessively detailed. Thus for example, traders' obligations in respect of the provision of appropriate information, written estimates, spare parts, servicing or the features of extended warranties would be included in relevant sectors. As afurther instance, approved codes should provide a means of banning arbitration clauses in some traders' standard contracts which oblige consumers to go to arbitration and deprive them of their rights of access to the court, including the small claims procedure or, in Scotland, to the sheriff court.

It should also be possible to facilitate the decriminalisation of particular areas of regulatory consumer protection legislation when a general duty and codes are in place by covering the same substantive points in codes. The Office does not see this as a weakening of consumer protection, but rather, given the proposed enforcement mechanism, it will enable the efficacy of the law to be improved to the benefit of consumers. (5.19–5.21)

Enforcement is envisaged as follows:

Local authority trading standards departments (and environmental health departments as appropriate) should be given a major role in enforcement. Without such a role for local enforcement agencies, which can act quickly on the basis of local information, a general duty would be unlikely to be effective in raising trading standards or improving redress. The Office proposes that in the event of a trading standards officer becoming aware, through complaint or otherwise, of instances of trading practices which he considers to be a breach of the relevant code, it would be open to the officer to make an informal approach asking the trader to comply with the code and, in a suitable case, ask the trader to give redress to aggrieved consumers. If the informal approach failed it would be open to the trading standards officer to serve the trader with a formal notice. This would set out the alleged breach of the code and invite the trader to propose a remedy, which would include an undertaking to comply with the relevant code provisions and an offer to give suitable redress. If the trader complied with the formal notice, that would be the end of the matter. If, however, the trading standards officer were unable to obtain a satisfactory response, he could take action in the local county or sheriff court seeking a court order requiring the trader to comply with the relevant sections of the code and, where appropriate, to give suitable redress. If the trading standards officer's case were successful the court would grant a mandatory injunction or interdict ordering the trader to refrain from breach of the relevant sections of the code, and would order redress to any consumers who had been injured by the breach of the code. Ultimately the sanctions for breach of the injunction would be a fine or imprisonment for contempt of court. In instances where financial compensation was not appropriate, an alternative sanction open to the court could be to declare the contract unenforceable. The above procedure could also be applied to breaches of the existing civil and criminal law.

In this way the trading standards officer would be enforcing the code and the general law in the public interest and also, in effect, pursuing a mass restitution suit on behalf of consumers. However, in cases involving matters of general importance or difficult questions of law or fact it should be open to the Director General of Fair Trading to initiate cases instead of the local trading standards officer, or to take over such cases at any stage of the procedure.

If there were persistent breaches of the general duty or the general law, thus indicating a course of conduct, it might in addition be open to a trading standards department or the Director General to seek an injunction from the court to require the trader to cease the conduct. (5.28–5.30)

Such a progressive universalization of consumer protection takes regulation of the market into a system more reminiscent of medieval courts, customs and conventions than of nineteenth-century *laissez-faire*.

Nor should the OFT's other role as regulator of big business be forgotten. It is also responsible, with the Secretary of State for Trade and Industry, for maintaining competitive markets by preventing the development of monopolies and attacking restrictive practices. It can refer takeover bids to the Monopolies and Mergers Commission, with the agreement of the Secretary of State, if it thinks that allowing them to proceed would affect the public interest and permit market dominance by the proposed conglomerate. It was the OFT that campaigned against the Stock Exchange and developed a case to take it to the Restrictive Practices Court, which precipitated the reregulation of the financial sector under the SIB. The OFT retains a role in monitoring the effectiveness of the new regime. It is notable that the OFT, one of the quangos, which as a category were vilified by the Thatcher administation in its first term as the embodiment of unnecessary interference, should not only have been exempted from the purge of them, but had its staffing and responsibilities increased. Regulation on both the large and small scale hence seems to be accepted as politically desirable.

Some of the reasons for this can be seen by considering the implications of consumerism more widely. The growth of affluence, remarked on in the 1950s by Galbraith,[5] has been sufficiently sustained to involve not mere spending power, but new expectations of security in the upper two-thirds of society which has come to benefit from it. Expectations of safety, reliability and durability have become entrenched. Housing is expected to be warm and dry, cars not to break down and to start even on frosty mornings, televisions not to explode, holiday travel to be a simple rapid transit to the sun, rather than a lengthy odyssey of dawdling trains and missed connections. This security has also, as has been remarked on in the chapter on financial institutions, its counterpart in finance, with ever more diverse financial arrangements underpinning the security of long-term participation in the consumer society. It is this expectation of security that has given rise to regulatory intervention to sustain it, and to the identification of cases where this fails as scandals.

It is not simply a question of demand for reliability from an enlarged constituency of more affluent consumers, however, but also of an increase in the rate of change, and in the complexity of the goods and services consumed. These changes have put the consumer in a position of inevitable ignorance and dependence in relation to the manufacturer and supplier. With the introduction of the radio in the 1920s it quickly became possible for children to build their own 'cat's whisker' receivers. Who today understands the functioning of a transistorized radio, still less of a television or video cassette recorder? Nor is this a purely technical matter, as Moore, discussing the background to the drive against white-collar crime in the United States in the late 1970s, explains:[6]

Recent changes in both the organization of the society and our determination to control the behavior of people within large institutions have vastly increased the extent of what is now perceived to be the white-collar-crime problem.

One significant change is the continuing elaboration of the network of exchange relationships in which individuals find themselves enmeshed. It used to be true that important economic transactions were conducted primarily either within a family or between the family and a small number of institutions. The transactions were relatively few, relatively simple so that neither side had a great deal more information about the exchange than the other, and conducted by individuals who expected to have long-term relationships, so that neither side would be willing to risk their relationship for a small advantage in a given exchange. Now, partly as the result of a continuing process of differentiation and specialization that occurs with the growth of an exchange economy, partly as the result of increased wealth that allows us to buy more complicated products, and partly as the result of a vast expansion of governmental activities paralleling the growth of the market economy, individuals find themselves dealing episodically in complex transactions with many different institutions. Moreover, many of these transactions are based implicitly or explicitly on trust, because one party controls much of the relevant information on which the transaction is based. An auto mechanic knows more about what he did to a car than a customer can easily discover. The owner of a building may know more about its real worth than an insurance company. A welfare client knows more about her qualifying characteristics than the case worker. And a fire inspector may know more about the fire regulations governing the grant of a license to a restaurant owner than the owner does. Thus the sheer number and complexity of the transactions conspire with the absence of an expectation of a continuing relationship to create enormous opportunities for fraud and exploitation . . ..

A second significant change related to but different from the elaboration of the exchange economy is the emergence of large institutions with discretionary control over resources and activities that are valuable (perhaps even vital) to other individuals. These institutions lend credibility and distribute authority among individual representatives. In doing so, they increase the opportunities for the *individuals* who represent the institutions to deceive and exploit other individuals who do business with or have an interest in the activities of the institution. An auto repairman working for a nationally recognized company can get away with a shoddy repair job more easily than an unaffiliated mechanic by hiding behind his organizational affiliation.

Whether one looks at long-term historical changes in society and economy, or at the particulars of individual sectors, then, there are sources of pressure for regulation. The role of the state is increasingly to act as guarantor of the security of citizens in their economic relationships. One way of looking at this is to review the active regulatory and interventionist role of the state, which undoubtedly exists and has been widely remarked upon.[7] In this book, however, emphasis has been laid by contrast on the part played by business itself in improving regulation and security. Under social democratic governments state intervention of a bolder sort is supposed to be favoured to constrain the exploitative and unreliable aspects of business, but it is subject also to the expectation that business will resist intervention, a matter which is usually presented as business wishing to preserve its privileges and remain unaccountable. Under recent neo-conservative governments in Britain and the United States, the state's role as guarantor has been more that of a stimulator of self-regulation than administrator of state regulation. As has been evident in the preceding chapters, business is necessarily a major partner in such regulation. Appreciation of this fact diminishes the apparent disparity between the two political approaches to the problem though, as is particularly evident in the more volatile political atmosphere in the United States, changes in political climate may be translated into considerable changes in the style and extent of regulation over the short term.

In the longer term, business will continue, by small and, on the micro-level haphazard, increments to be made more accountable, and as part of that process business offences will come to be increasingly carefully evaluated and possibilities for them circumscribed by ethical and regulatory innovation, and by special institutional arrangements, and the continuing perpetrators of them will be more and more likely to suffer exclusion from the market, not only as individually unacceptable but as a threat to the common good.

NOTES

1 Reiss, 'Selecting Strategies of Social Control over Organisational Life', in K. Hawkins and J. M. Thomas (eds), *Enforcing Regulation,* Kluwer Nijhoff, 1984.
2 That is, the company, not an individual in it, for present purposes.
3 For a fuller account of this point, see M. J. Clarke, 'Insurance Fraud', *British Journal of Criminology,* 1989, no. 1.
4 The Office of Fair Trading published its discussion paper, *A General Duty to Trade Fairly,* in 1986.
5 The relevant works by J. K. Galbraith on the social and economic development of western industrialized societies are *The Affluent Society,* Penguin, 1962, and *The New Industrial State,* Penguin, 1969 (revised edn, 1975).
6 The comments by Moore on the changing nature of market relationships in contemporary western industrialized states are to be found in H. Edelhertz and C. Rogovin, *A National Strategy for Containing White-Collar Crime,* D. C. Heath, 1980, pp. 26–7. See also H. Edelhertz, *The Nature, Impact and Prosecution of White-Collar Crime,* National Institute of Law Enforcement and Criminal Justice, US Department of Justice, Law Enforcement Assistance Administration, 1970.
7 See for example R. Baldwin and C. McCrudden (eds), *Regulation and Public Law,* Weidenfeld and Nicolson, 1987.

Index